Ralph Shanks

+

Lisa Woo Shanks

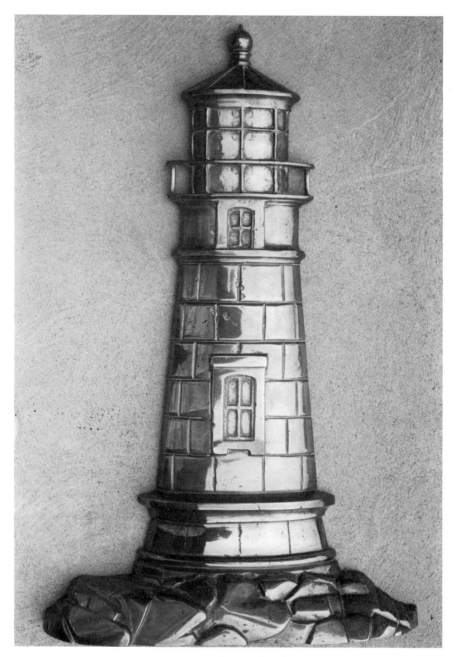

Large metal logos were mounted on the bow and on the stern of many U.S. Lighthouse Service tenders. (U.S. Coast Guard Academy Museum)

Cover: Point Bonita lighthouse with heavy surf breaking, 1975. (R. Shanks)

GUARDIANS OF THE GOLDEN GATE

Lighthouses and Lifeboat Stations of San Francisco Bay

Ralph Shanks
and
Lisa Woo Shanks, editor

The U.S. Lighthouse Service flag

Costaño Books   P.O. Box 355   Petaluma, California 94953

COSTAÑO BOOKS
P.O. BOX 355
PETALUMA, CALIFORNIA 94953

By the same author:
Lighthouses of San Francisco Bay
Lighthouses and Lifeboats on the Redwood Coast
The North American Indian Travel Guide

Library of Congress Catalog Card Number: 89-81047

ISBN: 0-930268-08-3 (soft cover)
ISBN: 0-930268-09-1 (hard cover)

DEDICATED TO OUR PARENTS:
Rev. Ralph C. Shanks, Sr.
Viola Lacewell Shanks
Dr. Jennie Woo
In memory of Dr. Stephen "K.K." Woo

Mile Rocks
by Lisa Shanks

Fort Point Coast Guard Station's 44-foot motor lifeboat off the Golden Gate Bridge, C. 1972. (U.S. Coast Guard)

GUARDIANS OF THE GOLDEN GATE: LIGHTHOUSES AND LIFEBOAT STATIONS OF SAN FRANCISCO BAY

TABLE OF CONTENTS

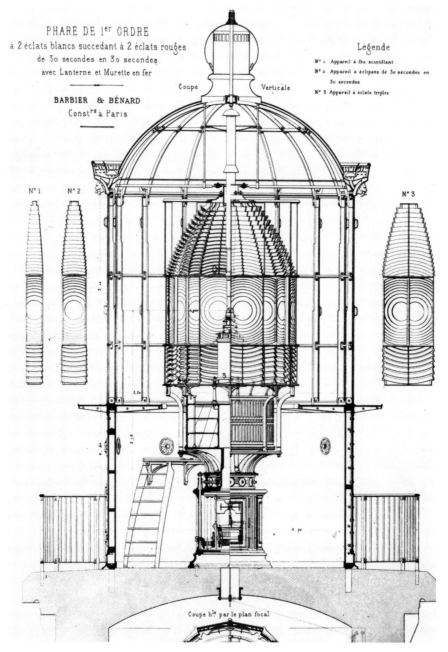

PHARE DE 1er ORDRE
à 2 éclats blancs succedant à 2 éclats rouges
de 3o secondes en 3o secondes.
avec Lanterne et Murette en fer

Coupe   Verticale

BARBIER & BÉNARD
Const.ds à Paris

Légende

N.° 1   Appareil à feu scintillant
N.° 2   Appareil à éclipses de 3o secondes en
        3o secondes
N.° 3   Appareil à éclats triples

N° 1   N° 2   N° 3

Coupe h.te par le plan focal

A Lens of the First Order

A MESSAGE FROM
REAR ADMIRAL RICHARD A. BAUMAN, U.S. COAST GUARD

The personal kindness of Ralph and Lisa Shanks made a recent trip to the California lighthouses a memorable occasion. Like every lighthouse enthusiast, I was anxious to visit all the lighthouse structures that are still in existence, whether still maintained by the United States Coast Guard or by others. The Shanks' knowledge and experience in lighthouse matters made my pilgrimage highly enjoyable and complete. I was sure that their research in depth had identified each and every light. Their providing of stories and histories that make each of our lighthouses fascinating and unique heightened the enjoyment of each visit. In recording the stories of dedicated service by the United States Coast Guard and its predecessor services, the United States Lighthouse Service and the United States Life-Saving Service, the Shanks have contributed significantly to the maritime history of the California Coast. In these bicentennial years of the Lighthouse Service and the United States Coast Guard, a book detailing the history, dedication and valor of light keepers and life savers of the unique waters of San Francisco Bay is most appropriate.

I have spent many hours being entertained and fascinated by Lisa and Ralph Shanks, both in person and in their writings. *The waters of the Golden Gate could have no finer chroniclers.*

Rear Admiral Richard A. Bauman, USCG (Retired), served as First Chief of the U.S. Coast Guard Office of Navigation. He was responsible for the nation's 70,000 maritime aids to navigation and was also Commandant of the First U.S. Coast Guard District.

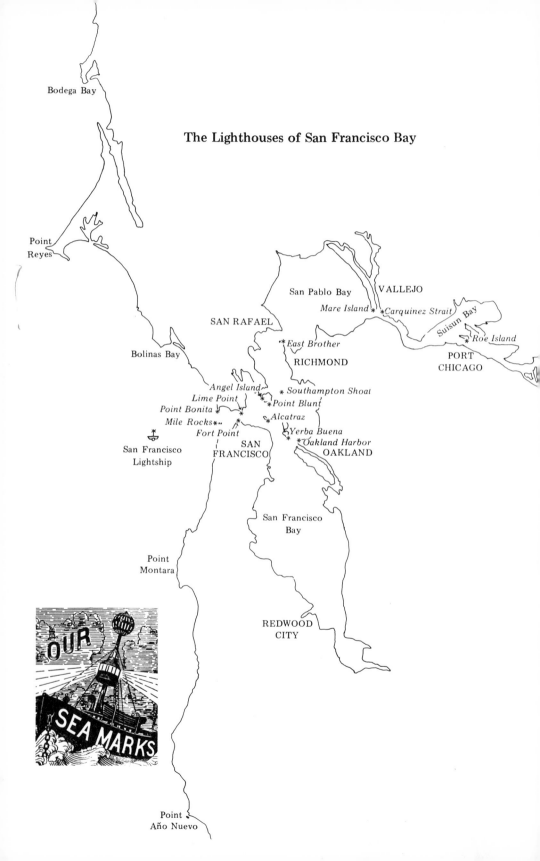

The Lighthouses of San Francisco Bay

Bodega Bay

Point Reyes

Point Reyes

San Pablo Bay

VALLEJO

Mare Island * *Carquinez Strait*

SAN RAFAEL

Suisun Bay

Roe Island

Bolinas Bay

East Brother

RICHMOND

PORT CHICAGO

Angel Island
Lime Point
Point Bonita
Mile Rocks
Fort Point

Southampton Shoal

Point Blunt

Alcatraz

San Francisco Lightship

SAN FRANCISCO

Yerba Buena
Oakland Harbor

OAKLAND

San Francisco Bay

Point Montara

REDWOOD CITY

Point Año Nuevo

OUR SEA MARKS

PREFACE

I have been around California lighthouses all my life. I first climbed the steps to a lighthouse lantern room in 1949 under the guidance of Wayne Piland, keeper of Crescent City lighthouse up near the California-Oregon border. Keeper Piland taught me how the lighthouse operated from the top of the tower to the depths of the basement. He cared deeply about his profession and its vital importance to mariners. He taught me about the sea by actions and by words.

One of my most vivid memories from childhood is of Wayne Piland, my younger brother Don and me launching the station life raft on the treacherous shore of Crescent City Lighthouse's island. "You almost always launch from the south side of a California island, Ralph," Wayne Piland advised me. We launched among huge boulders, many taller than I. Don and I climbed in the raft first. Keeper Piland, in his hip boots, was almost knocked off his feet by the surf. It was instantly clear—without a word being said—that I was to handle the raft if Wayne Piland should be knocked down or lose his grip on the raft.

That was a big responsibility when you are only eight. But climb aboard Keeper Piland did and we rowed over the low, broad swells and around the island to the north. There were massive rocks off the lighthouse and on their vertical sides we could see starfish. There was one particularly spectacular starfish we all really wanted to see, but it was high up on a rock and firmly attached. The keeper gave me the oars and I held the raft carefully, stern first, to the rock despite the surge. Piland stretched up high and retrieved the coveted starfish. The light keeper loved and respected marine life and we all admired the big starfish. Back we rowed, over the low swells, through the violent surf to the boulder strewn beach. Landing was easier, skillfully handled by Wayne Piland. It was a skill I wanted very much to master.

I learned a great deal those first days at a lighthouse: respect for the power of the sea, admiration for its strange and wonderful creatures, a bit about boat handling, and a first lesson about how to operate a lighthouse. This was a fascinating life, but a no nonsense life since you soon learned that people's lives depended upon a reliable lighthouse.

Every time we were in Crescent City, I begged my parents to take us to visit Keeper Piland and his wife, Martha, at their lighthouse. We returned many times and every occasion was a thrill. It began a friendship between light keeper and boy that never wavered. Over 40 years later, Wayne Piland and I were still friends.

I didn't know it at the time but this was an ideal introduction to California lighthouse keeping. Crescent City Lighthouse was built in the original 1850s style of the state's very first beacons. It was by then the last sentinel in the state to be operated as a one-keeper family station, as many early day lighthouses had been staffed. Crescent City Lighthouse was a near duplicate of the original Alcatraz Island sentinel, the first American lighthouse on the Pacific Coast.

It is strange, but I never intended to write about lighthouses. I always felt more at home in a lighthouse lantern room or on board a Coast Guard vessel than writing. But during the 1960s and 1970s, the Coast Guard began automating and unmanning California's lighthouses. Many light stations were being abandoned to the weather and to vandals. Lantern rooms and lenses were being removed, the ultimate desecration of a lighthouse. Some stations were still active but were closed to the public. The Coast Guard suddenly found itself with many beautiful, historic buildings in its care and no clear plan as to their preservation. The American people, who had visited the light stations during over a century of manned operation, suddenly faced no trespassing signs.

As I visited both contemporary Coast Guard light keepers as well as the old veterans of the U.S. Lighthouse Service, I felt a deep sense of loss. It is a loss I feel yet to this day. The keepers, their wives and children all began sharing the stories of their lives at the lighthouses. I began recording the stories of the Lighthouse Service and Coast Guard keepers and their families. As I had visited the large majority of California lighthouses while they were still actively manned light stations and knew so many keepers, I found that there seemed to be no one as qualified or interested in recording this fascinating aspect of California's maritime history. Having been trained in California lighthouse matters since childhood, having the blessing of many lighthouse friends, and having a master's degree in sociology, all combined to offer me no excuse for not recording the history of our great California lighthouse keepers and Coast Guardsmen. I began to feel as much at home writing books as I did in the light towers.

My first book was *Lighthouses of San Francisco Bay*, published in 1976. When the book came out, Karl Kortum, director of the National Maritime Museum in San Francisco, sagely told me, "Ralph, as soon as you write a book, all kinds of new information will come to you." Karl was right. Since I wrote *Lighthouses of San Francisco Bay,* many more lighthouse keepers, Coast Guardsmen, and their families have been interviewed, and numerous sources of new written information have been uncovered. Repeated visits to lighthouses and lifeboat stations have also provided a wealth of information. Many gracious lighthouse and life-saving enthusiasts, librarians, researchers, and others have provided valuable help as well.

Thus, in this new book, *Guardians of the Golden Gate: Lighthouses and Lifeboat Stations of San Francisco Bay,* my wife, editor Lisa Woo Shanks, and I again bring you the classic stories and historic photographs from *Lighthouses of San Francisco Bay*. These accounts have been enlarged as new information and participants have been encountered. Best of all, we also have found dozens of new stories to enrich our knowledge of San Francisco Bay Area lighthouses and lifeboat stations. We have also added dozens of previously unpublished photos for your enjoyment.

The book includes an important section on the surfmen of the U.S. Life-Saving Service and the U.S. Coast Guard. Throughout the book there are exciting accounts of search and rescue operations. But beyond this, we have included the amazing history of the U.S. Life-Saving Service in California, forerunner of the Coast Guard's search and rescue branch. We also try to draw your attention to 6 particularly historic Coast Guard Lifeboat Stations which stand today: Point Reyes, Fort Point, Humboldt Bay, Arena Cove, Pt. Arguello, and Bolinas Bay.

For those of you who have read *Lighthouses of San Francisco Bay*, I hope you will understand why I left all the classic stories in for new readers. For you veterans, I hope the wealth of new information and the countless wonderful stories graciously shared by dozens of lighthouse keepers and Coast Guardsmen and their families please you. It has taken over 12 years to research this book and bring it into print for you.

Join us now as we climb the iron stairways of the sentinels and relight the ancient wicks. There are watches to be stood and beaches to patrol. There are new lighthouse keepers with whom to share the watches. There are new Coast Guardsmen and women with lifeboats prepared to pass through the surf. Let's take the lantern and walk on down the beach. They are there, on watch, awaiting our arrival.

Yerba Buena by Lisa Shanks

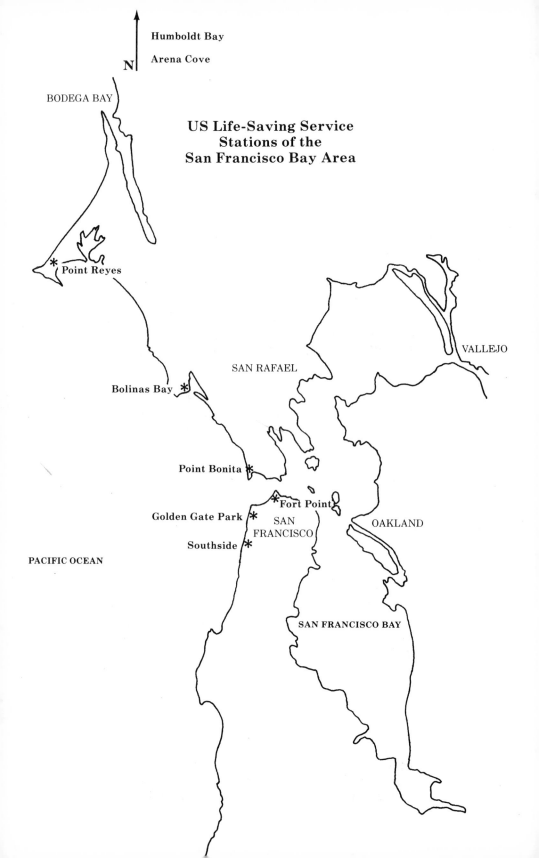

N

Humboldt Bay

Arena Cove

BODEGA BAY

US Life-Saving Service
Stations of the
San Francisco Bay Area

* Point Reyes

VALLEJO

SAN RAFAEL

Bolinas Bay *

Point Bonita *

*Fort Point

Golden Gate Park *

SAN
FRANCISCO

OAKLAND

Southside *

PACIFIC OCEAN

SAN FRANCISCO BAY

INTRODUCTION: LIGHTHOUSES AND LIFEBOAT STATIONS

California's coast is rich in maritime adventure. The earliest sailors were the California Indians. Such tribes as the Chumash, Gabrieliño, and Yurok, frequently ventured out to sea. But Native American travel was almost solely by daylight. The Spanish followed the Indian sailors and, although they did sail at night, built no lighthouses nor life-saving stations in California.

By the early 1850s, the California coast was still dark. No lighthouses guided mariners despite a growing population and increased commerce. Neither was there any organized rescue service. Mariners navigated with little assistance and if they wrecked they could expect almost nothing in the way of help.

It wasn't that navigational aids or life-saving services were unheard of in 1850. Lighthouses had been invented in Africa at least by 280 B.C. and probably existed well before that date. Africa, Europe and Asia could all boast lighthouses since ancient times. Lighthouses had reached the Atlantic coast of the United States by 1716 when Boston Light was completed.

The world's first organized life-saving service manning lifeboats had begun in China prior to 1750 on the Yangtze River, upstream from Shanghai. In 1824, the British followed the Chinese example and established their first life-saving institution which evolved into the Royal National Lifeboat Institution (R.N.L.I.), and today remains Britain's lifeboat service. In the United States, the Massachusetts Humane Society, established in 1785, erected the first American life-saving station at Cohasset in 1807.

But California had none of these. Spain and, later, Mexico owned the region and California was a distant and unimportant part of both country's empires. All of this changed in 1849 when gold was discovered and in short order America seized California from Mexico. This resulted in a tremendous increase in shipping along the Pacific Coast, particularly in California. The very center of this trade was San Francisco Bay.

The first chain of permanent buildings constructed in California had been the Catholic missions. Twenty-one in number, the Spanish began erecting them in 1769 and completed the task at Sonoma in 1823. Today, they remain among California's most historic and treasured buildings.

But a second chain of structures, equally beautiful and possessing their own fascinating history, was begun by the Americans in 1852 and was not completed until the 1930s. These were California's lighthouses.

Swirling seas and a distant breaking beach isolate dangerous Mile Rocks lighthouse in the Golden Gate, C. 1960. (U.S. Coast Guard)

Like the missions, the lighthouses were erected to aid in the settlement and development of California. Similarly, both chains were built to last. Most of the missions and most of the lighthouses still stand today. Both were begun for humanitarian and economic reasons. The missions had the function of converting the California Indians to Christianity and providing a native labor force for the colonizers. The lighthouses were constructed to safely mark the sea lanes for maritime commerce, thus saving the lives of countless voyagers and their cargoes.

There were also important differences between the two chains. The missions had the stamp of Spain and Mexico upon them and have always remained Latin institutions. The lighthouses, on the other hand, have always been American, with a heavy mark of the New England Yankee.

Beginning at Alcatraz Island, the Americans constructed 60 lighthouses in California. Thirty-six of these remain today, and although some are sadly altered or have been allowed to fall into disrepair, over two dozen are perfectly preserved and rank with the best examples of American lighthouse architecture.

The most highly developed lighthouse system on the entire Pacific Coast was on San Francisco Bay. The Bay had more lighthouses within its confines than any other comparably sized area on the Pacific Coast. Not only was development intensive, it also began earlier here than anywhere in the West. The first West Coast district headquarters of the U.S. Lighthouse Service was established on San Francisco Bay. The first American lighthouse of the Pacific Coast was built at Alcatraz Island in 1854. The first West Coast lighthouse depot in the West was on the Bay, and beacons from the Mexican border north to Oregon were, at one time, all serviced from Yerba Buena Island. The first fog signal on the Pacific Coast was here, too, at Point Bonita. Finally, the variable character of the Bay itself was to give rise to an almost unparalleled diversity of lighthouse architectural styles. Probably only Massachusetts Bay and Chesapeake Bay ranked with San Francisco Bay in their wide array of harbor lights.

The sailor's guidebook, *The Pacific Coast Pilot*, describes San Francisco Bay as "the largest harbor on the Pacific Coast of the United States." It is, the *Pilot* adds, a harbor which "is more properly described as a series of connecting bays and harbors of which San Francisco Bay proper, San Pablo Bay, and Suisun Bay are the largest." On these waters there is extensive foreign and domestic shipping and large numbers of pleasure craft. These vessels ply a highly variable body of water. There are deep-water channels and muddy shoals, low marshlands and high, bold headlands. There are gale winds and sudden, unexpected calms. Dangers include incredibly strong currents and numerous rocks, islands, and shoals. All these hazards to navigation are often shrouded in fog. There is a summer fog which blows in from the sea and a winter fog, locally known as "tule fog", which originates in interior marshlands.[1] These physical and climatic characteristics combine to make San Francisco Bay one of the most challenging bays in America.

The diverse character of the land and the water meant that early mariners faced countless difficulties in navigating the Bay. It also meant that navigational aids, particularly lighthouses, had to be built

---

[1]Tule is a tall reed which grows in marshy areas of both salt and freshwater.

In a scene repeated countless times along all of America's coasts, the U.S. Life-Saving Service goes to the rescue. The surfmen believed that regulations said you had to go out no matter what the conditions, but the regulations said nothing about your chances of coming back alive. The motto of the rescuers thus became "You have to go out, but you don't have to come in." A sign stating this motto hung in the boat room at Humboldt Bay Coast Guard Lifeboat Station at least as late as the 1970s. In this photo the crew of the Klipsan Beach, Washington, Life-Saving Station go the aid of the Alice in 1909. (National Maritime Museum)

in locations which differed widely from one place to the next. Variable topography required that the lighthouses be constructed using a great array of architectural and engineering techniques. The result was fascinating! There were tall towers and short ones; beacons combined with dwellings and others separated from the living quarters; stations on shore, on islands, on rocks, and even in the water. There were lighthouses of iron, wood, cement, rock, and brick. Some stations were cozy family light stations, while others were lonely, isolated places.

Despite the diversity, the beacons of San Francisco Bay all had certain things in common. As with lighthouses everywhere, they were built to warn of a danger or to mark a channel, or both. Lighthouses perform these functions in several ways. First, they show a light. The major requirements of the light are that it is bright and that it can be readily distinguished from other lights in the vicinity. In the early days, brightness alone was enough to distinguish a beacon, and lighthouses often displayed fixed lights (a steady, non-flashing beam). Later, as more lights came into use, it was necessary for almost all lighthouses to show lights which flashed in some identifiable pattern. Mariners came to carry a book, called a *Light List*, which gave the various flashing characteristics of all the West Coast's sentinels.

Making the light both bright and causing it to flash were not easy matters. Early lighthouses were illuminated by oil lamps, and these, of course, cast a rather feeble, steady beam. The problem of making the light appear both bright and flashing was solved by a Frenchman, Augustin Fresnel, in 1822, using gigantic lenses often consisting of hundreds of prisms. When California's lighthouses were built, they were equipped with Fresnel lenses.

At the time California became a state, America's lighthouses were under the jurisdiction of the Treasury Department's fifth auditor, Stephen Pleasonton. By the mid-nineteenth century, Pleasonton's reign had received so much criticism that control of the lighthouses was taken out of his hands. On October 9, 1852, Congress established a nine-member Lighthouse Board made up of engineers, scientists, and military men to administer a civilian organization which would come to be called the U.S. Lighthouse Service. This organization would operate virtually all of the lighthouses in the United States from 1852 until it was merged into the U.S. Coast Guard in 1939.

The new Lighthouse Board set about improving and enlarging the American lighthouse system. A naval officer, Washington A. Bartlett, was sent to Paris to acquire 63 Fresnel lenses to be used in modernizing existing lighthouses and in equipping new stations on the Pacific Coast, an area devoid of navigational aids at that time. Part of Bartlett's original shipment of lenses was sent to California, and lenses of the Fresnel type would come to be used at virtually every light station on the California coast.

All of California's lighthouses were in the 12th (later, in 1910, re-numbered the 18th) U.S. Lighthouse Service District, with headquarters in the old Customs House in San Francisco. While some unlighted buoys and other supplies were kept at small "buoy depots" at Terminal Island in Los Angeles Harbor, at San Diego's Ballast Point, and on Humboldt Bay's North Spit, the 12th District's main supply depot for California's lighthouses, lightships, and lighted buoys was on San Francisco Bay's Yerba Buena Island. Pier 15 in San Francisco supplemented the island lighthouse depot as a facility for loading tenders.

The new lenses were magnificent. They were composed of hand ground glass prisms and glass "bull's eyes" mounted in a gleaming brass framework. On large lenses there were over 1000 individual pieces of glass, and at night all the lenses gave the appearance of gigantic, glistening diamonds. An oil lamp was placed inside the lens, using a glass chimney to carry smoke up to a ball-shaped vent on the lighthouse roof. At night, the lamp was lighted, its diverse rays being focused into powerful beams by the prisms. The Fresnel lenses were so efficient at focusing the lamp rays that beams could often be seen for over 20 miles at sea.

For some lighthouses, an immovable fixed lens with a steady light beam was sufficient to warn mariners. But for most, some sort of flashing pattern had to be created so there could be no question as to which lighthouse was in sight. To create a flashing effect, the entire lens was usually placed on wheels or ball bearings which ran in a track at the base of the lens. A clockwork drive, powered by a weight, was used to rotate the lens. Several times a night, keepers would rewind the weight to keep the lens turning. Such flashing lenses had their prisms and bull's eyes arranged in panels. As the lens turned, light beams showed steadily from each panel, but to the mariner at sea the light appeared to be flashing. The effect was created because each time the panel lined up with a viewer, the viewer could see a flash of light, but in between the panels the light appeared to go dark. It was an ingenious device and is still in use today.

Fresnel classified his lenses by order, the largest being the first order and the smallest the sixth order. The following chart indicates the major types and their approximate size.

Mile Rocks third order lens. (R. Shanks)

Order	Height	Inside Diameter
First	7' 10"	6' 1"
Second	6' 1"	4' 7"
Third	4' 8"	3' 3"
Third and $1/2$	3' 0"	2' 5 $1/2$"
Fourth	2' 4"	1' 8"
Fifth	1' 8"	1' 3"
Sixth	1' 5"	1' 0"

Large first or second order lenses were used primarily at coastal lights where it was important for the light to be seen from many miles out to sea. Smaller order lenses were used most often in harbors, fourth and fifth order lenses being the most common sizes used on San Francisco Bay.

In addition to a light, most California lighthouses had a fog signal. The fog signal might be a whistle, a horn, a bell, a siren, or even a cannon. All fog signals had the common feature of emitting a patterned sound warning during foggy weather. Light lists also included fog signal characteristics; and just as mariners could identify a lighthouse by its flashing characteristic, they could also recognize it by the number, duration, or frequency of blasts emitted by the fog signal. On San Francisco Bay, fog was the worst hazard to navigation, and all of the light stations were equipped with fog signals.

Lighthouses also aided the mariner on clear days as day marks. For those unfamiliar with the coast, early light lists often included illustrations of light stations to aid in identification. The distinctively shaped lighthouses provided unquestionable confirmation of a ship's position.

Today, modern lighthouses also aid the seaman by means of a radio beacon, a device which, like lights and fog signals, sends a repetitive signal by which mariners can fix their position. Thus, lighthouses now broadcast their warnings using radio waves as well as light and sound waves.

The old-time lighthouses were staffed by at least one and sometimes as many as five attendants. These attendants were called keepers, or less formally "wickies", referring to their duty of trimming the wicks of oil lamps. Lighthouse keepers have been stereotyped as being only white men. In actuality, there were many women keepers, and under the Coast Guard; Asian Americans, Black Americans, American Indians and Hispanic Americans were commonly lighthouse keepers. These men and women served with admirable records.

Today, all stations in California have been converted to automatic operation and have been unmanned. While some have been completely closed down, most light stations are still in use as important navigational aids. The active stations are still under the jurisdiction of the 11th Coast

Guard District's Aids to Navigation Office located at 400 Oceangate Blvd., Long Beach, CA.

Although all of the lighthouses in California are now unmanned, most will be very necessary as aids to navigation during the coming years. Modern technology has not rendered lighthouses obsolete. As one responsible oil tanker pilot told me, "There is nothing like a lighthouse to give you complete certainty of your position."

No navigational aid, be it a lighthouse, radar, loran, or buoys, has ever been able to completely eliminate shipwrecks. In 1989, in a matter of weeks, the United States witnessed four oil tanker wrecks resulting in severe damage to our environment. During the same period, a Soviet ocean liner rammed an iceberg, sending passengers and crew to struggle for survival in lifeboats and on ice floes. We sometimes hear the false claim made that lighthouses are no longer needed today with all the electronic navigational aids available to mariners. Yet repeated wrecks and frequent statements by seafaring men and women refute this notion. With record numbers of boaters afloat, many with limited knowledge and navigational equipment, the need for our lighthouses and buoys is greater than ever. With ships now carrying cargo capable of unprecedented environmental damage, this is no time to downgrade America's lighthouse system. I have had bar pilots, oil tanker pilots, commercial fishermen, yachtsmen, and Coast Guard personnel all tell me of cases where lighthouses assisted them at critical moments when navigating. When the historic sailing vessel *C.A. Thayer* was brought from the Pacific Northwest to San Francisco Bay for preservation, it was Mendocino County's Point Cabrillo lighthouse that warned of an approaching lee shore at the last moment and saved the ship. When it was proposed that the Golden Gate's Point Bonita lighthouse be relocated, it was the San Francisco bar pilots, who bring enormous cargo vessels into the harbor, who most strongly protested.

Lest we forget the dangers and frequency of shipwrecks, I have included a section on the rescue work of the early U.S. Life-Saving Service. Parent of the Coast Guard's search and rescue operations, the United States Life-Saving Service was founded in 1871 to provide an organized and continuing effort to protect the crews, passengers, and cargo of ships in distress along the more traveled and dangerous portions of America's coastlines.

The U.S. Life-Saving Service was organized similarly to the Lighthouse Service. Headquartered in Washington, D.C., it too divided the United States into districts. Its geographically largest district was on the Pacific Coast and comprised California, Oregon, Washington, and Alaska. Most life-saving stations had a keeper (the officer-in-charge) and a crew of six to eight surfmen. The keeper directed most rescues, ran the station, and trained his crews. During the early days, the stations were equipped with only unpowered pulling boats which had to be

A surfman and his bride. The Life-Saving Service provided no disability pay and no life insurance. If her husband drowned, a wife was left destitute. Nor was family housing provided, except for the keeper. The number six on the surfman's shoulder indicated he was the sixth ranked among a six to eight man crew, undoubtedly new to the Service. The couple would have faced hard times and nights of worry during fearful storms. In many ways, the wives were as courageous as their husbands. (Author's collection)

A large breaker lifts a Life-Saving Service lifeboat into the air during a surf drill on the bar. Drills were held in the surf on the nation's roughest bars and off our most dangerous beaches. In the background is a train building the harbor entrance jetty. Coquille River Life-Saving Station, Bandon, Oregon, C. 1900. (National Maritime Museum)

rowed and with beach carts that had to be hauled over the sands by the men themselves.

The Life-Saving Service was a civilian organization, operating in California from 1878 until 1915. In 1915 it was merged with the Revenue Cutter Service to create the modern Coast Guard. During the Life-Saving Service era, 1871—1915, rescue stations were generally called "life-saving stations". After 1915, the Coast Guard usually referred to its marine rescue facilities as "lifeboat stations". Most life-saving stations originally launched their boats by hand while lifeboat stations were equipped with a marine railway for launching its lifeboats. Having a marine railway (often called a launchway) was an important development in rescue work since it eventually allowed stations to be equipped with heavy motor lifeboats.

The life-saving stations and lifeboat stations equal the lighthouses in historic importance and fascination. Sadly, a smaller proportion of these historic rescue stations survive today than do lighthouses. Only six remain in all of California. Humboldt Bay Lifeboat Station, near Eureka, is still active and in Coast Guard hands. San Francisco's Fort Point Lifeboat Station was active as late as 1990 and, hopefully, will become a part of the Fort Point National Historic Site of Golden Gate National Recreation Area. Point Reyes Lifeboat Station, with one of the last two operational lifeboat marine railways on the entire Pacific Coast and an operating 36-foot motor lifeboat, is now owned by Point Reyes National Seashore. Bolinas Bay Life-Saving Station is the College of Marin's biology station and its lookout tower a private residence. Arena Cove Life-Saving Station, in the town of Point Arena, is privately owned, reportedly to become a bed and breakfast inn. Its lookout tower is owned by PG&E. Point Arguello Lifeboat Station still stands on the shore of Vandenberg Air Force Base near Lompoc. It is used as a base recreational facility. All are historic treasures equal to lighthouses in importance.

Most lighthouses and lifeboat stations were built at unusually spectacular points along the coast, often at locations of important events in early California history. Some sites are botanically or anthropologically significant, and all offer rare vistas for the traveler. In recent years the National Park Service, the Coast Guard, the California Department of Parks and Recreation, many historical societies, and other organizations, businesses, and individuals who care about our maritime heritage, have made significant progress in preserving our lighthouses, lightships, and lifeboat stations.

As will be described in this book, many San Francisco Bay lifeboat and light stations are architecturally unique and many have played key roles in maritime history. All have fascinating stories. If the reader comes to share the author's love of the old beacons and rescue stations, then the book will have succeeded.

* * *

Note to the reader: All locations mentioned in the book are in California unless otherwise noted. We hope to make this a three-part book series. If you would like to be notified of future books, please send your name and address to: Costaño Books, P.O. Box 355, Petaluma, CA 94953.

With lanterns in hand two beach patrolmen set off in opposite directions after exchanging "checks" (tokens) showing they have met at the ends of their respective patrols. Such exchanges of checks occurred on Ocean Beach in San Francisco at a post (west of about Ulloa Street) when Golden Gate Park and Southside stations' patrolmen met. (U.S. Coast Guard Academy Library)

First Alcatraz Lighthouse in its later days. A wooden addition had been built to provide more space in the little lighthouse, February 1908. (U.S. Coast Guard)

ALCATRAZ ISLAND

Prior to California's statehood, its aids to navigation were primitive and few. Open fires and a few oil lamps dimly and sporadically marked the Pacific Coast. The discovery of gold in the state brought an unprecedented increase in shipping beginning in 1849. By 1852, funds had been appropriated by Congress to provide the West Coast with much needed light stations.

The nine-member U.S. Lighthouse Board was created during this period. The Board set about modernizing lighthouses by substituting highly efficient Fresnel lenses for less efficient Argand lamps and reflectors. A contract was also issued by the U.S. Secretary of the Treasury to build seven lighthouses in California and one at Cape Disappointment, Washington. A sailing ship, the *Oriole,* was chartered and, after a difficult voyage around Cape Horn, arrived in California. The ship was loaded with lumber, machinery, tools, and skilled workmen, ready to begin lighting the Pacific Coast.

Scouts had been sent ahead to determine the best location for each beacon. Alcatraz Island, with its strategic position just inside the entrance to San Francisco Bay, was chosen as the first construction site. Work began in rainy December at the very summit, near the southeast end of the island. By the time the summer fog began to roll in eight months later, the station was nearly complete.

The sentinel was the prototype of the Lighthouse Service's new design, a California cottage lighthouse, which featured a dwelling surrounding a short tower.[1] Eventually, seven California lighthouses would be erected with basically the same California cottage lighthouse plans. Although providing a rather compact living and working area, the circular stairway to the lantern was but a few feet from the keeper's bedroom and tending the light did not require a long walk, often through foul weather, as was common with other designs. The design was adopted with the assumption that the station would be operated

---

[1]The California cottage lighthouse has been previously called a Cape Cod cottage style lighthouse. The dwelling portions' architectural style appears to have its origins in Scotland, rather than Cape Cod. Nearly identical houses can be seen in Scotland today. The name "Cape Cod" has been used in lighthouse books in recent years when referring to this type of light. No such lighthouses were ever built at or near Cape Cod. Most of these structures were built in California. "California cottage lighthouse" is a more accurate term. California light stations originally equipped with California cottage style lighthouses included: Point Loma, Santa Barbara, Point Conception, Point Pinos, Fort Point, Alcatraz Island, and Crescent City. A few similar lighthouses were built in Washington and elsewhere but lacked the architectural uniformity of the California stations.

Alcatraz Island showing the prison beginning to overshadow the original lighthouse. The California cottage style lighthouse is at the very summit of the island. The fog bell house is the little building furthest left, C. 1900. (U.S. Army, Presidio of San Francisco Museum)

by one keeper. The little structure was really adequate only so long as the beacon remained a one-family operation. The building was two stories high in addition to an ample basement. Through the very center of the building, running from the basement up through the roof, was the tower. Its circular staircase provided access from one story to another and the dwelling was actually built around the tower. Above the level of the dwelling's roof, the tower held the lamp-cleaning room and atop that was the lantern room. The 50-foot lighthouse was painted white with a black lantern room and black trim, a paint scheme that remains common on California lighthouses even today.

From mid-1852 until well into 1854, the lighthouse was conspicuous only during the day. The new French third order lens did not arrive until 1853 and budgetary problems delayed installation. Finally, on June 1, 1854, the fixed (non-flashing) white light was shown and the first American lighthouse on the Pacific Cost was in operation!

It soon became apparent that the California coast was subject to fog of almost unrivaled frequency, which often rendered the light ineffective. Only two years after establishing the light, a fog bell had to be added. The bell was rung by hand, and the task of tending the light and ringing the bell during the recurring fog may have been too much for the poor keeper. At any rate, the lighthouse inspector repeatedly found him absent from his post, and he seems to have earned the dubious distinction of being the first light keeper in California to be fired.

The first Alcatraz keeper was one of the few unreliable wickies in the entire history of California light attendants. His successors at Alcatraz certainly did better. They also had much easier duty when machinery was later installed which, powered by a clockwork mechanism that only had to be wound once every four hours, automatically struck the bell at

The first American lighthouse on the Pacific Coast. Built atop Alcatraz Island on San Francisco Bay, this pioneer sentinel was also the first built in the California cottage architectural style with a light tower surrounded by a dwelling, 1908. (U.S. Coast Guard)

prescribed intervals.

By 1886, Captain Leeds, a former sailor, was in charge of the light. Leeds took real pride in his station and spent a great deal of effort in making improvements. He added several rooms onto the lighthouse and modernized the existing ones. He also constructed a two-foot high wall around the beacon and filled it with good, rich soil for gardening. Leeds' previous gardening attempts may have led him to be one of the first to call Alcatraz "The Rock".

By the 1890s, Leeds had an assistant, C.E. Engelbrecht, and the men divided the night into two watches, changing at midnight and alternately taking the first half of the night. The island's post office was also located at the lighthouse during Leeds' tenure.

In 1901, a new fog signal station was added at the northwest end of Alcatraz. Here a small, frame bell house was erected to hold the new, 3000-pound, mechanically struck fog bell. The following year, a new flashing lens replaced the old fixed (non-flashing) one. San Francisco was becoming a metropolis and the fixed light was too easily confused with other bright lights around the Bay, and so its days came to an end. Technically of the fourth order, the new lens consisted of relatively small panels with "bull's-eye" shaped prisms mounted in brass.[2]

The change to a flashing lens probably was prompted by a general upgrading of San Francisco's navigational aids after the loss of the *Rio de Janeiro* in 1901. Inadequate fog signals were blamed for the tragic wreck at Fort Point Ledge. Later that year, two of the North Pacific Coast Railroad passenger ferries, the *San Rafael* and the *Saucelito*, collided off Alcatraz and the *San Rafael* went to the bottom. The Alcatraz fog bell had done its duty well, however, and negligence on the ferry captain's part was blamed.

The last keeper of the West's first lighthouse was George W. Young, a tall gentleman with a snow-white beard, who, in his seventy years, had wandered "every part of the globe except the Poles". Young had been in the Lighthouse Service for 22 years and came to The Rock from the Farallon Islands.

Young had three assistants and they stood four-hour nightly watches in addition to beginning their daily work at 8:30 each morning. Each evening when the sun disappeared in the west, the sundown gun would boom at the military fortress below the light, announcing sunset. In a few minutes night would sweep over the Bay and the old keeper would begin his labors. He would climb the winding stairs to the lamp-cleaning room, then up an iron ladder, through a little trap door, and into the lantern room. He would raise the yellow curtains from the windows, remove a covering from the lens apparatus, light a lamp, and place it inside the lens. Then Young would grip the crank and wind the seventy-pound clockwork weight. After a brake was released, the lens began slowly revolving and the pioneer lighthouse would serve mariners another night.

If fog threatened, Young and his assistants had a "new-fangled" electric attachment that allowed them to start or stop the mechanically struck fog bells without even leaving their quarters. Young summed

---

[2]The Lighthouse Service records indicate, and some writers have claimed, that the original Alcatraz lens was transferred to Cape St. Elias lighthouse in Alaska. A lens from this lighthouse is on display in the Cordova town museum. This lens is not the original Alcatraz lens since it is reported to be a flashing type lens, not a fixed type lens as originally used at Alcatraz. The original Alcatraz lens was exhibited in San Francisco in 1915 at the Panama-Pacific International Exhibition's Lighthouse Service display. It may have served in Cape St. Elias for a time later, but must have been removed. Perhaps a reader can locate it.

The first American lighthouse on the Pacific Coast was Alcatraz's beacon, a California cottage lighthouse with a lighthouse surrounded by a keeper's dwelling. Captain Leeds, principal keeper, poses in the foreground, while his assistant stands on the lantern room balcony. (San Francisco Public Library)

Construction of the second Alcatraz Island lighthouse, 1909. This lighthouse is the one which stands today. (U.S. Coast Guard)

up his life at Alcatraz, "It's a pretty slow life here, but when you've wandered around the world for over half a century, it's good to have a nice, quiet berth (when) the pleasant memories of the past come to you in the silence of the night . . ."

On April 18, 1906, the night wasn't so silent. The infamous San Francisco earthquake struck, throwing down a chimney from the lighthouse and slightly cracking the structure. But the sentinel survived, perhaps in part because of improvements that had been made back in 1868. Around that time, extensive repairs were needed, so new brickwork was added to the tower, a new gallery floor built, and the glass in the lantern room reset. Some of this reconstruction work probably made the building safer.

The fog bell houses were relocated several times and more modern bell striking devices installed periodically. The increasing presence of the Army on the island had its influence too. A real effort was made to keep the light station grounds and buildings attractive and clean "so as to conform in neatness to the military post in which it is situated". The Lighthouse Service, with its demanding inspectors, was not about to allow Alcatraz Island Light Station to become subject to complaints by some Army officer.

Alcatraz Island had become the site of an extensive military prison in the 19th century and its buildings were ever increasing in size and number. By 1909, the prison had so overshadowed the beacon that a new lighthouse was begun. The new lighthouse soon towered above the east side of the old sentinel. It, too, was a fine structure—an octagonal reinforced concrete sentinel rising majestically 84 feet above the ground and over 200 feet above the Bay. Inside, beautiful iron spiral stairs led far up to the lamp-cleaning room and a vertical ladder ran from there into the compact lantern room. The lens was transferred from the old structure to the new and the role of the West's first lighthouse ended. The 1906 earthquake had cracked the stone tower and toppled its chimneys, but it was the rising prison walls which forever closed out its friendly rays.

The grim penal institution continued to grow as it was transferred from military to civilian administration. At the base of the tower, keepers' dwellings had been built in two wings, with an oil room and carpenter shop underneath. Next door were the homes of the warden and the prison doctor. Considering the not-too-select company Alcatraz offered, with hundreds of America's most hardened criminals sharing The Rock, the lighthouse area was the elite neighborhood of the island.

There was generally little contact between light keepers and prisoners. But during the 1920s, according to an old lighthouse yarn, one of the Alcatraz light keepers became very interested in all the infamous criminals on the island. His interest led to long hours of reading detective stories and looking carefully at pictures of the criminals. One day he looked down on a line of passing prisoners. The keeper saw one he recognized from his reading!

The wickie called out to the guards, "Hold that line! I've spotted one that's wanted!" The prison officials thought the keeper was crazy. Everybody locked-up on Alcatraz was wanted. But it turned out the observant wickie was indeed correct. The criminal was wanted for murder. He was serving on a lesser offense under another identity, a rather creative method of "hiding out". The inmate eventually admitted the murder under questioning.

Keepers' children rode the prison boat to San Francisco to attend school. The same boat made runs to Fort Mason with each change of guards. Keepers' wives, intent upon shopping, caught a bus filled with departing guards and rode down the winding prison street to the landing. From a gun tower above the landing, a key would be lowered to the boathouse and everyone would climb aboard the launch. All passengers were counted both when leaving the prison island and again upon reaching Fort Mason. In those days, the wives typically went shopping about once every three weeks, and milk and bread had to be frozen to keep. After dinner, garbage could not be routinely tossed away. Anything which might be worked to create a weapon had to be tossed into a special garbage security location. There, it was beaten, broken, and cast into the Bay.

If a prison break was attempted, the keepers were told to lock their doors and windows and remain inside. (A special door led directly from their quarters into the lighthouse.) During searches, they were not allowed to leave the island. In 1946, the prison's worst escape attempt and riot occurred. Many guards were captured and rioting convicts seized control of cell block "D", just 150 feet from the light station. Keeper Edward Schneider remembered that "bullets whizzed around us" and things became so extreme that the U.S. Marines were called in. The Marines landed and stormed the cell block amid bullets, exploding hand grenades, and a raging fire. By the following day, the "Battle of Alcatraz" was over and the authorities were again in command.

Large signs warned that any vessel coming within a certain distance of Alcatraz Island would be fired upon by guards. For Bay pleasure boaters, Alcatraz offered special hazards. In 1950, two couples and another man found themselves in a very scary situation. Their cabin cruiser broke down in the early morning off Alcatraz in heavy fog. Abandoning their drifting boat, they managed to climb ashore on the rocks of Alcatraz. There they sat, "scared to death" that they might be shot by guards confusing them for participants in an escape attempt.

The second Alcatraz lighthouse was necessarily much taller than its predecessor. Keepers lived in the dual-winged dwelling and used the curved lower story as a carpenter shop and oil room. (National Archives)

Alcatraz had a well-earned reputation as a no-nonsense prison where you didn't take chances. After shivering and shaking for hours, a guard finally spotted the five stranded mariners as the fog lifted. Fortunately, he was a man who asked questions before he shot. After a bit of explaining, the Coast Guard was called and a rescue boat carried the five to safety.

No one came to know the island better than Keeper Edward Schneider. He spent 28 years on "The Rock" tending the light and fog signals. He was a big 270-pound man who saw much action during his tour of duty. He was there when a Northwestern Pacific ferryboat ran aground in 1931 and when a freighter hit the island in 1946. He vividly recalled the 1946 prison riot and how quickly it seemed to end. He especially enjoyed Christmas when he played Santa Claus for the guards' children.

It was around Christmas time in 1953 when Assistant Keeper Ron Ferguson and his wife Carmen received orders transferring them to Alcatraz Light Station. Ferguson had begun his career as a seaman at the Point Reyes Lifeboat Station operating 36-foot wooden motor lifeboats on rescues in Drake's Bay and out in the Gulf of the Farallons. Because there were no quarters at the lifeboat station for enlisted men's wives, Ferguson arranged a transfer to a family station, Point Montara lighthouse on the San Mateo County coast. He expected to spend the rest of his Coast Guard career at peaceful Point Montara light. But he was stunned one day to receive notice that in three days he was to report to "The Rock" to become Keeper Schneider's assistant.

Ferguson recalled, "I was very surprised but we loaded our things in an old International panel truck. We reported to Fort Mason pier in San Francisco, right at the foot of Van Ness Avenue," the pier that stands immediately west of the curving Municipal Pier. There they awaited the arrival of the prison boat for their journey to Alcatraz.

When the boat arrived, Keeper Ferguson showed the guard operating the prison boat his orders. Ferguson immediately realized he was being assigned to an extraordinary place.

"Oh, your name is Ron Ferguson," the guard commented.

"Yeah, that's my name," the young assistant keeper replied.

"The prisoners said your name is RICK Ferguson."

"What are you talking about?" Ferguson asked.

"The prisoners knew you were coming a week ago."

"I just found out three days ago and the prisoners knew it before I did?"

"That's the prison grapevine. They'll be upset, though, because they got your first name wrong," the guard concluded.

When the boat arrived at Alcatraz, Ron and Carmen Ferguson's belongings were loaded on a bus and they were driven up to the lighthouse. Once there, Ferguson reported to Head Keeper Schneider. Schneider lived alone on the light, his family gone. There was another couple living at the light station, an assistant keeper and his wife and baby.

The Fergusons moved right in and Ron spent his first day cleaning up his new quarters. He carefully lined the garbage can with newspapers and threw out all the tobacco packages left by the previous keeper, a pipe smoker.

"The following morning there was a knock on the door and a guard was standing there. He proceeded to admonish me for lining the garbage can with newspaper." The guard declared, "First of all, they can put notices in the newspaper that would be information to the prisoners if they happened to get a hold of it . . . so no more newspaper lining." The guard continued, "Second thing, don't throw tobacco away because that's considered money by the prisoners on the island." It was becoming clear that Alcatraz was a unique light keeping assignment.

Mr. Ferguson soon found that Alcatraz Island light keepers were generally restricted by prison policy to the light station itself. But Alcatraz could be a very fogbound place and there were fog signals located at each end of the island. There were times when the fog horns would need maintenance and a keeper had to cross the prison to reach them. "If I ever had to go to the ends of the island where the fog signals were located, I had to wear my Coast Guard uniform and notify the officer of the guard. I had to designate the time I was going to leave the lighthouse and the direction I was going. He would notify the watch towers. Then I would proceed along, directed by hand signals from the guards in the watch towers to stop or move forward," Ferguson stated. When he had to go to the fog signals, Keeper Ferguson had to cross the prison yard but this could only be permitted when no prisoners were there. As he crossed the island, electric gate locks would be opened for him so that he could pass from one area to another.

The prison guards played an important role in the operation of the fog horns. Alcatraz Light Station was a compact station with the dwelling attached to the lighthouse via a special door. Keepers stood watch in their quarters in the dwelling. In the central hallway, outside the quarters and at the base of the lighthouse, was a switch which turned on the fog signals. There was also a telephone here which the watch stander was to answer. Since the light station was located on the eastern end of the island, if you were in the dwellings, it was difficult to see fog approaching from the Golden Gate. The people with the best view were the guards in the watch towers. They regularly telephoned the light keepers to report changing weather conditions, particularly approaching fog. The phone would ring and it would be a guard saying, "This is guard tower (number so and so) calling. It's foggin' up down here." Keeper Ferguson remembers, "We'd say 'OK' and throw the switch starting the fog horns and they'd call back in a couple of hours or so when the fog was gone and we'd shut it off."

Keeper Edward Schneider inspects the lens atop the second Alcatraz Island lighthouse, C. 1950. (Treasure Island Museum)

On rare occasions there was excitement on the island when a boater disregarded Alcatraz's signs warning mariners to stay well off the island. When the signs were ignored by the curious, the keepers would hear the guards firing warning shots to drive intruding boats away.

Light keepers could have guests, but even that might not be routine. Keeper Ferguson and a visiting friend were standing outside the lighthouse one day waiting for the prison boat to go ashore. There was a signal that came just five minutes before the boat was ready to leave. You weren't supposed to leave your quarters for the boat until you heard the whistle. But Ferguson and his friend were deep in conversation and they just automatically started to move down toward the boat as they talked. It was a couple of minutes before the signal was to sound. All of a sudden they heard the word, "Freeze!" and that was it. It was back to the lighthouse until the whistle blew.

Light keeping on Alcatraz had become rather easy duty by 1954. Occasionally the Fresnel lens had to be polished, the fog signals had to be tended and periodically repaired, and there was a bit of routine maintenance. Keeper Schneider was popular with the young Coast Guardsmen and allowed them and their wives to go ashore virtually any night they wanted. Carmen Ferguson worked in San Francisco and commuted daily to her job by the prison boat. The frequent prison boat trips made shopping and entertainment in the City easily accessible. Keeper Schneider felt he had everything under control and asked little of his crew beyond standing watch and carefully maintaining the light and fog signal.

Assistant Keeper Ron Ferguson felt Alcatraz light was the best duty he ever had. "It was just so good there. It had the greatest view of the Bay. In the evenings, it would be so nice. You could hear people's voices and music drifting over from San Francisco," Ferguson reminisced.

Head Keeper Edward Schneider expressed similar feelings when he retired, "I guess no matter where I am, I will remember the big Alcatraz light . . . it's been a good station and it has been a good duty." Both Schneider and Ferguson left Alcatraz and others took their place tending the beacon.

Finally, early in 1963, the prison was closed and the lighthouse keepers had the island to themselves. They could walk freely along the shore and fish where they pleased. Pets were now permitted, and a can of beer could be enjoyed without worrying about its disposal.

These pleasures did not last long, however. In November 1963, the lighthouse was converted to automatic operation and the station unmanned. The light was subsequently serviced and monitored both by the Fort Point and the Yerba Buena Island Coast Guard stations. The old lens was removed and a new double-drum reflecting light was installed. Fog signals remained at each end of the island, the easterly one still in a small bell house-like structure. Fog detectors automatically started and stopped the fog horns while the light operated continuously.

In 1970, a group of American Indians landed on the unoccupied island and claimed the abandoned prison facilities under an old law which specified that excess government lands be returned to Native Americans. The Federal Government rejected the Indians' claim, but law-enforcement officials did not force the issue and the Indians remained in control. They utilized electrical power supplied to the lighthouse. In an attempt to drive out the Indians, Federal officials turned off the beacon's electrical supply and the lighthouse went dark. Coast Guard buoy tenders placed lighted buoys at each end of the island. This action brought immediate protests from mariners and the San Francisco Board of Supervisors, but Federal officials of that period apparently believed that subduing the Indians was more important than maritime safety. The light remained dark until the Indians themselves relighted it on the eighth of June, with the help of several prominent San Franciscans concerned about maritime safety who smuggled a generator over by boat and carried it up to the lighthouse. The First Americans said they had lighted the sentinel so that it could be a symbol to all tribes of Indian determination to "achieve their just claims and the recognition of their rightful dignity".

Unfortunately, during the late stages of the Indian occupation, fire broke out, damaging the lighthouse and destroying the keepers' quarters. Smoke billowed from the base of the tower, giving it much the same appearance as when the Seminoles burned Cape Florida light in 1836. Within a few months, the persistence of the Federal Government and the extreme hardships of living on The Rock combined to force the Indians from Alcatraz Island.

According to newspaper reports, Indian veterans of the Alcatraz protest told an intriguing story. On the night of the lighthouse fire, none of the Indian people were living in the buildings which burst into flame. However, a mysterious boat was seen rapidly leaving the island just as the fire started. Arson is strongly suspected by some of the Native Americans. With no pumps or water to fight the fire, there was little the Indian people could do but watch it burn.

Happily, today the lighthouse is fully restored to normal operation. Its 200,000-candle-power beam still serves as one of the West's major lights. Its interior still boasts the beautiful spiral staircase. The National Park Service tour route passes directly beneath the soaring Alcatraz lighthouse. In the museum, the 1902 lens is on display. The tours capture much of the character of America's toughest prison and offer close inspection of a symbol of hope on an island where hope was so often lost.

Alcatraz lighthouse burning after a fire broke out during Indian occupation of the island. The tower survived, but damage was severe. (U.S. Coast Guard)

Under the watchful eyes of Keeper Fred Zimmerman, a San Francisco Bay ferryboat passes Yerba Buena's beautiful Victorian lighthouse. The sentinel's fifth order lens was typical of those which lighted the inner bay. To the right of the lighthouse can be seen the flat-roofed oil house. C. 1950s. (U.S. Coast Guard)

YERBA BUENA ISLAND

The first San Francisco Bay mariners were the Ohlone and Coast Miwok Indians, so knowledgeable and highly skilled that they could navigate the Bay using "balsas", small boats made of bundles of tule reeds. Remembering that the swift currents sometimes swept sailing vessels out of the Golden Gate and that the choppy waters still occasionally sink small craft, the feat of handling reed boats using only double-bladed paddles places the Ohlone and Coast Miwok among the best of the Bay's mariners.

The Ohlones frequently traveled from one shore to another, often stopping at a 350-foot high, oak-studded island conveniently located between the San Francisco peninsula and the "Contra Costa". Little more than 140 acres in size, the island rises steeply from the Bay and then turns to a less rugged interior. When the Spanish colonialists first visited the island, they undoubtedly landed at the little cove on the island's east side. The Spaniards named the island "Yerba Buena", meaning good herb, in recognition of the refreshing, curative virtues of a native California mint which grew there in abundance.

The Ohlones had taken no more than acorns, and the Spanish left no more than a name; but when the Americans arrived in 1849, they introduced goats and began to chop down the oak trees. Although goat-herding squatters continued to live there for years, the island's strategic mid-Bay location soon caused it to be designated a military reservation. By the 1870s, the Army had chased the squatters off, and soldiers and goats had the island to themselves. Then, a disastrous fire swept the barracks, and the Army moved out. The goats became so numerous that the Americans began calling the place Goat Island. It was a name that would stick for decades.

Early mariners had to use whatever markers were available to navigate San Francisco Bay, and Yerba Buena Island was always an important seamark. Early navigational charts advised mariners to line up the north end of Yerba Buena Island with the soaring grove of redwood trees that then grew on the East Bay hills. By following this course, a ship could be steered safely past notorious Blossom Rock, a deadly menace just out of sight beneath the Bay's surface. Certainly a lighthouse was needed on such an important island.

By this time, San Francisco and Oakland had become major cities, and travel between them was heavy. Yerba Buena was at the very heart of the Bay Area and more ferry boats passed its shores than any of the other Bay islands. Any inadequately marked island would be a hazard to navigation, but Yerba Buena was especially dangerous because of its proximity to several ferry boat routes. Thousands of commuters, as well as all transcontinential railroad passengers, used the ferry lanes off Yerba Buena. With an annual passenger count running into the millions, the island could not remain unmarked.

In the 1870s, Yerba Buena's extreme southeast point was acquired for a lighthouse reservation. Clearing the land was not particularly difficult, since the goats and woodchoppers had long been at work. The light station would require only about two and one-half acres, located above a 50-foot high cliff. Soon materials were landed, and a bell house was mounted right on the face of the cliff. To equip it, a fog bell, probably the old veteran that had been brought in by ox cart in the 1850s, was transferred from Point Conception. Just behind and a little above the bell house, a concrete platform was poured and twin fog signal buildings were erected side by side, each holding ten-inch steam whistles and coal-fired boilers. A large water tank and coal house stood on each side while a stairway led up to the octagonal frame lighthouse. Although only 22 feet high, the tower was a lovely Victorian structure complete with an ornamental pediment above the doorway, fancy woodwork at each of its many corners, and a decorative railing around the balcony. A fifth order lens was brought down from Yaquina Bay lighthouse in Oregon when that station was replaced by a new beacon on Yaquina Head. The fixed light was shown from a white tower with a black lantern room accented by lead-colored ornamental trimmings. A typical flat roofed California style oil house was built nearby.

About 80 yards above the hill, a two-story frame dwelling with similar ornamental trim housed the two keepers and their families. One family occupied each level. The lower story was large with two bedrooms, but some head keepers preferred to live in the less spacious upper level. Behind the residence, there was a little laundry room and outhouse. Except for the lighthouse, all the station's buildings were white with red roofs.

Fog was the biggest hazard at Yerba Buena, and the fog bell had arrived in 1874, a year before the lens. The bell, however, was not to serve as the principal sound device, but only to back up the steam whistles if they became disabled. The bell's clockwork was kept wound anyway, its weights ready to descend the cliff face to activate the mechanical striker every ten seconds. On October 1, 1875, the light and whistles began operation, serving such a heavily traveled route that eventually the San Francisco *Chronicle* would report that "Ferry boats carrying 18,000,000 people passed by it."

The island had been abandoned by the military and was still wild and rugged in the late 1870s. There was no school and no regular transportation ashore. One lighthouse family solved the problem by teaching their three daughters how to sail, and the skillful young women daily sailed their sloop to school in San Francisco.

Lovely guardian of the Golden Gate. Yerba Buena Island lighthouse in the 1930s. Photo by lighthouse keeper Irving Conklin. (U.S. Lighthouse Society)

Fog approaches Yerba Buena Island light station's dwelling. Perhaps a keeper on watch in the upper gabled room will start the fog signal soon. (U.S. Coast Guard)

Yerba Buena Island Lighthouse Depot during the early days of operation. Note buoys, chains, and shops. The Depot was soon expanded and lighthouse tenders and lightships were berthed here. (U.S. Coast Guard)

The Lighthouse Service's depot on Yerba Buena Island with the tender **Sequoia** *moored at the wharf. The historic depot still stands, now used as Coast Guard Base San Francisco's buoy depot. The depot deserves inclusion in the National Register of Historic Places, June 1930. (U.S. Coast Guard)*

Besides a lack of educational facilities, another annoying—and exhausting—inconvenience was the water problem. The well was below the fog signal station at the new Lighthouse Depot to the east. The steam whistles consumed gluttonous quantities of water, and the wickies had to hand-pump every drop of it up to the tank. This situation continued well into the 1880s, a period which saw only one major improvement at the station—a new derrick was added to the landing beside the bell house.

By now, Yerba Buena was referred to as "Goat Island", and the depredations of the hooved beasts, coupled with the woodchoppers' activities, had left the island with few plants larger than a shrub. Oakland poet Joaquin Miller began urging replanting the island, and on November 27, 1886, the island hosted California's first Arbor Day. The day was a success, and each year the light station's trees gained in stature, so that today a small forest shelters the residence.

By 1900, some of the trees were ten feet tall and the island had changed in many ways. The bell house had been removed and a new bell apparatus installed which allowed more room for the landing platform. In common with some other stations, the two smokestacks of the fog signal building had been torn down and a single massive brick chimney did the work. The cliff itself would soon change character, too. To give greater visibility to the station, it was completely painted white, a feature that would last almost as long as the trees.

The 12th Lighthouse District established its Yerba Buena Island Lighthouse Depot near the light station in 1873. The depot was the heart of the 12th District and serviced all the light stations, lightships, and buoys along the California coast.

Yerba Buena Lighthouse Depot was staffed with a keeper, blacksmith, blacksmith's helper, and a watchman. For years this crew was supplemented by the 26 officers and crewmen of the lighthouse tender *Madroño*. The ship spent hundreds of hours there annually, taking on supplies for her treks up and down the coast supplying light stations and tending buoys. By 1890, she was supplying 28 light stations and was required to make at least four calls a year to each of them for inspections and to bring keepers their pay. The ship was literally a lifeline for many light stations. The *Madroño* often steamed over 10,000 miles a year, supplemented only by her own steam launch and by the *Hazel*, a little seven-ton, wooden, screw launch that helped service San Francisco Bay stations. When the *Madroño* was laid up for repairs at Mare Island or San Francisco, supplies just didn't go out.

The first West Coast tender, the *Shubrick*, had arrived in 1857 and was followed by the *Manzanita* in 1870 and the *Madroño* herself in 1885. All had come by way of Cape Horn, as did the *Columbine* seven years later. Two lightships had come the same way, numbers *76* and *83* arriving in 1905. (Not all these vessels served California

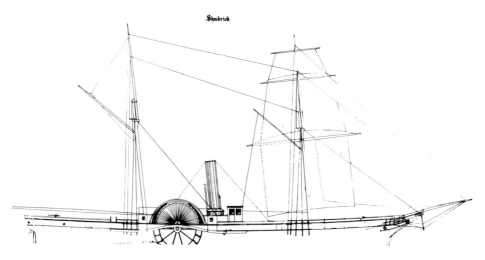

Original plans for the Lighthouse Service's tender Shubrick. *She was the first steam powered lighthouse tender and the first tender on the Pacific Coast. (National Archives)*

Lighthouse tender Shubrick, *first steam powered American lighthouse tender and first lighthouse tender on the Pacific Coast. (U.S. Lighthouse Society)*

light stations, some being assigned to the 13th District in the Pacific Northwest.)

Then, in January 1909, a veritable fleet arrived in San Francisco. Termed "The Lightship Flotilla" by the press, it consisted of three lightships and three lighthouse tenders. They had been built at Camden, New Jersey, and the 135-foot lightships and the 190-foot tenders *Sequoia, Manzanita,* and the *Kukui* had braved a 124-day voyage and 14,000 miles to reach San Francisco. The lightships could not make over eight knots on the trip, and the tenders had to regulate their speed accordingly. Out of Callao, Peru, the lightships were towed by the tenders for several hundred miles in order to save coal. Arriving at San Francisco, all required some repair but soon were off to their new duties. Two of the lightships, *Numbers 88* and *93*, and a tender were sent to the Pacific Northwest to become, respectively, the *Columbia River* lightship and the *Swiftsure Bank* lightship. One tender, the *Kukui,* was stationed at Honolulu. The *Relief* light vessel *Number 92*, and the tender *Sequoia* both made San Francisco their home port. With two lightships, *San Francisco, Number 70* and *Blunts Reef, Number 83*, already assigned to the 12th District, there were at times as many as four Lighthouse Service vessels tied up at Yerba Buena. The old Columbia River lightship, *Number 50*, the Pacific Coast's first lightship, was sent to Yerba Buena Island temporarily and served briefly as a relief lightship in California. Then she was sent to Astoria, Oregon, where she was decommissioned and sold.

Two tenders (the *Madroño* and *Sequoia*), two relief lightships (*Numbers 76* and *92*), and two "on station" light vessels meant that Yerba Buena Depot was a busy, growing place with much coming and going. Buoys lined the piers and wharves, and the tenders were equipped with buoy docks, fifty feet in length, to be used in placing the new acetylene-lighted buoys along the coast. These floating docks were tied alongside the tender as platforms for the crew to stand on while they worked on certain buoys in calm waters.

When the Lightship Flotilla had arrived in 1909, John P. Kofod was the assistant keeper up the hill at the light station. Kofod had been born in Denmark, worked as a glazier creating stained glass windows for churches, and had followed his uncle, a keeper at Lime Point Fog Signal Station, into the Lighthouse Service. As was customary, Kofod had to begin his career at difficult, isolated coastal light stations. He served at Point Sur on the lonely Big Sur Coast and at windy Point Reyes north of San Francisco. Coming to Yerba Buena Island was to have pleasant long-term consequences for the family especially since a Navy base had been established there, too. Kofod's daughter would meet and marry a young Navy radioman stationed on the island and eventually Kofod's grandson, Walter Fanning, would be born in the second story of the keeper's dwelling. The birth was duly recorded in the log book which

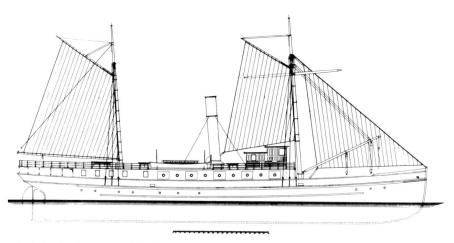

Original plans for lighthouse tender Madroño. *(National Archives)*

was kept in a little stand-up desk. A family wedding for yet another relative was held alongside the two-story keepers' residence, adding to the happy family memories.

Mr. Kofod served at Yerba Buena until 1914 when he was transferred north on San Francisco Bay to East Brother lighthouse. Then, in 1925, he returned to Yerba Buena as head keeper where he served until 1929.

Grandson Walter Fanning experienced many of the joys of island lighthouse life during these years. The famed San Francisco Bay ferryboats between Oakland and San Francisco constantly used the light station for guidance. The numerous ferries of three railroad companies—the Southern Pacific, Western Pacific, and the Key System—carried countless passengers by the light. With constant marine traffic, the fog signal had to be kept ready for use at all times, no small feat in the days of steam whistles.

Fast moving San Francisco Bay fog could arrive with surprising speed. It would take 45 minutes or so to start a steam fog signal if there were no fires going in the fire box. It takes time to heat water, of course, and during such a time ships could be struggling blindly through the fog. At some stations, a bell was rung until steam was built up. At Yerba Buena, experienced keepers kept the boiler fires banked, mounded and covered with ashes so that it would burn long and slowly. When the keepers saw approaching fog, they would stick a metal hoe in the fire box and spread out the fire, throw in a few shovelfuls of coal, open the draft, and in 10 or 15 minutes they had a full head of steam. A timing mechanism opened and closed a valve to activate the whistle which would scream every 16 seconds for an ear piercing four seconds.

The lighthouse tender Madroño *was for decades the mainstay of many light stations. Here, she is servicing a buoy. A floating "buoy dock" can be seen in the water directly below the ship's stack. (U.S. Coast Guard)*

If this procedure wasn't fast enough during the early years, a backup fog bell was rung until steam could be produced.

Yerba Buena's most charming custom involved the big 10-inch diameter fog whistles. Each New Year's Eve, Keeper Kofod would take his grandchildren down to the fog signal. Around midnight there might be a dozen ferry boats at or near the island. The steam whistle would be fired up with a shovelful or two of coal and while a head of steam was building up, Kofod would station the children beside the big whistle lever. Grandfather Kofod would then stand at the fog signal building window and watch as each ferry passed close by. Upon his signal, the children would raise the fog whistle level three times, producing the traditional salute of three long blasts. It was a thrill to hear each ferryboat respond.

There were other exciting times. Southeasterly storms would toss the ships about in the Bay and during one storm a disabled ferry crashed violently into the Key System pier in Oakland.

It could be thrilling, too, when the keepers had to whitewash the high, rocky cliff below the light station for increased visibility. Using ropes, the wickies lowered themselves down the steep cliff face. They climbed all over the rocks spraying paint out of a wooden barrel, using a hand pump as they made their way across the face of the cliff.

Sometimes excitement was accidentally created. There was no electricity at the station in those days. So Walter Fanning's father, using his knowledge of electricity gained as a radioman, decided to rig up a battery powered electric light system for the keepers' dwelling. Batteries powered the lights and for awhile it looked as if the 20th century had come to the island. But not for long. The system short circuited and caused a fire in the attic. The Navy fire department rushed to the dwelling and saved the Kofod's home. For decades the fire's cause was a family secret.

The Navy personnel were good neighbors. During Christmas, Lighthouse Service families joined the Navy people for an annual party. All the children were invited and everyone enjoyed the Christmas tree, singing, and exchanging of gifts.

The Lighthouse Service children knew most of the Navy youngsters since by this time they rode to San Francisco to school on the gasoline launch *Castro* or a tug. These vessels also carried island personnel and supplies back and forth between the island and San Francisco's pier 14.

Wayne Piland knew the supply boat run from Yerba Buena to San Francisco quite well. In 1919 he was just out of Navy boot camp and had been assigned the job of "Boat Orderly" on the vessel. Each morning, Monday through Friday, the light keeper's daughter would ride the boat to school. She was about 15, not much younger than Piland, and they talked frequently. Piland tried to visit the light but a high fence and big signs forbid Navy personnel from visiting the station. He could get within shouting distance, but that was about it. He probably never dreamed that later he would become the head keeper here.

But 1918-19 were not good years at Yerba Buena. The Spanish influenza epidemic was ravaging the globe and a military base was a poor place to try to weather a disease that would kill 20 million world-wide and over a half million in the U.S. On Yerba Buena, funerals seemed an almost daily occurrence, sometimes with six to nine caskets. The first one to die had their casket placed on the traditional field piece. The rest of the caskets were loaded into a truck which followed along behind.

One day, Piland's best friend, Navyman George Warren, came down the hill and told Piland he wasn't feeling well. Warren went off and Piland boarded the morning boat for his duty run to San Francisco. Two days later Piland was on the supply boat helping load one of the caskets going ashore and just happened to look at the little white card on the end. It said "George Warren".

The tragic influenza epidemic eventually passed and life slowly returned to normal. The lighthouse tender *Madroño*, with its big wooden pole boom, and her counterpart, the *Sequoia*, with its long lattice steel boom, continued to swing buoys and supplies on board, and to steam up and down the California coast serving light stations. These two tenders (plus, in later years, the *Lupine*) would make "the shortest tender run" as the wickies called it. It was just a few hundred yards around the point from the Yerba Buena lighthouse depot to the Yerba Buena light station landing. Alternately, a whale boat full of supplies would periodically be rowed around the point to the landing in front of the fog signal. There a stiff leg derrick, powered by a steam winch, would use a sling to haul up sacks full of coal. Food came up the "goat trail", the path from the depot to the light station. Milk was a local product since Keeper Kofod kept two cows. A large garden was planted and artichokes seemed to do especially well.

When John Kofod retired in 1929, it brought to an end the many childhood adventures his grandson Walter had experienced on the island. There had been a little beach accessible by a rugged trail west of the lighthouse. Walter had spent many hours beachcombing here. There, too, on the west side was the little old graveyard where long ago some foreign seamen had been buried. Or, he could sit and watch the Navy parade ground and the activities there. When Keeper Kofod retired, he pronounced Yerba Buena the "best station on the coast."

But, for some later keepers, Yerba Buena was perhaps a bit too close to all the activity of the Lighthouse Service depot. One day, Keeper Albert Joost rowed the five miles from Yerba Buena Island north up San Francisco Bay to Southampton Shoal lighthouse. He had come to this offshore light station to talk with young Ole Lunden, the assistant keeper. Mr. Joost asked Ole if he would like to trade jobs. Ole thought about the small, unreliable boats the Lighthouse Service had issued Southampton Shoal's wickies to cross the often choppy, swift moving waters to shore at Tiburon. Foremost in his mind was getting his wife, Bernice, out of the risky twice weekly trips ashore. Lunden told Joost that the exchange of jobs would be fine if the District Office would approve. Late in 1930, the trade was completed and Ole and Bernice Lunden moved to Yerba Buena Island.

The Lundens found a beautifully landscaped station with many positive features. The lens was a fixed, non-flashing type with no weights to wind. Watches could be stood while sitting in the dwelling. As assistant keepers, the Lundens had been assigned the upper story. There was a little sitting room in the residence's gable. When he was on watch, Ole could see not only the lighthouse but all over the Bay. The sitting room became his favorite spot.

The Navy Commissary on the island was open to the keepers, reducing the need to go ashore frequently. Besides, when you did want to leave the island, reasonably large, reliable vessels were readily available. The only drawback were the wharf rats in the dwelling's attic.

For many years now, Yerba Buena had been known simply as Goat Island and early Lighthouse Service documents sometimes refer to it that way. But, about 1931, a move was made to rename the island Yerba Buena. When this was officially approved, the island people all held a celebration. A sailor dressed up as a goat and everybody pushed him into the Bay, symbolizing the name change. From then on it was Yerba Buena Island. "Goat Island" had disappeared.

By 1931, ferry service ashore was being provided by the Navy tugs *Castro* and *Vigilante* as well as other boats. With so many Navy personnel coming and going, Lighthouse Service people from both the light station and the lighthouse depot had almost hourly trips ashore available.

But a threat to the light keepers' jobs seemed to loom ahead. Construction on the San Francisco-Oakland Bay Bridge was about to begin and the span would pass through the island. The Lighthouse Service planned to automate the lighthouse and transfer its keepers upon completion of the bridge. The beacon and fog signal could then be controlled from the adjacent lighthouse depot. With the 1930s Depression worsening, Keeper Lunden decided to seek a transfer to Point Vicente lighthouse in Los Angeles county, a sentinel which seemed to have a more promising future.

Work on the huge bridge took several years, the span being completed in 1936. Suddenly island dwellers had unlimited access to Bay Area cities. In 1939 transportation was further improved when rails for the Key System electric trains were added to the bridge and now both automobile and railroad transportation ashore were available. During this period, a large landfill project was completed and Yerba Buena Island had a new neighbor—Treasure Island, site of the 1939 Golden Gate International Exposition. Treasure Island was designed to become an airport and the China Clippers, famed trans-Pacific amphibious passenger planes, began arriving and departing.

As it turned out, none of these changes led to lighthouse automation. The light remained manned as the 1940s began. That young Navy man mentioned earlier, Wayne Piland, had returned to Yerba Buena. He now wore a different uniform, that of the U.S. Lighthouse Service. He also had a wife and two children and a wealth of experience gained as a keeper at Point Arena, Punta Gorda, Humboldt Bay and—most recently—Point Sur. He had transferred to Yerba Buena from lonely Point Sur to provide better educational opportunities for his children.

Piland had no doubts he was getting a good station. He even had a light keeper and his wife visit him from the Pacific Northwest. They exchanged small talk for a while and then the visiting wickie enthusiastically praised the wonderful fishing at his distant light. It soon became apparent that the couple wanted to transfer to the Bay Area, preferably to Yerba Buena. Try as he might, Piland couldn't discourage the man and the visitor's anxiety for a transfer became more apparent. Finally, he had to come right out and say that he "wasn't interested and that Yerba Buena was one of the best stations on the California light list!" Piland's stepfather served on the lighthouse tender *Cedar* and had visited this distant lighthouse. He came back describing gale force winds and terrible isolation. There was no way Wayne Piland would trade Yerba Buena for that life.

All the lighthouse families faced adjustments in July 1939, when the Lighthouse Service was merged into the Coast Guard. The transition was not an easy one. Old time keepers were now under the command of less experienced and often younger Coast Guard officers. The change was made especially painful when orders were issued to collect the beautiful, historic brasswork lamps, dustpans, and even a few lighthouse lenses and send them to Yerba Buena Island lighthouse depot. There they were broken, smashed and tossed into scrap bins for recycling. Some lighthouse families simply disobeyed the order and kept their precious old brass light keeping lamps and tools. (Modern day Coast Guard people strongly criticize such a foolish order and most join the lighthouse families in working to preserve our lighthouses.)

The early 1940s were tense times to be at Yerba Buena. World War II began and San Francisco Bay was unsurpassed in its importance to the war in the Pacific. Battleship Row was southwest of the island and aircraft carriers with deckloads of planes also regularly passed by.

When the War began, America was woefully unprepared. As the War progressed, there were periodic nighttime blackouts when all of the Bay Area's lights had to be extinguished if an air raid was feared. When an air raid warning sounded, the lighted buoys in the harbor presented a problem. Buoys were placed as guideposts and they could lead friend as well as foe. There was no way to turn the buoy lights off without going from one to another by boat. So when a blackout warning was sounded, soldiers were lined up and down the San Francisco-Oakland Bay Bridge with orders to shoot out the buoy lights. This was a fast, but dangerous and inefficient, method of putting out the buoy lights.

Strangely, during the blackouts, when the entire Bay Area was in darkness, the Key System electric trains would still be running across the bridge with all their lights on. They could be seen high above the light station. They reminded Wayne Piland of "giant, luminous caterpillars in the sky" against a background of totally blacked out cities.

There were many blackouts during the War and it was necessary to build an automatic system for turning off the buoy lights. All those soldiers up on the bridge firing away were a far greater danger to the Bay Area than an invasion that would never come. As a result, an automatic system for turning off the buoy lights was installed and the gun smoke disappeared from the bridge.

Piland served at Yerba Buena until 1946 and then was transferred north to Crescent City light through 1953. Crescent City was the last of the state's original lighthouses still to be operated in the early manner as a one-man station. It could be a wild place with waves frequently showering the tower and sea water running down the lantern room ladder. When the Coast Guard first considered automating the Crescent City lighthouse in 1948, Piland fought back. He called several newspaper reporters to try to build public support for the continuation of the Crescent City light as an active station. Articles appeared in newspapers describing the historic station. Piland urged that civilian keepers be used to man lighthouses instead of enlisted men.

"The results would be much better," he explained, "both for the personnel and in terms of the quality of service rendered to the government."

Piland was first, last and always a Lighthouse Service man, and when the Coast Guard had taken over in 1939, he had lived through a difficult transition period. He was never afraid to speak out and some Coast Guard officers resented it. But the Admiral in charge of the 12th Coast Guard District admired him. When Crescent City light was finally automated in 1953, Piland had orders to transfer to Point Montara. But the Admiral overruled that and said, "It would be nice to have Piland at Y.B.I." So the Piland family returned once again to Yerba Buena.

The Coast Guard years had begun and Wayne Piland's crew were all enlisted men. As had been the general practice for nearly a century, head keeper Piland lived downstairs in the dwelling. His two assistant keepers lived upstairs. One day Keeper Piland was inspecting the assistant keepers' quarters upstairs. He heard strange, snapping sounds coming from the bathroom. There, in the bathtub, was a baby alligator, something which confirmed Piland's opinion that his Coast Guardsmen needed more training. It wasn't too many weeks before the alligator was getting quite large and he had to order the assistant keepers to get rid of it. Alligators were officially banned at Yerba Buena.

Yerba Buena light station was to experience something far more mysterious and frightening than any alligator. One quiet night, an assistant keeper was upstairs, alone, on watch. The man sat at the table reading. He unexpectedly heard the dwelling's front door open and steps coming up the stairs. Then, at the top of the stairs, the assistant keeper heard the door open and then close.

"The Old Man (Officer-in-charge Piland) must think I'm asleep on watch," the assistant laughed to himself. He then wondered why Piland would be spying on him since it would be totally out of character. The assistant keeper turned around, ready to laugh at Piland, only to have his mirth turn to terror. Wayne Piland was not there. No one was there.

U.S. Lighthouse Service Superintendent Captain Harry W. Rhodes in his office in the Old Customs House in San Francisco. As superintendent of the 18th Lighthouse Service District from 1912 through 1939, Captain Rhodes was in charge of all the state's lighthouses and lightships for nearly three decades. He was the inspector for all of California's light stations and visited them frequently. (U.S. Lighthouse Society)

The buoy tender Blackhaw *returning to Coast Guard Base San Francisco on Yerba Buena Island. This 180-foot long vessel is the modern equivalent of the old lighthouse tenders. (U.S. Coast Guard)*

The ghostly steps continued. They passed by the wickie and entered the upstairs quarters. Like the lower story front door, the upper story door was locked. Yet the assistant now, again, heard the *locked* door open and then close. This was too much for the assistant keeper. Terrified by the ghostly presence, he ran down the stairs and clawed at the front door, too panicked to even turn the doorknob. Finally getting the door opened, he stood alone outside the residence and just shook. Later, his courage returning, the assistant forced himself to go back upstairs and investigate. No one—nothing—was to be found. No human being could have gotten through those locked doors. The next morning, the frightened assistant keeper told the story to Piland, showing him the claw marks the assistant had left on the door.

By the late fifties, the light station itself had changed somewhat. Half of the fog signal building had been removed and only one peaked roof, now holding an air horn instead of a steam whistle, remained. The landing was gone, not needed since the bridge had been completed. The lighthouse was unaltered except for the substitution of an iron-pipe

The buoy tender Blackhaw *is one of the Coast Guard's strong right arms. She has just lifted a large whistle buoy on board her buoy deck to bring it ashore for maintenance. A new replacement buoy can be seen forward. At this time, it was raining, the deck was slick with sea slime and water, and the ship was working in maximum seas of about four feet. The deck crew was using extreme caution as the huge buoy was chained down on the rolling deck. A false move could easily lead to a crew member being crushed. Buoy tender crews are among the hardest working people in the Coast Guard. In the Gulf of the Farallons, 1985. (R. Shanks)*

railing on the balcony and an electric light bulb in the lens. The old lens still gleamed in the tower and one of the station's most prized possessions, the original kerosene lamp, had been carefully handed down from keeper to keeper, its brass still shining after nearly a century of use. Even the "lure", the pear-shaped chimney in the lantern room, remained, although with electricity, there were no longer oil fumes and smoke to be carried away.

During this period, the position of officer-in-charge had been held by such proud men as Fred Zimmerman and Wayne Piland, two of the finest of the old civilian keepers. Wayne Piland was the last civilian keeper of both Crescent City and Yerba Buena lights. He retired in 1958 after serving five years on his second tour of duty on the island. The Coast Guard continued operating the beacon with a three-man crew until automation occurred in July 1958.

Yerba Buena Island light station in 1976. The station changed little in a century. The lowest structure was the fog signal building, the highest was the keepers' residence. Trees were planted on California's first Arbor Day. (R. Shanks)

The Lighthouse Service Depot much as it looks today. Now, however, the buoy tender Blackhaw *has replaced the earlier tender shown here, the* Magnolia. *(U.S. Coast Guard)*

By now, the island—and the Bay Area—had become so urbanized that some mariners had trouble distinguishing the light. Whatever the problems of mariners, birds could readily find it and an increasing number made blind assaults on the lantern room windows, sometimes causing serious damage. As a result, the lighthouse was floodlighted in 1957, the first West Coast beacon where this technique was tried. The experiment easily solved both problems.

The old Yerba Buena Lighthouse Depot had grown to become "Coast Guard Base, San Francisco" after 1960. Newer ships had long since replaced the Lightship Flotilla. Light vessels continued to use the depot until 1971, when they were replaced by large navigational buoys. Lighthouse tenders spawned buoy tenders, and for some years two were based there, the *Blackhaw* and the *Red Birch*. At present, the venerable *Blackhaw* is still based there. Built in 1944, this 180-foot black hulled beauty is much loved by her crews. The days of the tender runs up and down the coast are not yet gone, as the *Blackhaw* still serves buoys and a few light stations from San Luis Obispo north to St. George Reef. The wharf is still lined with buoys, and the resemblance to the early days is striking. The industrial facilities are much expanded now, and 82-foot and 95-foot patrol boats are sometimes moored nearby along with 41-foot and 44-foot rescue craft. The historic 1930 art deco Lighthouse Depot still stands today, now called the Buoy Depot.

Above the handsome historic buoy depot, the priceless old lighthouse still shines, its original lens proudly bearing the name "Barbier & Fenestre Constructeurs, Paris, stamped in brass over a hundred years ago. The dwelling and serene grounds retain their traditional flavor and beauty. The grand old residence has become the home of a series of distinguished Coast Guard admirals and their families, a high tribute to the esteem in which the station is held. Through recent decades, the grand old residence has served as the home of the admiral commanding the Coast Guard operations first in northern California and more recently for the entire Pacific Coast. This selection of the light station as the home of the Pacific Coast's highest ranking Coast Guard officer gives an indication of the prestige in which it is held. It is a lighthouse that can boast of having its beautiful Fresnel lens often cleaned by an admiral.

It is hoped that an occasional "Open House" could be held at the light station allowing visitors to tour this exceptional light station and the adjacent depot. Perhaps each admiral and wife occupying the stately dwelling could generously set aside a few days a year when tours by reservation might allow visitors to enjoy the fine lighthouse and grounds. Many yachting people who sail San Francisco Bay consider it the most ideal home in the entire Bay Area. Most of the light keepers and admirals who have lived here agree with them.

Here, on a windy day, waves shoot over 50 feet into the air as they break below Point Bonita lighthouse. The sentinel's ancient lens, which once guided clipper ships filled with pioneers, now leads modern container ships into the harbor, 1975. (R. Shanks)

POINT BONITA

Point Bonita is a spectacular steep and narrow formation of grey rock which extends for a half mile off the Marin Headlands. It forms the outer reaches of the north entrance to San Francisco Bay and its significance to mariners was learned early.

By 1850, Congress had already received a recommendation from the Coast Survey that a lighthouse be placed on Point Bonita as soon as possible. Funds, as usual, were slow in coming. The steamer *Tennessee*, heavily laden with passengers, met with disaster when she ran ashore north of the point during heavy fog. Miraculously, the ship grounded on one of the few beaches along the southern Marin coast, and all aboard were saved. (The scene of the wreck still bears the name Tennessee Cove.) Had the ship struck closer to the point, the steamer would have encountered offshore rocks and vertical cliffs, and the story would then have had a more tragic ending. The funding delays had almost proven disastrous.

Any doubts about the need for a light station at Point Bonita had, by now, vanished. Serious consideration was given to building a lighthouse at Point Lobos in San Francisco on the southwest side of the Golden Gate and plans were even drawn. These tentative plans called for a California cottage style lighthouse of the type later built at Crescent City, Point Loma, Point Pinos, and elsewhere. But local mariners knew the coast the best and they argued in a petition for a beacon on the opposite shore at Point Bonita, noting that "the Light at Point Lobos . . . could not be approached in thick weather, without great risk of coming in contact with dangerous rocks . . . Point Bonita can be safely approached within 150 yards . . ." Richard Hammond, Superintendent of Lights at San Francisco, concurred and forcefully expressed his concern, "The erection of a lighthouse at Bonita Point . . . is of great moment and importance to the commerce of this port . . . and is essential to the safety of vessels approaching this harbor." No one could reasonably argue with that, considering the broken wreckage that marked the Golden Gate. In March 1853, Congress appropriated $25,000 to build Point Bonita Light Station. Seven thousand dollars of this was spent placing an order for a second order Fresnel lens from Paris.

The fixed (non-flashing) second order lens purchased meant that lighthouse authorities were quite serious about the need for a powerful and effective light at Point Bonita. A nearly identical second order lens was also purchased for Boon Island lighthouse, nine miles off York Harbor, Maine. Boon Island is New England's tallest lighthouse at 133 feet and many Coast Guardsmen today consider it the most treacherous station to land on in the entire state of Maine. That both Boon Island

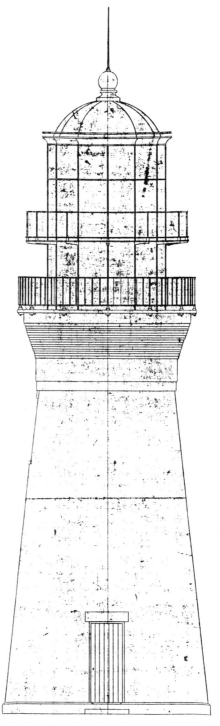

Original plans for the first *Point Bonita lighthouse, 1855. (U.S. Coast Guard)*

and Point Bonita were to be equipped with the same type lenses at the same time indicates that the Lighthouse Establishment, so often ignorant of West Coast needs and conditions, knew Point Bonita needed to be a major light station. First and second order lenses were expensive and they were reserved for the most important coastal stations.

In May 1854, the Lighthouse Board directed 12th District Lighthouse Inspector Campbell Graham to give his full attention to the construction of Point Bonita Lighthouse. This was no small order. Point Bonita was isolated and landing at Bonita Cove could be tricky. Besides, Graham had ongoing construction work at lighthouses all the way from Washington state to southern California.

With such a heavy workload and so much pressure from the business community and government to get a new Pacific Coast lighthouse system in operation quickly, there was probably little time for reflection. Inspector Graham visited Point Bonita and selected its highest hill as the lighthouse site (near where the Coast Guard radar antenna stands today). This would later prove a mistake, but Americans were largely new to California and had limited knowledge of the region's natural environment.

Along the low shores of the East Coast, taller was better as far as lighthouse sites went. On the West Coast, where cliffs routinely soared hundreds of feet above the surf, higher wasn't to prove better. Higher was to prove foggier. And fog rendered even first and second order lenses invisible.

But these weren't major considerations in the mid-1850s. Ships were ramming rocks and sinking, the public and government were howling, and Inspector Graham and his associates had many lighthouse construction jobs on their hands.

Graham generally liked the site at Point Bonita. It was, of course, high—260 feet above the sea. The cliff top was narrow and would have to be cut down about 10 feet to provide a large enough level area for the new beacon. There was, though, "a luxurious growth of grass and wild flowers." And, "the soil is remarkably fine and well adapted for cultivation."

Graham didn't like the landing because 50-foot cliffs on the Bonita Cove side of the point would mean "considerable difficulty" in bringing supplies ashore. He noted that the seaward face of the point was "almost perpendicular and composed principally of rock." If he had been there on a day when the surf was running high, he might have added that the Pacific hits the point with such force that the breakers literally sound like artillery fire.

A local contractor was hired but soon backed out of such a challenging job. A new firm, Hofras and Cowing, was hired and they tackled the lonely cliff top. Work progressed now and eventually a conical masonry light tower, topped by a very handsome lantern room with an umbrella-shaped roof, was completed. The beacon was built with loving care, even with the addition of iron gargoyles in the form of American eagles at each of the rain spouts, a feature also used at Farallon Islands light, 23 miles offshore to the west. The new Point Bonita lighthouse was 56-feet high and stood awaiting its second order lens. Rains and heavy seas delayed the landing of the lens at Point Bonita for nearly a month. But, in March 1855, it was successfully brought through the surf and landed. On May 2, 1855, it was first lighted and Point Bonita became an operating lighthouse. The lens looked like a glistening diamond and shown forth from its lighthouse crown 306 feet above the sea.

Early visitors marveled at the neatness and order maintained in the tower. The lamps burned five quarts of oil each night, and reporters commented that nary a drop marred the spotless interior. The oil was stored in large tanks near the entrance to the tower (possibly inside the little shed that stood nearby), and each evening the required amount was drawn off and the keeper began his nightly rounds. He ascended a flight of stairs in the masonry portion, then entered the multi-sided watchroom, where he kept his tools, glass chimneys, and other supplies. Up another short flight of stairs was the lens with its prisms and reflectors, "the latter so dazzling bright that it was impossible to look closely at the lens on sunny days".

The lone keeper and his family lived on the same hill, a short distance to the north, in a one-and-a-half-story brick and stone cottage, stuccoed a gleaming white. Most of the early California lighthouses (including the first structures at Alcatraz and Fort Point) had been built with a tower literally surrounded by a cottage, so that the light tower emerged from the dwelling roof. Point Bonita's residence was basically of the same California cottage architectural style, except that the tower was never placed within the dwelling but stood some distance away. Virtually the same plans and technique were also used at Farallon Islands Light Station.

The view from the station was unparalleled and the sea air stimulating, but, for keepers, the first years at Point Bonita were ones of extreme isolation and loneliness. Transportation was so poor that the keeper shortly wrote his superiors complaining that,

> There are no inhabitants within five miles from this point, from San Francisco to Point Bonita; there is no direct communication but by chance, a sailboat may be procured at an expense of $5, and from $2 to $5 for freight.

It was typical of the early lighthouse system to make no provision for transportation other than occasional visits by the lighthouse tender, and poor pay always remained characteristic of the job.

Point Bonita was unusual in the near record amount of fog found there, and Lighthouse Service administrators felt that some sort of noise maker had to be established as a fog signal. In mid-19th century

A rare photo of the first Point Bonita lighthouse atop the narrow headland. High fog forced the sentinel's relocation to the point's lower tip in 1877. (Bancroft Library)

The first keepers' dwelling at Point Bonita. (Bancroft Library)

America, some of the noisiest devices in existence were cannons, and it was decided that an Army-surplus siege gun would make a dandy fog signal. A hefty, eight-foot long 24-pounder was acquired from the Benicia Arsenal and a new keeper, Sgt. Edward Maloney, U.S. Army, Ret., was hired. Sgt. Maloney was an experienced cannoneer, and he readily agreed to the assignment. The sergeant was to fire the cannon (minus ball, of course) once every half-hour during foggy weather. With Point Bonita averaging over 1000 hours of fog annually, the old campaigner had his job cut out for him.

On August 8, 1856, the cannon went into service, and the Pacific Coast had its first fog signal. On foggy days it boomed forth on the hour and half-hour, sending its warning echoes across the Golden Gate. However, Point Bonita's fog had a way of lasting longer than almost anywhere. It would last day and night without respite, and soon the faithful sergeant was writing his superiors:

> I cannot find any person here to relieve me, not five minutes;
> I have been up three days and nights, and had only two hours'
> rest. I was nearly used up. All the rest I would require in 24 is
> two, if I could only get it.

The lighthouse inspector eventually sent the exhausted Maloney an assistant. Lighthouse Inspector Hartmann Bache was very sympathetic to Edward Maloney's plight. First of all, he personally knew how isolated Point Bonita was. He had informed his superiors that for some time he didn't have any idea how well the new fog gun was working as he'd found it impossible to get to Point Bonita himself. He recommended buying the station a boat instead of leaving its personnel in isolation. A boat would be handy for a stranded visiting lighthouse inspector as well.

He also ordered the station's head lighthouse keeper, Edward A. Colson, or the first assistant keeper, to relieve Maloney. Apparently, the Lighthouse Service had hired Maloney as a fog signal attendant and not as one of the regular light keepers. The light keepers didn't see operating a fog signal as one of their tasks. This problem was soon ironed out when Bache ordered Colson or his assistant to aid Maloney in his cannoneering. Forever after, California light keepers manned the fog signal as well as the light.

Problems at the new station were rampant. The keepers began complaining about the very low pay they were receiving for an isolated and difficult job. Mariners also began complaining. Not about pay but about the fact that they couldn't hear the fog cannon. Bache took a steamer out the Gate and listened. It was true. You couldn't hear the fog cannon when it was fired.

Soon Bache was complaining too. The price of gun powder was high in San Francisco and rising. Because of improper installation of the lens, the glass chimneys used for the lamps in the lighthouse lens were breaking by the dozen. Keeper Colson was falsely accused of incompetence by the Lighthouse Board.

Bache had by now, of course, provided Sgt. Maloney with additional help, but the West Coast's pioneer fog signal attendant had enough—he resigned. Maloney was not alone. Although Keeper Colson had been vindicated of charges of incompetence over the mysterious breaking chimneys incident, he was fed up, too, and resigned as well.

The personnel problems were enormous. During one nine-month period in 1855-56, the station went through seven keepers. Dissatisfaction was almost as great over on rocky Alcatraz Island light station. During the same period, five of its keepers had quit. The West Coast had the beginnings of a new lighthouse system, but

Point Bonita lighthouse's fog cannon. This was the first fog signal on the Pacific Coast and was the grandparent of all those fog horns, bells, gongs, whistles and sirens which later guided mariners in thick weather. It is shown here on display at Coast Guard Base Alameda on its original carriage. Today the historic fog cannon remains at Coast Guard Island, Alameda, but a new ship's style gun mount has replaced the proper mounting. (Golden Gate National Recreation Area)

Point Bonita's second order lens is the largest on San Francisco Bay. Built in France in the 1850s, it was brought around Cape Horn in the hold of a sailing ship. The ladder at left gives an idea of its large size. (R. Shanks)

it wasn't working very well. Low pay, isolation, non-existent transportation, and an unrealistic and insensitive Lighthouse Board were the real issues.

Things finally did improve a bit out at Point Bonita. A mechanically struck fog bell arrived and was installed at the base of the lighthouse. It was a scientific wonder whose clockwork drive required little beyond winding once every six hours. By August 1856, the new 1500-pound fog bell was clanging away. It was much more effective than the cannon and made life much easier for everybody. Surprisingly, the fog cannon was not immediately discontinued. It remained until 1857.[1]

Transportation remained a problem at Point Bonita. A boat was purchased for the keepers, probably a 14-foot Whitehall. It didn't last long. It was soon wrecked on the rocks of treacherous Bonita Cove and the keepers were as isolated as ever.

During those long, lonely years of the 1860s, the silent fog had repeatedly enveloped the lighthouse in a manner which would spell its doom. Lighthouse engineers had built most of California's first beacons on the highest reaches of the coastal headlands, unaware that California fog is frequently a high fog which shrouds the upper headlands while leaving lower elevations clear. At 300 feet above the sea, the Point Bonita beacon was often so covered by high dense fog that it was invisible from the straits below. Lighthouse authorities decided that the tower would have to be abandoned and a new lighthouse established at a lower position at the less foggy tip of Point Bonita. A new fog signal building would also be placed nearby.

Point Bonita's tip in those days was called "Land's End". To reach Land's End meant crossing the steepest and narrowest section of the point. The area was particularly dangerous because some of the rock was so unstable that big chunks of the point would suddenly break off and fall a hundred (or even two hundred) feet down to the crashing surf. As if this were not enough, elsewhere the rock was so hard that it was almost impossible to penetrate.

Nevertheless, the Lighthouse Service decided that the light and fog signal must be relocated at the tip. A crew of workmen was assembled and brought to the point. When they arrived and saw Point Bonita's cliffs first hand, a goodly portion of the crew quit, refusing to work on the crumbling cliffs. Eventually, however, a full crew was obtained and noticeable progress began.

A narrow path was slowly cut along the point above Bonita Cove. The cliffs were so dangerous that only a very narrow trail could be cut. In such a restricted space, only one or two men were able to work at a time, which slowed progress considerably. Landslides and slip-outs occurred throughout construction, and this necessitated rebuilding some sections. At times it was a "nip-and-tuck" operation where the crew had to cross a 100-foot deep chasm on a single, unsupported plank using only a rope to hold onto. About two-thirds of the way to the end of the point, they encountered a massive rock which resisted cutting. A precarious

---

[1]The fog cannon may have been a failure but its historic value was recognized early. It was the first fog signal on the Pacific Coast, and, as such, was preserved by the Lighthouse Service and later the Coast Guard. It remains today on display at the Coast Guard Base on Coast Guard Island in Alameda. Perhaps some day it can be reinstalled at its historic location at Point Bonita.

wooden walkway, which hung above the surf, had to be fastened to the outer edge of the rock. Beyond the rock, the opposite conditions were encountered. Here, the point was weathering badly and unstable rock kept slipping away.

Despite all, a secure trail was finally completed. Work then turned to leveling the portion of Land's End overlooking the cove for the fog signal building. The fog signal would require many tons of coal to fire her boilers, and this would necessitate some sort of landing. Finding a suitable spot was a problem but, fortunately, a solid, stable rock was discovered which jutted out into the cove over deep water. The rock was well below the trail and workmen had to be lowered to the site by ropes. Once there, they built a landing platform with a boom for unloading supplies from the tenders and a combination railroad track and stairway which connected the landing to the trail above.

Work now centered on providing a power source for the railroad. At the top of the track, a steam-powered winch operated a cable system which pulled little coal cars up the track at a respectable 45-degree incline. A more ancient mode of transportation took over at the trail—horse cars ran along a track to where the fog signal building was under construction. Once the fog signal was complete, both the horses and the steam engine would do a lot of puffing, since the signal's boiler fires would consume over 75 tons of coal a year and every last chunk of it would be hauled along the railway.

The new fog signal was a siren. Not an ordinary siren, but a giant among sirens. The siren's trumpet alone was 16 feet long with a mouth 30 inches in diameter. Inside the siren itself, a disk containing 12 holes was powered by a small machine which spun the disk at the rate of 2200 revolutions per minute. Steam was forced into the siren, and as it escaped through the whirling holes, a great wail was created.

The siren, however, was soon subject to Point Bonita's tricks. It had not been in operation long when, during a storm in 1874, the bank holding the fog trumpet gave way and fell into the sea. The next year, Land's End had to be leveled further and the fog signal building moved back from the edge of the cliff.

Relocating the fog signal building was not the only major reconstruction. Access to Land's End was greatly improved when a 118-foot long tunnel was carved through the massive rock which had previously resisted cutting. The tunnel was handcarved by highly skilled Chinese-American construction workers, many of whom had extensive experience in tunnel construction from building the West's railroads. The tunnel eliminated the precarious walkway and also allowed the railroad to be extended from the landing track through the tunnel and up the hill to where the keepers resided. A one-horse cart, built to fit the narrow tunnel, brought supplies up to the dwellings.

The newly reconstructed lighthouse at the tip of Point Bonita overlooks a passing steam schooner north bound for the Redwood Coast, C. 1877. (U.S. Army Museum, Presidio of San Francisco)

The construction of a steam-powered fog signal meant that the station staff had to be expanded. Most stations with steam fog signal equipment needed four keepers. The original keepers' cottage, even with its two-room addition, was inadequate to house everyone assigned to the station. Thus, two handsome frame houses were built alongside the original 1856 residence.

It was an age of steam both for fog signals and tramway winches, and steam required water. Even the attractive residence grounds con-

Point Bonita lighthouse keepers operating the derrick at the landing near the point's tip. The foundation of this landing can still be seen below the trail between the tunnel and the suspension bridge. Later, the Army and the Life-Saving Service established a substantial pier landward in the cove. (U.S. Coast Guard)

tributed to the operation of the station. The keepers' lawn was dug up and a reservoir constructed there (undoubtedly largely underground). The reservoir was fed by a spring in the ravine, the water being pumped up to the site by a windmill.

In 1877, the reconstruction program culminated with the relocation of the lighthouse. The seaward portion of Land's End was leveled and a low, rectangular, one-story masonry building constructed. It contained three rooms: an oil room, a storage room, and a sitting room. The center room was built with fortress-like walls, since it would bear the weight of the tower. Both the lantern room and the polygonal iron watch room of the original lighthouse were placed on top of the new structure. The original beacon's masonry portion, about half its height, remained and was enclosed with a brick cap to serve as a day mark. The new lighthouse, painted white with a black lantern room and sporting double balconies, was an aesthetic success. The old lantern room, with its eagle's head gargoyles and antique roof, blended with its new base to

Point Bonita's wonderful foot tunnel hand carved in 1877 by skilled Chinese-American workers. Chinese-Americans were very important participants in California maritime history, being the Bay's first commercial fishermen and crewing many American trans-Pacific sailing ships and steamers, 1982. (U.S. Coast Guard)

become one of California's most beautiful lighthouses. On February 2, 1877, the three circular wicks of its lamp were lighted by Keeper John Brown, and the second order lens again marked the Golden Gate. It was rather amazing to have a lighthouse with its *upper* half built in 1855 and its *lower* half built in 1877. The lighthouse was 33 feet high.

Teddy Roosevelt's famed Great White Fleet used Point Bonita lighthouse as a navigational guide during its 1908 visit to San Francisco Bay. (Harry Dring)

The new lighthouse at Point Bonita represented a highly significant West Coast adaptation of lighthouse construction. It was, like its predecessor, a short tower equipped with a large lens, built to mark a very high headland where fog was a major problem. Such a beacon was typical of many of California's major coastal light stations which were generally equipped with first or second order lenses. Excellent examples came to be built at Cape Mendocino, Punta Gorda, Point Reyes, Farallon Islands, Point Sur, and Point Conception, as well as Point Bonita. These short, powerful sentinels contrast with the more narrow, relatively small, low-power lights so common in Maine, or the tall towers of the Middle Atlantic states and the South. They are true California lighthouse classics.

The distinctive new lighthouse at Point Bonita continued to show its fixed white light through the closing decades of the 19th century. Then, shortly after the turn of the century, another major reconstruction project occurred at Land's End. A new brick fog signal building was erected in front of the lighthouse, replacing the older fog signal building nearby. Work on the new fog signal had been slowed because the brick manufacturers, well aware of the rough winter sea conditions at Point Bonita, refused to deliver materials directly to the point until the weather improved in April. The new structure was so well designed that it enhanced the beauty of the lighthouse by mirroring it both in style and strength. Completed in August 1903, the fog signal building housed a steam siren of the first class which emitted an ear-shattering, five-second long wail every 35 seconds during foggy weather. The building was painted white with a red roof and had been designed to meet the peculiarly West Coast situation of short lighthouses. Fog signal buildings at the beginning of the 20th century often had large masonry smokestacks to

keep the smoke from the boiler fires away from the lighthouse. Since Point Bonita's fog signal was in front of the short lighthouse, a tall stack would partially obscure the light. As a result, a long pipe had to be built from the fog signal building to the stack which was erected in back of the lighthouse. The big, white chimney thus towered behind the lighthouse, and more than one mariner may have wondered if he was seeing double.

The fog signal wasn't all that was new at Point Bonita. In 1899, the U.S. Life-Saving Service would open its new Point Bonita rescue station. No lighthouse could eliminate all maritime disasters, of course, and shipwrecks continued at the Golden Gate. Three life-saving stations had been built south of the Golden Gate in San Francisco: Fort Point, Golden Gate Park, and Southside stations. These protected San Francisco's Ocean Beach and the south side of the Golden Gate. But the north shore had no rescuers except Point Bonita's light keepers.

To be sure, the Point Bonita wickies made heroic rescues. In 1874, the tug *Rescue* rammed the rocky headlands and the light keepers were able to save eight of the nine-man crew. Two years later, they fished a pair of soggy survivors of a capsized boat out of the cold waters.

In 1887, the schooner *Parallel* was washed toward the rocks of Point Lobos to the south. Her crew abandoned the ship in terror and rowed to Point Bonita light station for help. They had good reason to leave their drifting vessel. Her cargo was among the most dangerous imaginable—kerosene, hay, and over 40 tons of highly explosive black gun powder. Any owner who loaded a ship with that combination of cargo was criminal indeed.

The abandoned *Parallel* drifted onto the rocks, coming ashore near the Cliff House in San Francisco. The dedicated surfmen from Golden

February 1913 view of the entire point from Bonita Cove. This photograph hung in the Point Bonita light station office for many years. It was presented as a gift to the author by officer-in-charge Bob Grass. (Author's collection)

Gate Park Life-Saving Station immediately went to the rescue, trying to save the ship. The surfmen had no idea of the *Parallel's* deadly cargo and went on board to save her and protect the ship from looting. The sea began pounding the schooner against the cliffs and then the inevitable happened. With three surfmen on board, the *Parallel* exploded. Debris flew up to a mile away and all three surfmen were seriously injured. The *Parallel's* crew, perhaps wanting to get away from the whole ugly scene, were fed by the light keepers and quickly left for Sausalito.

In 1895, the schooner *Samson* was anchored in Bonita Cove. A gale arose and she began dragging anchor toward the point's jagged cliffs. The light keepers saw the trouble and the deadly potential of a helpless ship, high winds, and vertical cliffs. They began blowing the fog signal, trying to attract the attention of the life-saving lookouts and patrolmen across the Golden Gate at Point Lobos. But the wind and sea drowned out the noise.

Conditions worsened and the wind blew so hard that the light keepers had to crawl on their hands and knees to keep from being blown off the cliff. Fort Point Life-Saving Station's lookout eventually saw the wreck and surfmen arrived at Point Bonita after a valiant effort, but sailors were already drowning in front of the light station. Finally, the Fort Point surfmen saved one boatload of crewmen and the Point Bonita lighthouse keepers struggled down the cliff and pulled three more sailors to safety from the pounding breakers.

The day after Christmas in 1896 was cold at Point Bonita, with rain squalls and a gale wind blowing. Keeper George D. Cobb kept his eye on the sea, especially on days such as this one. Suddenly, he saw a sailboat capsize and its three occupants go into the water. Cobb rushed to lower the little lighthouse boat from its davits, no easy task since it was exposed to the full fury of the wind. Successfully launching the station boat, he began rowing toward those struggling in the water. Rowing was very difficult because the station boat was designed to be

handled by no less than two oarsmen and Cobb was alone. Making matters worse, he had to work his way past offshore rocks, through heavy seas, and contend with gale winds. Reaching the sailboat, he found two sailors alive, but unconscious. Pulling wet, unconscious people on board was extremely hard but Keeper Cobb managed anyway. He then found that a third victim had drifted in among the rocks. This man, too, was unconscious and was being battered against the rocks by the heavy seas. Cobb rowed over and got him on board too. This was a bloody job since the third man had been cut by the rocks and was bleeding badly. Now Mr. Cobb had to work his boat back to safety, a task made harder by the additional three men on board. But again, George Cobb succeeded and all made it ashore safely. The happy ending was that all three sailors recovered and Keeper Cobb received national recognition when he was awarded the Life-Saving Service's silver medal.

But not all such rescues ended so happily. In February 1891, the *Elizabeth* had stranded at Rocky Point, between Point Bonita and Muir Beach. This region was northwest of Point Bonita and it was always a terrible place for a shipwreck. As the *Coast Pilot* advised, "From Point Bonita to Rocky Point, the coast is very rugged and broken. The cliffs, which are the seaward termination of spurs from Mount Tamalpais, rise to heights of over 500 feet and are intersected by deep, narrow valleys stretching inland."

The Golden Gate Park Life-Saving Station's lookout had seen distress signals earlier from the lookout at San Francisco's Point Lobos. The seas were so heavy at San Francisco's Ocean Beach that the Golden Gate Park crew couldn't launch their lifeboat. So they had telephoned Fort Point Life-Saving Station and that crew had set out in their lifeboat through the Golden Gate to the rescue. Seas here were terrible as well, and giant waves swept the officer-in-charge, Captain Charles Henry, out of the lifeboat and drowned him.

With fog signal building in front of the lighthouse and the stack for the boiler fires behind it, Point Bonita can be seen as it looked during the first quarter of the twentieth century. The portion of the lighthouse from the lower balcony upward was from the original 1855 tower. (U.S. Army, Presidio of San Francisco)

Bonita Cove with the Point Bonita Lifeboat Station's boathouse and the government pier. Along the shore in the distance the Lighthouse Service's landing can be seen precariously mounted on the cliff, 1939. (U.S. Coast Guard)

The conditions by now had become so fearsome in the Golden Gate that the surviving surfmen were forced to return to Fort Point. When the Fort Point and Golden Gate Park surfmen finally reached the *Elizabeth* by an overland route across southern Marin County a day later, the surfmen found 29 dead, 11 survivors, and a totally destroyed ship.

Wrecks such as the *Elizabeth* pointed out the need for a life-saving station on the north side of the Golden Gate. There had been a life-saving station on the north shore at Bolinas Bay from 1881-1885, but it had burned and would not be rebuilt until 1915. As a result, Point Bonita's lighthouse keepers had been the sole rescuers on the north shore of San Francisco Bay for years now. Clearly, with increasing shipping, they needed help.

Thus, in the summer of 1899, work had begun on the new Point Bonita Life-Saving Station. Building the life-saving station wasn't easy. Plans called for a one-and-a-half story building with attached lookout tower. Two boathouses were to be built, Boathouse A on Bonita Cove and Boathouse B on the ocean side near Rodeo Lagoon. Rough waves in Bonita Cove slowed foundation work on Boathouse A and very hard rock held back progress at Boathouse B on the ocean side. But, in September 1899, work was completed and a particularly beautiful station was soon in operation.

Now the Golden Gate and its immediate approaches had three life-saving stations on the south shore—Golden Gate Park, Southside and Fort Point—and Point Bonita on the north shore. Point Reyes had received a life-saving station in 1889 and Bolinas Bay station would be eventually rebuilt. Thus, mariners ultimately were able to count on help when they needed it from three rescue stations on each side of the San Francisco Bay approaches. Considering the number of shipwrecks and their magnitude, six life-saving stations seemed none too many.

When a vessel was in distress, the Point Bonita lighthouse keepers would sound five or six short sharp blasts on the fog signal followed by a prolonged blast—the standard signal used by California light keepers to alert nearby life-saving stations.

Point Bonita was a well equipped life-saving station. It had a lifeboat, surfboat, breeches buoy, a line throwing Lyle gun, and a beach cart with a team of horses for hauling the rescue boats to remote locations. There was an officer-in-charge, the keeper, and six to eight surfmen. Early boats were rowed using 18-foot long oars, but by the end of the first decade of the 20th Century, "power motor lifeboats" were being added to many life-saving stations. This increased the station's range and efficiency tremendously.

The first motor lifeboat on the West Coast was assigned to Cape Disappointment, Washington, in 1905, and the second probably to Humboldt Bay, California. Fort Point was the first station in the

Bay Area to receive one, in 1907, and Point Bonita the second. Two local stations, Golden Gate Park and Southside, would never get motor lifeboats because the surf at San Francisco's Ocean Beach was too heavy to allow a marine railway to be built as a launchway. Other California stations—Point Reyes, Arena Cove and Bolinas Bay, were all eventually equipped with the new 36-foot motor lifeboats. Although there have been design modifications over the years, self-bailing and self-righting motor lifeboats still remain the backbone of Coast Guard rescue operations.

While the Point Bonita surfmen had fine new quarters and a nice frame dwelling had been previously added for the light keepers, the original 1856 keepers' dwelling was still in use in 1906. The years had not been kind to the structure. Its upstairs was uninhabitable and the lower story dank, small, and unpopular with the keepers. The Lighthouse Board had requested funding to replace the old dwelling for years but to no avail. On the morning of April 18, 1906, the dwelling's career came to an end.

An assistant keeper, a single man, lived in one part of the 1856 dwelling and another assistant keeper, Hermann Engel and his family, lived in the other. When the great San Francisco earthquake hit that morning shortly after 5 a.m., Mr. Engel was on watch at the lighthouse. The rest of the Engel family and the third assistant weren't so lucky. They were asleep in the aged dwelling.

Suddenly, the great quake began shattering the rigid stone and brick dwelling. Its gable ends were shaken out, walls cracked, large segments of the walls came tumbling down, and chimneys toppled. The third assistant keeper reacted first, urging the neighboring Engel family out of the house. Everyone scrambled out of the building amidst falling debris and rising dust.

The assistant keeper ran off to tell the head keeper what had happened and the surfmen came running up the hill to the rescue. Fortunately, everyone was safe. The upper floor had apparently sheltered the occupants from falling brickwork and saved everyone's lives. It is a credit to the amazing dedication of the Lighthouse Service personnel that Keeper Engel remained on watch at the lighthouse, undoubtedly terribly worried about his family. The lighthouse itself, sturdily built upon one of the few solid rocks at the point, had suffered no damage. A surfman came down to the light to tell the keeper his family was safe.

Other dwellings were less damaged so the immediate problem was where to house the two keepers. The surfmen fed, housed and cared for the keepers and their families at the Life-Saving Station. The surfmen saved what they could from the dwelling, including furniture. Eventually, the third assistant keeper moved into the abandoned siren house at the tip of the point and the Engels into an old Army engineer's office. With characteristic lack of speed, it was nearly two

Point Bonita Life-Saving Station with its soaring lookout tower, 1961.
(U.S. Coast Guard)

years before the Lighthouse Service completed a new dwelling for assistant keepers.[2]

Interestingly, the old abandoned lighthouse tower atop the hill survived the 1906 earthquake just fine. The lantern room was long gone, now mounted atop the new lighthouse base at the point. But the Lighthouse Service still liked having the old capped tower atop the Point's highest hill. It could be seen for long distances, both at sea and from the harbor. Thus, it made a fine day mark to navigate by in clear weather. Mariners used it to take their position when entering the Golden Gate during daylight.

---

[2]Keeper and Mrs. Engel's daughter, Norma, wrote of these and other fascinating events in her book, *Three Beams of Light*, which is highly recommended. She recalled how the Point Bonita keepers carried broom handles as props to prevent being blown over on windy days and avoid flying off the cliffs. She tells such stories as how one wickie fashioned harnesses for his little children so if they fell over the steep banks, they wouldn't fall very far. He lived in the dwelling built at the point's extremity on the siren house site. The yard terminated in steep cliffs and the home site was quite perilous. Later, the Engels transferred to Ballast Point light on San Diego Bay and on to more adventures.

Point Bonita Life-Saving Station's motor lifeboat Majestic *on launchway at Bonita Cove. The lifeboat was pulled by winch up and down the marine railway on the railroad-type carriage it is shown riding on. The remains of this marine railway may still be seen on Bonita Cove below the trail to the lighthouse. (Golden Gate National Recreation Area)*

But the Army had come to the Point some years earlier and built massive fortifications for artillery. They hadn't liked the 1856 dwelling either and wanted the Lighthouse Service to tear it down well before the 1906 earthquake took care of that. But now, in 1907, they were after the old lighthouse, too. The War Department demanded that the old lighthouse be removed for "a fire control project." Just how the old masonry lighthouse could have been a threat to national security is a mystery. But, anyway, the Lighthouse Service very reluctantly agreed and eventually the historic tower was razed. The Army had begun what was to be a long and sad record of needlessly destroying historic Coast Guard buildings in the state while at the same time preserving its own historic structures.

With the Lighthouse Service, the Life-Saving Service, and the Army at Point Bonita, the area was covered with buildings. So many people were living there that eventually a school was established and the custom of children going to classes in distant Sausalito discontinued for a time. High school age young people always had a long trek, taking the train from Sausalito to, at various times, either San Rafael or Mill Valley. A new road had been built through the Throckmorton Ranch and the isolation of the early years was now fading.

In 1922, five great searchlights were established—one each at Lime Point, Fort Miley, and the Presidio, and two were installed at Point Bonita, one just seaward of the new fog signal building (where the structure can still be seen today). The powerful searchlights were encased in small, galvanized-iron houses with large windows. It was claimed that the Army-operated searchlights could find a vessel 12,500 yards at sea and were designed for military use and to aid lost ships which occasionally steamed about the harbor entrance in confusion. Searchlight drills were held with all the lights operating simultaneously. During these drills, the government tugboats *Golden Gate, Argonaut*, and *Hartley* steamed around the strait, while the operators of the searchlights attempted to find them.

With all these lights around, it was decided to update Point Bonita lighthouse's signal. As established in 1855, the Point Bonita was a fixed, not a flashing lens. This meant that the light simply shone all night, never varying its character. This worked fine during the early days when there were few lights with which the sentinel could be confused. But now there were many lights in the area and Point Bonita needed to flash a distinctive signal. An occulting device, called an eclipser or shield, was installed within the lens. Clockwork driven, the shield rotated within the lens, periodically blocking its light and making the light appear to go dark for a set interval. A light, as in Point Bonita's case, would appear to shine, for example, 25 seconds and then go dark for five seconds as the shield passed by. The lamp in the lens, of course, would be burning steadily; it was just the revolving eclipser that made the light appear to go dark. This was a standard Lighthouse Service method of converting older fixed lenses into flashing ones. Point Pinos lighthouse at Pacific Grove, CA, was similarly equipped and kept its eclipser on hand for emergency use into the 1970s. Electricity with its automatic flashing devices eventually rendered eclipsers obsolete, except as a backup system powered by a clockwork drive and weights in case the electrical system failed. Typically, these early lenses were converted to occulting lights—that is, lights which are on longer than they are off—the opposite of flashing lights which are off longer than they are on.

Of course, this new fangled modern equipment didn't mean the end of shipwrecks. On January 8, 1915, the steam schooner *Eureka* was capsized by immense waves, thrown onto the rocks and began breaking up. Assistant Keeper Alexander Martin went to the rescue. Taking a rope, he lowered himself over 100-feet down the sheer cliff toward the *Eureka* in a heroic attempt to rescue those on board. The line was too short, however, and Martin dangled literally at the end of his rope. There was no choice but to climb back up the cliff, bravery and good intentions not withstanding. Fortunately, the Point Bonita life-saving crew soon arrived in their boat and, in a daring rescue, were able to save nearly everyone on board. Martin's attempt had been a courageous one as well and was typical of those who lived at Point Bonita.

Alex Martin and his family lived in the dwelling at the point's very tip, near where the suspension bridge is today. Assistant Keeper Martin got plenty of experience with those high cliffs beneath his home. Things always seemed to be falling in the water. The family cat fell over the cliff. So did his daughter Dorothy. One day Martin's light keeper's hat was in the water and the family thought Alex Martin had fallen in. But it was just his hat and, like Dorothy, Alex Martin was safe. There were always surprises, always changes at Point Bonita.

Assistant keeper at Point Bonita light calling in the weather at the watchroom which once stood atop the lighthouse just seaward of the lantern room. Meteorological equipment and log books dominate the scene, 1975. (R. Shanks)

The year 1915 saw another change at Point Bonita. The life-saving crew suddenly found themselves members of a new organization when the Life-Saving Service and Revenue Cutter Service merged to form the modern Coast Guard.

The light keepers continued to be employees of the Lighthouse Service, an organization some of the wickies considered none too generous at payday. By 1917, many Pacific Coast light keepers found their salaries intolerably low, and some began a campaign to make Congress and the public aware of their plight. Soon, a petition was drawn up and sent to every keeper along the coast for signing. It read:

To the Congress of the United States:

Your petitioners, employees of the United States Lighthouse Service, appealing to your fairness and sense of justice, respectfully and earnestly ask you to alleviate our indigent circumstances by granting an increase in salary enabling us to maintain a decent standard of living under present conditions.

The annual salary appropriation, not to exceed an average of $600 for each Lighthouse Keeper established by Act of Congress about forty years ago, has remained stationary, while living expenses have increased more than one hundred percent, during which time employers in general have granted their help a corresponding increase in pay.

Lighthouse Keepers being stationed at isolated places are often taxed with the additional burden of having to board their children in distant communities in order that they may attend school, many being deprived of the benefit of an education, as an average salary of $50 per month will not allow it.

There are instances on record where Lighthouse Keepers have remained on station for a number of years, the salary being insufficient for them to take advantage of the allowed leave of absence and after many years of faithful and efficient service, no provision being made for a pension, their dependents are left in dire circumstances.

The duties of a Lighthouse Keeper being in a measure similar to those demanded of a Coast Guard Station Crew and fully as important, hazardous and strenuous, are deserving of a compensation equal to that allowed surfmen in the Coast Guard Service and we feel justified in respectfully urging you to grant us the same.

The light keepers certainly deserved more adequate compensation, but the job continued to remain underpaid. Twenty-two years later, however, the wickies did achieve equality with the surfmen when, in 1939, the Lighthouse Service was incorporated into the Coast Guard.

The late Thirties were the twilight of Lighthouse Service operations. Such veterans as Stephen A. Hicks were still there. Keeper Hicks had arrived in 1935 from Point Arguello light in Santa Barbara County. He had an interesting career, having worked in the far North for the Hudson's Bay Company. He'd been whaling for a time, but much preferred light keeping. The Hicks family felt fortunate to live in the big dwelling and not be stuck out in the precarious little house at the point's tip. Assistant Keeper George Watters and his family lived out there now and erosion had continued around the residence. It wasn't too many years before the dwelling would have to be abandoned.

Having the Army on the Point could be annoying. Keeper Hicks had his garage on property that the Army had taken over. Every time he or his wife wanted to get their car, they had to go through the whole, "Halt, who goes there?" routine. Getting an education was a bit easier and Keeper Hick's daughter, Barbara Hicks Clough, recalls attending the station's own little red one-room schoolhouse.

The first winter of Coast Guard operation, 1939-40, saw some foul weather. There was destruction all along the Point. Landslides swept down the cliffs near the boathouse and many feet of trail were lost. It was even worse out at the lighthouse. The area where the suspension bridge now hangs was a paved trail at that time. The rock gave way and the trail fell into the Pacific. The opening that resulted left the lighthouse inaccessible, and a breeches buoy had to be rigged to cross the chasm. Point Bonita was one of the few mainland lighthouses in history to be reached by breeches buoy, a device designed to remove sailors across raging surf from wrecked ships. Eventually, a wooden causeway was built, and the sentinel could again be visited without an aerial ride. Later, the causeway was replaced by a wonderful suspension bridge, a miniature of the Golden Gate Bridge. This added another distinction to the station. It became the only Coast Guard lighthouse to be reached by suspension bridge. The assistant keeper's dwelling that had been built on the point just east of where the suspension bridge now hangs, finally had to be abandoned as cliffs crumbled away.

That harsh winter had seen worse than crumbling cliffs. On December 3, 1939, the motorboat *Pinto,* with 12 people on board, capsized on the Potato Patch Shoal about a mile off Point Bonita during a storm. The Point Bonita Life-Saving Station crew responded immediately in their 36-foot motor lifeboat. Heavy seas smashed the *Pinto* to pieces and swept those struggling in the water away from the Coast Guard rescue boat. But all the wreckage in the water gave the survivors objects to hang onto and the motor lifeboat crew went in among the storm tossed wreckage time after time until all 12 were saved. For this heroic rescue in the storm swept seas, four Point Bonita surfmen received a total of one gold and three silver life-saving medals. Officer-in-charge Chief Cecil M. Thomas received the gold medal. Such high awards were only given to

Point Bonita Life-Saving Station (with its prominent lookout tower) had neighbors in this 1950s Coast Guard photo. Light keepers dwellings had been built on the life-saving station's grounds by the Coast Guard. (Golden Gate National Recreation Area)

crews who placed themselves in great danger to save the lives of others. There are few more dangerous places than the Potato Patch Shoal when the bar is breaking.

The passing years saw more changes. The old steam siren had long been replaced by compressed air horns, and the fog signal building now had generators, air compressors, and a huge air tank instead of boilers. The light was electrified and thus required less maintenance. The familiar sight of the tender *Madroño* steaming into Bonita Cove with supplies had become just a memory since the road to Sausalito had been improved and supplies would evermore arrive by land. The lighthouse's appearance changed slightly, too, when a watchroom was built atop the roof, just seaward and below the lantern room. Here, Coast Guardsmen could keep watch on the station and the harbor entrance. In later years the balcony was removed from the tower, and this fact encouraged some visitors to describe the lighthouse as looking like a ship, since the watch room platform resembled a ship's bridge. The interior also encouraged such description since there were ship's ladders and even railings covered by fancy rope-work.

By now, the Coast Guard had developed fast motor lifeboats, and the need for so many life-saving stations near the Gate was diminishing. As a result, the Point Bonita life-saving station was closed down (reportedly in 1946). This meant a dramatic decrease in the number of people living at the Point. The school was no longer in existence and the boat house, most of the dwellings, and even the life-saving station were eventually torn down. To house the keepers, the Coast Guard built three new cottages near the life-saving station site. One of the residences housed three bachelors, while the other two each served a family.

The last of the Lighthouse Service veterans were gone by the early 1950s and the Coast Guard now completely staffed the light station. One of the officers-in-charge during that decade was Chief Frank E. Swanson. His crew put in a 70-hour work week combining station maintenance and long watches. The fog horn was a compressed air diaphone horn and it let out a blast that sounded like "Bee-oh!" According to maritime historian Jim Gibbs, the Point Bonita fog signal was the one used in a once famous radio soap commercial of the period. Listeners were urged to avoid "body odor", nicknamed "B.O." for its initials. The commercial used the "Bee-oh!" sound of the Point Bonita fog horn to warn listeners to use their brand of soap and avoid embarrassing "B.O."

During the Fifties, Point Bonita suffered from more than the threat of body odor. Fog increased substantially for at least several years and storm waves pounded the Point, sometimes climbing a hundred feet high. Chief Collins, stationed there during the period, recalled huge storms, "Some were so large that they washed up over The Saddle", the 100-foot high natural causeway connecting the mainland to the foot tunnel. This was the only large open section of trail from the dwellings to the lighthouse and on rough days the surf booms like thunder here.

In 1967, even larger waves hit the Point. Storm waves often unleashed their full fury at Point Bonita. During the January 1967 storm, officer-in-charge Joe Belisle reported waves "crashing right on top" of the lighthouse—130 feet above the sea!

Through the 1960s, light keeping duties became easier, although tourism increased to almost unmanageable proportions. Many weekends would see hundreds of visitors tour the fascinating old sentinel, and serving as tour guides became a major part of the crew's duties. Eventually, the station attracted so many visitors that the Coast Guard was forced to close the station to the public, a sad loss to all.

However, serving the public had its humorous aspect too. When the 1964 Alaskan earthquake triggered a seismic wave, "tidal wave" warnings were broadcast all along the north Pacific Coast. Officer-in-charge Belisle never forgot the telephone call he received following the "tidal wave" warnings. A worried mother wanted to know if her son would be safe if he tried to ride the wave in on his surfboard. The answer was, of course, negative, but by the time the wave hit the Golden Gate it was relatively small and did not cause the terrible damage suffered by ports in Alaska and at Crescent City, California. It was storm, not tidal, waves that made Point Bonita's surf so spectacular.

During the 1970s, I visited the lighthouse often. I had friends among the keepers and often led school and college tours of the station as well. I particularly enjoyed visits which allowed me to relax and spend time talking with the crew. The lighthouse looked much as it did in 1877 and was nicely complimented by the fine fog signal building in front of it. The classic lens, super typhon fog horns, and a radio beacon all actively aided mariners. Watches were still frequently stood during the day and always at night. A watchroom was just seaward of the lighthouse lantern room, and it was one of my favorite places. From here you could see the Pacific swirling around the lighthouse on both sides and look far out on the San Francisco Bay bar. Most of the Point Bonita crew became very familiar with all the ships that regularly called at San Francisco Bay and could identify them far offshore. The watch room was very comfortable with a couch, table, chairs, desk, phone, television set, and great picture windows revealing the whole maritime scene. I spent many hours there.

Weather recording equipment was mounted on the wall above the desk. Every four hours, it was necessary to "call in the weather" to the Weather Bureau. This was a telephoned report of wind speed and direction, temperature, visibility, and sea height. All this was easy during the day, but at night estimating the height of the sea and visibility could be tricky. You could tell visibility by identifying which buoys you could see flashing out on the bar. But sea height on a dark night had to be judged only by the sound of the surf.

Routine maintenance was a regular feature of duty during the day. Painting the lantern room roof its traditional handsome black involved making a loop at the end of a sturdy rope and tossing it over the ball atop the lantern room roof. This gave the painter a line he could grasp as he worked his way around the top of the lighthouse. It was an old lighthouse keeper's technique dating back over a century. Once a week the fog horn's big compressed air tanks had to be "bled" to rid them of excess moisture. Whenever the fog rolled in, the horns had to be started—a deafening task when the station was boxed in by heavy fog.

Trail maintenance was another common duty. When I first came to Point Bonita in the 1960s, there was a lower trail from the residences over to today's main trail. This has fallen into the sea and largely disappeared. You could also see many parts of the old life-saving trail that led down to the boathouse site on Bonita Cove. This path has almost disappeared as well. Efforts in recent years have succeeded in making the main upper trail by the cisterns into a fine access to the lighthouse.

The trail to the Point has been a dominant feature in the lives of everyone who has worked here since it was built in 1877. It was always, "Shall we walk down to the lighthouse now?" or "I have to walk down to the lighthouse to go on watch now." It was always the trail that connected work with social life. It was always the trail that was the route to duty.

The trail, the winds, the crashing sea, the old Coast Guard boathouse marine railway, the remnants of the wharf, the wind dwarfed vegetation, the cave-like tunnel so carefully carved by the Chinese-American workers, the suspension bridge, and the beautiful lighthouse and fog signal building made the trek to Point Bonita unsurpassed nationally. *Motorland* magazine called it, "Probably the most magnificent setting of any lighthouse in the country."

The social center of Point Bonita lighthouse was, for at least three decades, the two-story building which was the sole survivor from the Life-Saving Station. Partly dug into the hillside, it now served as a garage in its upper story (perhaps the beach cart and breeches buoy apparatus were originally kept here). Its lower floor, however, opened toward the Coast Guard residences and here many a long conversation took place. The station office was on the lower level and for years its files still contained the old Lighthouse Service Bible, the original plans for the life-saving station, and instructions for operating a breeches buoy. A 1913 photo of the whole Point hung on the wall. There was also a combination workshop and recreation room with a pool table here as well. I could always count on a cup of coffee served in a heavy mug and some good Coast Guard sea stories.

The men were a varied group. I liked them all. There were a series of three officers-in-charge that I recall. Harry Hoffman was the first; he was older and more formal, and he ran the station quite traditionally. His successor, Bob Grass, was younger, more informal and very casual. Bob had come to Point Bonita from a motor lifeboat station and he seemed to miss the challenge of the North Pacific surf and the rescue calls. His assistant keeper, Harry Lent, had also been a crewman on a 44-foot motor lifeboat. The following account illustrates the type of experiences some of the lifeboatmen had encountered prior to coming to Point Bonita.

Harry Lent had been stationed at Depoe Bay Lifeboat Station in Oregon before coming to Point Bonita light. He was assigned to a 44-foot motor lifeboat crew there. These Coast Guard 44-foot motor lifeboats (and their kin the 52-foot motor lifeboats) are probably the best rescue craft in the world. They are self-bailing and self-righting and contain watertight compartments. If they capsize, they'll turn right side up again. If they are hit with huge seas, they'll bail themselves out. If a rock punches a hole in one, the other watertight compartments will keep the boat afloat. (They are called *forty-fours* or *fifty-twos* because of their length.)

So, if a Coast Guard rescuer has to be out in terrible sea conditions he or she can't do much better than a *44* or *52*. During a fierce 1973 storm, a man had been washed off a beach near Depoe Bay, Oregon. Despite the severe sea conditions, Harry Lent and several other Coast Guardsmen were sent out in 44-foot motor lifeboat *44373* to search for the victim. Massive 20 foot waves rolled across the sea making progress difficult on the water. Since winds were not too high, a Coast Guard helicopter was ordered to join the search. As the search continued, conditions in the air were tolerable, but on the sea, they were worsening. Suddenly, a wave larger than the rest, a good 30-feet high, hit the *44*, burying it in solid green water and capsizing the lifeboat. When the boat came up and righted itself, a crewman was missing and much of the equipment was damaged. Then a 25-foot high wave hit and again capsized the *44*. A third giant comber crashed down and the *44* went over yet again. Lent recalled solid green water, the cabin tearing away, and his safety belt disintegrating in his hands. Lent surfaced and saw that soon everybody from the *44* was in the water except the coxswain, John Greeten, who had a hold on the lifeboat's wheel and was trying to steer it despite having the boat's superstructure torn off. Then a fourth wave cruelly smashed the *44*, turning it over again. When the boat righted itself, the coxswain still remained on board. Greeten desperately tried to locate his crew in the water. But the giant waves

Keeper's dwelling at tip of Point Bonita at east end of suspension bridge, 1930s. (Irving Conklin photo, U.S. Lighthouse Society)

continued to break. Twice more the *44* was capsized, finally violently tearing Coxswain Greeten off.

Now no one was on board the *44*, yet the battered vessel kept right on going, its engine performing as usual. The fact that the lifeboat was still running made it impossible for anyone to reach her to try to climb back aboard. Chief Dave Edwards, a veteran lifeboatman, was one of the crew in the water fighting the huge seas. He had watched as the monster waves continued to strike the motor lifeboat and roll it again and again. Chief Edwards recalls seeing the *44* capsize and right herself at least six times. Everything on the main deck, except the lower part of the coxswain's chair and the massive towing bit, had been swept away. Even the boat's cabin and towing reel were gone. He also remembers helplessly watching as the still operating *44*, completely crewless, moved quickly away from the crew, headed toward a distant beach.

With the surfmen struggling in immense, cold waves, the Coast Guard helicopter was now the lifeboat crew's only hope for survival. In one of the greatest helicopter rescues in Pacific Coast history, the helicopter crew acted quickly and competently to lift everyone to safety. The motor lifeboat's coxswain, John Greeten, had been able to hang on longest, being washed off after six capsizings, but he had been seriously injured and was semi-conscious. The helicopter crew lowered their basket and used it like a net to gently lift the coxswain aboard the helicopter.

The incredible *44* never did quit operating. Crewless, she eventually ran ashore on a rocky Oregon beach, her engine still operating. The Coast Guard salvaged her, repaired her and she is still in service today, most recently at the Umpqua River Lifeboat Station on Winchester Bay, Oregon.

Point Bonita lighthouse periodically faced waves of the size the lifeboat crew experienced off Depoe Bay, Oregon. But life was very different for the Coast Guardsmen at a shore station. Many of the Coast Guardsmen loved the slow paced life at Point Bonita light, but there was almost always one or two who longed to return to the lifeboat stations and the challenge of the North Pacific surf.

John M. "Jack" Dusch was the third officer-in-charge I knew and the one who became the best known. Jack had come to Point Bonita after duty as an officer on board a patrol boat in southern California. Watching for smugglers was one of his major assignments and he'd made one of the biggest Coast Guard "drug busts" on the coast.

One day, while on patrol in fine weather, he noticed a large, fancy sailboat. It struck him as odd that on such a nice day, a big sailing vessel should be rigged for heavy weather. So he decided to take a closer look. The crew running the sailboat seemed to be handling it poorly. Strange, too, he thought. If you have enough money to buy a boat like that, he guessed you'd either learn how to handle it well yourself or hire someone

Point Bonita is the only American lighthouse to be reached by a suspension bridge, a replica of the Golden Gate Bridge. For a spectacular walk to the lighthouse, probably no lighthouse in the country surpasses Point Bonita with its foot tunnel, high cliffs, suspension bridge, booming surf and vistas of the Golden Gate. Best of all, at the end of your walk is the national treasure of Point Bonita light station itself, 1975. (R. Shanks)

to do it for you. The thing that really aroused his suspicion though, was that as the Coast Guard patrol boat pulled near, nobody waved. In his experience, when the Coast Guard goes by, nearly everybody waves, "Hi, Coast Guard!" But not these people. So Dusch and his crew stopped and boarded the fancy sailboat and made one of the biggest "drug busts" in southern California. And all because the smugglers didn't wave.

Now Dusch was at Point Bonita. He found plenty of challenges here, too, especially from the wind. Keeper Dusch recalled, "On Memorial Day weekend, 1977, we lost (electrical) power out (at the lighthouse) one night and the (backup) generator failed to start. I came out with my engineer (George Pfeffer) and the (suspension) bridge was swaying so badly that when I was about one-third of the way across, I had to get down on my hands and knees and crawl the rest of the way across the bridge (to the lighthouse side). When I reached that side, I had to hang onto the life-line stanchions to keep from being blown off the rock (and into the sea). That particular night, we were logging 55 to 60 knot winds out here."

Jack Dusch was to preside over most of the final days of manned Coast Guard operations at Point Bonita. By 1979, Point Bonita was the last manned lighthouse in California and its fame spread fast. Dusch soon found himself giving numerous tours to local school groups as teachers wanted to give their students a last chance to visit a manned lighthouse.

The media, too, began to seek him out. At first it was the local papers and television stations, but the story caught on quickly, "California's last manned lighthouse." It was a media favorite. Soon, even all the major East Coast papers were carrying the story and Jack could be seen on local and national television. I worked with Lorri Coppola, Pamela Boss and Peter Rafalow to co-produce a documentary for Viacom cable television called "Point Bonita: Last Manned Lighthouse"—a title not quite complete, it should have said "Point Bonita: Last Manned Lighthouse in California". The narrative did explain this fact. Still, it won a national cable television award for best special documentary.

The news stories grew. At first the media accurately called Point Bonita the last manned lighthouse in California. But soon, it was last on the Pacific Coast, and later some just called it the last manned lighthouse, period. I kept expecting to read soon that Jack was the last light keeper in the world but fortunately, things calmed down. Actually, two Washington state lighthouses, Alki Point and West Point, remained manned longer than Point Bonita and some on the Atlantic coast were manned as late as 1990. At least one Alaskan light station was manned longer than Point Bonita also. Point Bonita, however, was last to be manned in California.

We even had to protect the media at times. One television cameraman from KRON-TV, totally dedicated to his job, climbed up on the foghorn and stuck his microphone up to it, happily awaiting the moment when Jack would blow the fog signal. Jack was inside the fog signal building being interviewed and was about ready to blast the horns. It was my custom to always check to make sure no one was near the horns when they were being demonstrated. The big compressed air horns could be heard for five miles out to sea, and if you got too close, they reportedly could shatter your eardrums. I had gotten too close to Point Conception's foghorns once years earlier and my skull literally vibrated. It was frightening. I'm sure glad I checked that day at Point Bonita or the San Francisco TV cameraman would have been blown right off the Point.

It soon became clear that there was considerable public interest in Point Bonita and plans were made to transfer the historic light station, upon unmanning, from the Coast Guard to the National Park Service. Park Service planners began studying how best to assume control of the light station and reopen it to the public.

This Park Service planning came as something of a personal miracle for me. My first marriage had ended and I was one very lonely maritime historian and teacher. While conducting a Davidson Middle School tour

Original plans for the first keeper's dwelling at Point Bonita. Virtually the same plans were also used at the Farallon Islands Light Station. (National Archives)

Original plans for the 1858 fog bell house at Point Bonita. (U.S. Coast Guard)

at Point Bonita one day, the Park Service assigned a member of its planning staff, Lisa Woo, to come along and learn about lighthouses. She was beautiful, intelligent, and very interested in lighthouses. Well, one thing led to another and our first date was spent visiting Keeper Sandy Tucker and his wife at Pigeon Point lighthouse. By special arrangement, we were allowed to operate Point Bonita lighthouse to gain full understanding of lighthouse life. Lisa and I stood watch all night, overseeing the light, operating the foghorns, and monitoring the radio beacon. It was extremely romantic at Point Bonita at night and the following year we were married. Lisa and our marriage may have been the most exciting thing to happen to us at Point Bonita, but a far more dramatic event was to occur December 31, 1979.

Early that winter morning, Crowley Maritime's seagoing tug *Sentinel* headed toward the Golden Gate bound for Hawaii. She was towing two huge barges, both heavily loaded. The National Weather Service forecast predicted heavy swells, which on the San Francisco bar led Captain John Maddux to expect very large swells of up to 15 or 20 feet. These would be heavy seas, certainly, but veteran tugboat skippers had coped with them before.

Once out the Gate and off Point Bonita, however, it became evident that conditions were much worse than expected. Entering the bar off Point Bonita about 5 a.m., Captain Maddux encountered swells that were, by his estimate, reaching 35 to 40 feet. These were gigantic waves that were more than his tow could handle. The tug's mate, George Irish, soon realized that they were in the worst bar conditions he'd ever seen anywhere.

Despite a relatively new towline, the immense waves snapped the towline to the barge *Kona* and Captain Maddux radioed both the Coast Guard and Crowley Maritime for help. The *Kona* was loaded with $2.5 million in general cargo, including lumber, beer, and paper.

The other barge, the 400-foot long *Agattu*, presented a much greater danger. Not only was she even bigger than the *Kona*, but her cargo was far more sinister. The *Agattu* was carrying 35 one-ton containers loaded with deadly chlorine gas. She was also carrying nearly 4000 pounds of a potentially explosive component of fertilizer. About 45 minutes after the *Kona* broke loose from the tug, the *Agattu's* line snapped as well.

Both barges began drifting directly toward Point Bonita. The *Kona* ran aground just north of the lighthouse, near the visitor overlook. The *Agattu* followed suit a bit to the north, between the overlook and Rodeo Lagoon.

The potential disaster was appalling. The Coast Guard announced that a vapor cloud of deadly gas 22 miles long and 6300 yards wide could be formed. If it drifted toward San Francisco, it would be virtually impossible to evacuate the entire population of 700,000.

The *Kona*, being nearer the lighthouse, immediately received a heavy battering by the sea. Waves began sweeping the barge, carrying away her cargo and breaking her up.

Miraculously, the *Agattu* had grounded farther north and was exposed to less heavy breakers. She also came up higher on the shore and thus her cargo was more protected. Nevertheless, the shore was evacuated and placed off limits. Military personnel living in the area were told to be ready to leave on five minutes notice.

Salvage helicopters were rushed to the scene, but foggy weather hampered any removal of the *Agattu's* deadly cargo. It wasn't until January 2, 1980, that the chlorine canisters were airlifted ashore. The

Coast Guard Cutter Taney *on the San Francisco bar in the February 1960 storm facing a wave estimated to be perhaps 100 feet high by some analysts at the Army Corps of Engineers. The* Taney *was 327 feet long and the wave's height may be determined by comparing the vessel's length to the distance from the wave's trough to its crest. (U.S. Army Corps of Engineers)*

landed canisters were placed under guard in a Fort Cronkite parking lot. Crowley Maritime sent 50 men and women to work at the salvage site. By Friday, January 4th, it seemed clear that the *Agattu* would not break up and the salvor felt that the danger was over. Lisa and I visited the Point and saw that the *Kona* was so badly battered that she already looked like an old shipwreck. Her cargo was completely gone, being salvaged, according to the Coast Guard, by as many as 100 boats wanting her lumber or beer. For the most part, the lumber was smashed by the sea and there were no reports of drinkable beer.

The *Agattu* was in fairly good shape. Her cargo was being airlifted off and plans called for refloating and saving her. It was a miracle that the cargos were not reversed or that the barges hadn't come ashore in the opposite places. If it had, we might have had a maritime tragedy that would have made the *Titanic* appear small in comparison.

Ironically, not too long after the near tragedy a Coast Guard Aids to Navigation employee wanted to close Point Bonita lighthouse and move its navigational aids further inland. He also wanted to turn out forever the classic second order lens, one of the last of its type operating in California. Fortunately, the San Francisco bar pilots were appalled at such an ignorant suggestion and thoughtful Coast Guard people halted the proposal.

In June 1980, Jack Dusch was transferred from Point Bonita lighthouse and Mark Van Buskirk became officer-in-charge. He was to be Point Bonita's last head keeper. The light station was soon automated, unmanned and transferred to the National Park Service. The Coast Guard retained control of the lantern room and fog signal building, however, for the lighthouse is still an important and useful navigational aid. As a ship's pilot operating between San Francisco Bay and Hong Kong told me, "It sure feels good when I see that light and know for sure where I am."

Today, the lighthouse is open to the public on certain days for tours conducted by the National Park Service. It is a part of the Golden Gate National Recreation Area—Marin Headlands. A variety of worthwhile tours are offered and visitor programs are being developed. There is the opportunity to participate in a docent's program and serve at this national treasure. Hopefully, a visitor center can be developed in one of the former keeper's dwellings to provide the public full appreciation of this unique and wonderful light station.

It is fitting that this very night as I write, both Boon Island, Maine, and Point Bonita are sending out their guiding beams using their original 1850s second order Fresnel lenses. Each guards one of America's great oceans. No light is as beautiful as the ancient French lenses in their proper setting—in the lantern rooms of great lighthouses. Point Bonita has one of the last active Fresnel lens in northern California. No lighthouse scene is as beautiful as a lighted Fresnel lens in a lantern room at dusk. The lens is a glistening diamond which produces a type of beam very different from the flash of reflecting beacons. Point Bonita's lens is the same lens which welcomed the great sailing ships from New England and from the Orient. It is the same lighthouse the bar pilots will watch tonight from the bridge of container ships.

Lighthouse Service logo honoring the end of the service in 1939. At left is a buoy tender, at center a lighthouse and at right a lightship. (U.S. Coast Guard)

FORT POINT

In 1852, work had begun on California's first lighthouses, Alcatraz and Fort Point. Alcatraz was soon completed and Fort Point was finished shortly afterward. Both were California cottage types with a tower in the center of the dwelling. The structures sat unused for some time, awaiting delivery of their lenses. Before the French-made lenses could arrive, however, the United States Army decided it needed to fortify the entrance to San Francisco Bay. Fort Point lighthouse had been built on the southern shore of the Golden Gate's narrowest place. Consequently, it occupied the most strategic position in the harbor. In the name of national security, the three-month old lighthouse was torn down. When the French lenses finally arrived in late 1854, Fort Point's was assigned to Point Pinos light on Monterey Bay, where it is in use today.

Fort Point lighthouse was thus the second beacon built on the California coast, and it was the third to be lighted. It did, however, achieve first place in one category—it was the first to be torn down.

Fort Point became the site of a massive fortress, Fort Winfield Scott. However, the need for a lighthouse remained. On a narrow ledge between the fort and its sea wall, a second lighthouse was erected. It was a four-sided, truncated wooden tower which stood 36 feet high. In March 1855, its white light first shone forth from its fifth order lens.

The site was a poor choice. The ocean began eroding the sea wall, threatening both the fort and the beacon. In order to repair the sea wall in 1863, the lighthouse had to be removed. The year 1864 found authorities at work on a third lighthouse. Fort Point thus had seen three lighthouses at a time when most West Coast points had yet to see their first.

The third sentinel was uniquely situated among California beacons. It stood atop a fort. The fort gave the light a respectable height of 83 feet above the sea, although the light tower itself was only 27 feet high. It was an iron skeleton tower firmly bolted to the bastion's stone roof. A circular iron stairway, exposed to the weather, led up to an enclosed watch room. The watch room was entered by a tiny hatch. Furnishings were those necessary to light keeping: a small table for trimming wicks, a five-gallon oil carrier stand, a clock stand, and the like. The room was attractively sheathed

Fort Point lighthouse stands proudly atop Fort Winfield Scott. The flat roofed oil house may be seen at right. 1930s. (U.S. Lighthouse Society)

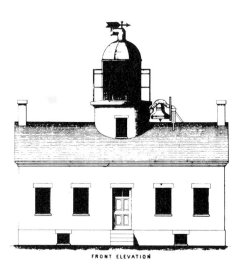

FRONT ELEVATION

The first *Fort Point lighthouse. These are the original plans for Fort Point's pioneer California cottage style lighthouse, 1850s. (National Archives)*

A rare drawing (dating from the 1850s) of the second *Fort Point lighthouse in the days before the sea wall was built. The sentinel stood directly in front of the fort, a factor which led to its early demise. (Fort Point National Historic Site)*

Beacon amid cannons. Fort Point lighthouse stands high atop San Francisco Bay's most formidable bastion. Below the light's balcony was the watch room, reached by a circular stairway unprotected from the Golden Gate's high winds. This was the third lighthouse to be built at Fort Point. (U.S. Army, Presidio of San Francisco)

James Rankin, distinguished keeper of the Golden Gate, wearing the handsome uniform of the United States Lighthouse Service. (Fort Point National Historic Site)

The Fort Point lighthouse crew built this manual winch to haul supplies up the steep bluff to their dwellings, 1908. (Fort Point National Historic Site)

with wood and had unique trapezoidal windows. It had a stairway that led up to the lantern room, which had a fourth order lens. The lens consisted of three panels and was equipped with parabolic mirror reflectors. The lens revolved on 24 ball bearings running in semi-circular groves. The clockwork drive was powered by a 70-pound weight which unwound down a 20-foot long drop tube. Every two and one-half hours the keeper on watch went to the crank and rewound the weight. The tower was painted white with a black lantern room. It made a handsome sight atop the fortress.

Besides the light, a small concrete oil house also stood on the roof. Its tanks held the oil burned by the beacon's lamp. At various times, fish oil, lard oil and kerosene fueled the light. Later, an oil vapor lamp came into use.

The original fog signal was a bell mounted on the side of the fort. It was reached by a ladder from the roof of the fort down to the bell's platform, where Stephens clockwork machinery mechanically struck the bell. The bell had a checkered history. Keepers had to risk their lives on the windswept ladder to reach it. Once at the bell, the wickies found they were beneath the mouths of cannons. It was a very unpleasant

Fort Point's fog bell was probably the most difficult to reach on the Pacific Coast. Keepers had to climb down the fort's side on the ladder (seen above the bell house) to reach the fog bell, a very dangerous route in high winds. The inadequacy of this fog bell was partially to blame for the wreck of the Rio de Janeiro *in 1901. (Fort Point National Historic Site)*

to be. By 1869, the bell had been thoroughly battered by guns firing over it.

The bell was also unpopular with mariners. They criticized it as being inadequate. For years they demanded improved fog signal equipment, a position supported by the Lighthouse Service. But Congress denied funds. Thus, the *Columbia* ran on the rocks in 1882; the *City of Chester* went down in 1888; and, in 1900, both the *Alameda* and the *LaMara* crashed into nearby rocks. In 1901, during thick fog, the passenger steamer *Rio De Janeiro* rammed Fort Point's submerged offshore ledge. Keepers heard the *Rio's* whistle blowing distress calls and commercial fishing craft sped to the scene. Italian-American fishermen saved dozens of lives, but the ship went down fast, and over 100 persons drowned.

Sadly, the tragedy could have been minimized if the highly skilled Fort Point Life-Saving crew had been called out sooner.

Fort Point light station was an integral part of a fortress. The three houses are the keepers' dwellings. Note the bridge leading from the upper dwellings to the fort. (U.S. Army, Presidio of San Francisco)

The surfman on watch at the lookout on the bluff above the fort thought little of the *Rio's* desperate whistle blasts calling for help. The surfman only notified the life-saving station after a fisherman arrived at the beach with the belated news of the terrible sinking. When the surfman finally called on his fellow lifesavers at the Fort Point Life-Saving Station, the highly acclaimed surfmen rowed to the scene in minutes, but it was too late for 130 people. Captain Hodgson, officer-in-charge of the Fort Point Life-Saving Station, was shocked at the crewman's actions and suspended him from duty.

The Lighthouse Board's report of the wreck was blunt and it offered a better solution. It stated that if the Federal Government had appropriated adequate funds for a modern fog signal, the tragedy would probably never have occurred in the first place.

The 3000-pound fog bell at Fort Point light had been faithfully operated. Whenever its machinery broke down, it was rung manually. If keepers were unavailable to ring it, their wives took over. Despite this dedication, the bell simply was not an adequate warning device at this location.

Finally, in 1904, a fog trumpet blown by compressed air was installed. Seven years later, this was further improved upon by substituting a siren. The fog signal building, near the light tower, was both uniquely situated and appropriate to its military setting. It stood atop a gun emplacement and had walls and roof a foot thick. It was probably the sturdiest building of its type ever constructed. Less sturdy, but equally faithful, was the battered bell. It remained on hand for emergency use.

The keepers lived on the bluff immediately south of the fort. Climbing down the steep bluff and crossing the windy gap to the fort was, according to old reports, "a very dangerous task during dark and stormy nights." The narrow gap between the bluff and the fort forms a natural wind tunnel that funnels the wind to hurricane force. With the idea of providing safer transit, a foot bridge was erected from the bluff top to the fort's roof. While it did provide more convenient access, the wind often blew so powerfully that the wickies were afraid to use the bridge lest they be blown off. Windstorms were so strong that the Lighthouse Service was forced to anchor the keepers' dwellings to the ground with cables. It was extremely bad when the keepers actually had to tie their houses down to prevent them from being blown away.

The light station experienced one of its worst storms in the late 1880s. The storm began by tearing shutters loose on the keepers' homes and shattering many windows. Families huddled in protected rooms to wait out the blow. At dusk, the keepers left their families to tend to the light. The wind was so strong that the bridge could not be used. The men crawled along the ground on hands and knees to get to the fort. The most dangerous part of the trip was climbing the open stairway up the tower to the watch room. Once inside they found that the tower was actually swaying. Despite being six stories above the fortress' rock floor, the keepers remained through the night tending the lamp. Unfortunately, their efforts were partly in vain, for during the night, a large ship (believed by the keepers to have been the *City of Chester*) went down off the Point.

Even during good weather, life was spartan. Supplies only arrived once every six months when the lighthouse tender *Madroño* landed at "Engineer's Wharf". For many years everything had to be carried up the steep bluff on the keepers' backs. Eventually, however, the wickies built a tramway up the headland, powered by a manually-operated winch. Supplies were kept in the oil house.

Fort Point's best known keeper was James Rankin. He came to the station from East Brother light in 1878. Rankin was to remain for the next 41 years, probably a record among California light keepers. He began a long tradition that led Rankin and his

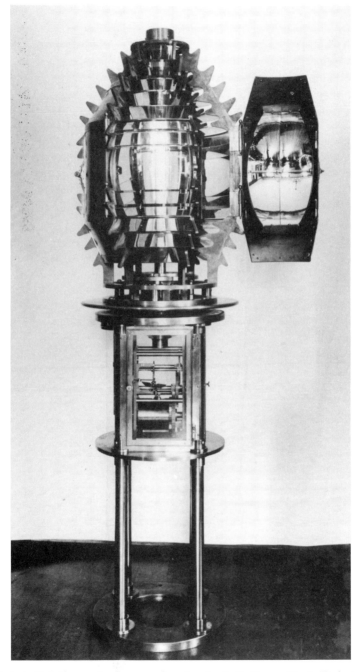

Fort Point lighthouse's lens prior to installation. Fort Point used both fourth and fifth order lenses during its active years. (U.S. Coast Guard)

descendants to dominate the Fort Point station for the remainder of its history.

Rankin was one of the grand, old-time light keepers who felt his basic responsibility was to save lives. He was always on the alert for shipwrecks, and people would return yearly to pay their respects and thank him for saving their lives. Rankin was kept busy pulling people from the water, in large part because of a quirk of the Golden Gate. The tide rushes in the Golden Gate and then, suddenly, the set of the current veers sharply toward Fort Point. The sea rams violently against the sea wall. It can sink a boat, drag a person across the rocks, and hurl him against the stonework. Even if a person survives the sea wall, the undertow can carry him out to sea.

A lookout was regularly stationed at the Point by the life-saving station. Since the majority of the time was spent simply watching the Bay, one early life-saving crewman would practice knot tying, using his life line. Unfortunately, it was at the conclusion of just such a knot-tying session that he heard shouts that someone was drowning. He grabbed his rope and raced to the sea wall, seeing a boy foundering offshore. Preparing to toss the boy a line, he looked at the hopelessly knotted mass in his hand and realized that his rope was useless.

Only the arrival of Keeper Rankin at that moment prevented tragedy. He had a ladder in one hand and a life preserver in the other. Nobody volunteered to help, so Rankin put the ladder over the side and climbed down the sea wall. Using the life preserver to stay afloat, he swam out and brought the boy to safety. The youngster recovered enough to say that his father was somewhere clinging to an overturned boat. The Fort Point life-saving crew responded to a telephone call and the surfmen saved the father. Both father and son recovered.

Even those on land sometimes faced danger at Fort Point. Two couples spent Sunday afternoon picnicking. After several bottles of wine, they began playing a portable Victrola and dancing. After a time, one couple decided the sea wall would make an exciting place to dance. It was. In a moment they had lost their footing and had fallen into the Bay. A fisherman saw the couple being swept seaward by the ebb tide. He ran to Keeper Rankin's house, shouting the alarm. Rankin and his son grabbed their trusty lifesaving tools, the ladder and a life preserver, and ran for the sea wall.

Alerted by Rankin's little granddaughter, both Assistant Keeper John Kunder and the girl's father, August Nagel, sprang into action. Perceiving the situation, they searched frantically for a rope. Unable to find it, the assistant keeper yelled to Nagel to grab the garden

Fort Point Life-Saving was new when this 1890 photo was taken. The station boathouse is just right of the pole and the station house is to the boathouse's right. Fort Point Life-Saving Station originally stood where Crissy Field is today and the station house was parallel to the beach. Both buildings were relocated 700 feet west about 1914 to make way for the 1915 Panama Pacific Exposition. During the move the station house was turned so that it is now at a right angle to the beach. (Golden Gate National Recreation Area)

hose and run for the sea wall. Nagel did just as he was told. He grasped the hose and started running. Unfortunately, everyone had forgotten that the hose was still attached to the faucet. Nagel only made it to the garden gate. His race to the rescue suddenly ended as the hose stretched taut and Nagel's forward progress ended. He flipped backwards and the blue in front of him changed from sea to sky.

Kunder and Nagel unscrewed the hose and made another start for the beach. When they arrived, Rankin had done it again. The couple was being helped up the ladder by the head keeper and his son. The lady's full skirt had acted as a parachute and had trapped a great amount of air, keeping her afloat. The husband, having no such advantage, had to swim. In order to make the exhausting swim to save the couple, Rankin had found it necessary to strip. When the Victorian

Fort Point Life-Saving Station with the boathouse closest to the camera and the station house at right. The boathouse doors faced away from the beach to make it easier to open them during high winds common at the Golden Gate, 1923. (U.S. Coast Guard)

lady saw Rankin, she became hysterical, screaming, "I've never seen a naked man in my life except my husband!" During this entire rescue, another of the picnickers repeatedly ran around the fort yelling, "Get a rope! Get a rope!"

The heroic keeper thus found himself standing by the sea wall, naked, with a shocked woman yelling and pointing at him, and a man continuing to circle the fort shouting for a rope for a rescue already completed. It was enough to make Rankin consider another line of work besides light keeping.

During his last years at Fort Point, the seventyish keeper saved a boy in 1918 and another youngster in 1919. At his retirement, the Commissioner of the Lighthouses wrote Rankin commending him for saving the lives of 18 people at Fort Point.

Fort Point was always manned by dedicated keepers. Assistant Keeper John Kunder drew the watch during the early hours of April 18, 1906. Suddenly, the great earthquake that was to destroy San Francisco began jolting the fortress. Kunder stayed at his post during and after the quake. Anyone who has felt the light tower shake on a windy day can only assume that Kunder was a man of pure courage. Fortunately, neither the lighthouse nor the fort sustained very serious damage. The chimneys on the keepers' dwellings were thrown down and

Fort Point Life-Saving Station's surfmen in 1908. From left to right they are surfmen Rodgers, Gunderson, Murray, Sullivan and Gunerson. Captain Cornelius Sullivan, second from right, assisted the author nearly 70 years later with his research. (Fort Point National Historic Site)

the footbridge displaced a short distance, but otherwise the light station remained sound.

Fort Point light station seems to have been a glorious place to grow up. The late Merriam Nagel wrote many fond accounts of her days there. Two generations of her family were born in the keeper's dwelling nearest the fort. There were spacious lawns, interesting paths, home cooking, beautiful sunsets, and the parade of ships. Helping clean the lens was a particular pleasure to her.

But there was another side to light keeping too. As Rankin neared retirement, his fame grew. A reporter from the San Francisco *Call* interviewed him. The reporter asked him what there was to see at the Point. Rankin replied:

> There is nothing here to see. There is the ocean and the sand and the guns and the soldiers. That is all. It grows monotonous. Always the ocean and the sand and the guns and the soldiers. As for the ships, one grows tired of them too. I have my family and my pleasures.

Asked what his pleasures were, Mr. Rankin replied, "I painted—sometimes. Come and see." He showed the reporter many pleasing landscapes he had done in oil. Virtually all were views from Fort Point.

Fort Point Life-Saving Station's lifeboat stands ready to assist as the steamer Progreso *burns at San Francisco's Fulton Iron Works, December 1902. (National Maritime Museum)*

Keeper Rankin points up one of the paradoxes of light keeping. While the work was often exhausting and sometimes monotonous, it provided a wonderful environment to develop close family ties, mutual dependence and appreciation, and a fine place to rear children. Even recently, many young Coast Guard families felt these same things and expressed a deep loss when their light station was automated and they were reassigned.

The last long-term keepers at Fort Point Light Station were George D. Cobb, Ralph Jordan and John Gonzales. Both Cobb and Jordan were already veterans of many years in the Lighthouse Service. A wickie usually didn't get a choice station like Fort Point until he'd spent some hard years at more remote locations up and down the coast. John Gonzales was a lucky exception to this rule. It was his and his wife Esther's first station.

Cobb was head keeper, a decorated veteran who had won a life-saving medal at Point Bonita. At Fort Point, Cobb lived in the lower dwelling nearest the sea wall and he always kept a life ring (preserver) hanging on his front porch. The station had that long history of people falling in the water and Mr. Cobb wasn't about to be caught unprepared.

His First Assistant, Ralph Howard Jordan, had worked the coast from Point Arena in the north down to Point Conception and Point Fermin in the south. His wife, Grace Alice Jordan, had served as assistant keeper at Point Fermin. Their daughter, Edith, had grown up at these lighthouses and came to know Fort Point well. Now an adult and married, she often returned to visit her parents.

The Jordans lived in one of the upper dwellings and Ralph Jordan had to cross the little bridge from the bluff to the top of the fort. Fort Point's notorious wind was especially tricky on that bridge, and on one blustery day, it whipped the keeper's eyeglasses right off his face. That slowed him down a bit until Edith's sister finally found them in a mud puddle.

The Jordan daughters had to help out in more ways than just hunting for eyeglasses. One night, only Mr. Cobb and Edith's father were on hand to run Fort Point light. The Second Assistant was on vacation. Keeper Jordan became quite sick and could not stand his watches. George Cobb was forced to assume the duties usually done by three men. After a time, it was clear that Cobb was becoming exhausted and couldn't continue to run the station alone. So the Jordan girls began

Fort Point Life-Saving Station's class E motor lifeboat. This may have been the first Coast Guard motor lifeboat on San Francisco Bay. At extreme left is executive officer Garner Churchill and to his left is Captain Beryl King, officer-in-charge. Surfman Harry Hoffman is fourth from right, 1927. (Harry Hoffman)

A guardian of the Golden Gate. A surfman oversees the harbor entrance from Fort Point Life-Saving Station's lookout tower. (Edith Hall Simons)

Fort Point Life-Saving Station's lookout tower is the two-story structure at left. Surfmen guarded the Golden Gate from this tower while light keepers likewise kept their watch from the lighthouse atop the fort. They were true Guardians of the Golden Gate. The Golden Gate Bridge's tollgate is now approximately where the lookout stood. (U.S. Army, Presidio of San Francisco Museum)

The Fort Point Life-Saving Station's 36-foot motor lifeboat frequently assisted aids to navigation work by performing such duties as transferring personnel at Mile Rocks lighthouse. (U.S. Coast Guard)

Heavy motor lifeboats had to be launched from marine railways such as this one at Fort Point Coast Guard Lifeboat Station. The building was constructed about 1919 to house 36-foot motor lifeboats. Note the lookout tower atop the roof. (Howard Underhill)

Fort Point Lifeboat Station with a 36-foot motor lifeboat on the launchway. A World War II Coast Guard woman looks longingly at the motor lifeboat. During her time of service, women were not allowed to operate motor lifeboats. Today, women have earned a respected place as skilled coxswains of Coast Guard motor lifeboats, C. 1940s. (U.S. Coast Guard)

standing their father's watches. If the fog came in, they were to call Keeper Cobb so that the fog signal could be started. Young Edith Jordan never forgot that sunrise when it was her watch and how thrilled she was to be running the Fort Point lighthouse. In earlier days, it was just such emergencies that launched many a wife or daughter in a career as a light keeper.

The Fort Point Life-Saving Station had been located about a half mile east of the Point since its establishment in 1889. This important Coast Guard station took part in many great rescues. To maximize their effectiveness, the surfmen who manned the facility had built the lookout up the bluff from the upper keepers' dwellings. Painted "barn red", it was a little room with a chair for the man on watch. Manned 24-hours a day, the keepers could see the endless rotation of watches as the surfmen walked through the keepers' yard to and from the lookout. Both the keepers and the surfmen had those long, often monotonous watches to stand, so on slow days they visited one another while on watch, playing cards both at the lookout and at the light station. When on duty, the keepers now stood watch either in the fog signal building or in the oil house where an easy chair was kept. From either place the light could be seen and they offered more space than the little lighthouse watch room. But space at Fort Point was soon to become cramped for a very different reason.

Work had started on the Golden Gate Bridge and the towering new structure would pass almost directly over the light station grounds. The bridge was to spell trouble in more ways than one for Fort Point Light Station, One day, Ralph Jordan was working in the fog signal building when he heard calls for help.

Responding to the hollering, Keeper Jordan climbed up on the fort's ledge-like wall for a look. He saw a man struggling in the water below the lighthouse. One of the bridge construction workers had fallen into the sea. Jordan "hit the phone" to call Cobb whose house was closest to the water. Cobb ran out of his house, grabbed his life ring, jumped into his car and tore off to the scene. Skillfully judging the current, he tossed the life preserver to the man and hauled him ashore.

The man's reaction to having his life saved was to get mad at Keeper Jordan for not tossing a life ring when he first saw him. Jordan patiently explained that there were no floatation devices at the fog signal. He added that he was too far away to have been able to throw anything that could have reached the fellow anyway. It was a situation James Rankin would have understood perfectly.

The light keepers witnessed the entire construction of the Golden Gate Bridge. As the monstrous bridge rose, the light station was diminished in importance. The Coast Guard's lookout had to be demolished (it stood near today's toll plaza). Esther and John Gonzales had their assistant keeper's dwelling moved twice to allow for cable anchorages as the suspension bridge grew. A construction pier was built out from the shore to the south tower of the Golden Gate Bridge. The new pier was a hazard to mariners; a boat rammed it.

The construction of the Golden Gate Bridge spelled the end of Fort Point as an active light station. The giant bridge arched almost directly above the lighthouse. When built, it blocked off the light and reduced the effectiveness of the fog signal. The light and fog horn had to be relocated offshore on one of the main bridge piers. On September 1, 1934, the lighthouse ceased operation. A week later, its last keeper, George D. Cobb, gathered his baggage and moved out of his home in the lower residence adjacent to the fort. His new assignment was Point Arena light.

Today, although the residences and footbridge are gone, the lighthouse still stands. Both the lighthouse and the fort have been

Coast Guardsman Ron Leist watches the Golden Gate from the look-out tower high atop Fort Point Lifeboat Station. Modern electronics equipment is valuable but so is an alert surfman maintaining a live watch on the harbor entrance, 1989. (Lisa Shanks)

included in the Fort Point National Historic Site, a unit of the Golden Gate National Recreation Area administered by the National Park Service. The old lighthouse has been accurately restored and repainted after many years of standing in rusty grandeur.

Fort Point may be reached by driving to the Presidio of San Francisco and taking Lincoln Boulevard to Long Avenue (turn toward the Bay). From the intersection of Long Avenue and Marine Drive, one can see Fort Point ahead. The fort and lighthouse can be visited daily until 5 p.m. A display of light keeper tools, photographs, and a small fog whistle can be seen here. From the fort's roof, visitors can closely inspect the lovely old sentinel. In the distance, the flashing lights of Point Bonita, Mile Rocks, Lime Point, Point Blunt, and Alcatraz Island lighthouses serve as reminders of the important role lighthouses still play on San Francisco Bay.

While visiting Fort Point lighthouse, it is also possible to walk along the beach east to see the historic Fort Point Coast Guard Life-Saving Station. This is another of the rare maritime treasures of the California coast. The original station was last used as the officer-in-charge's house. The original boathouse was last used as a garage. Both were built by the

U.S. Life-Saving Service in 1889. Only a few of the U.S. Life-Saving Service's historic stations still stand along the entire Pacific Coast. Two fine examples are at Arena Cove, Point Arena, California, and at Klipsan Beach, Washington. Both are in private hands. Another historic rescue station, Bolinas Bay, was designed by the U.S. Life-Saving Service, but was always occupied by the Coast Guard. It is now College of Marin's Biology Station in Bolinas, California. Point Reyes, Humboldt Bay, and Point Arguello Lifeboat Stations are other historic rescue stations in California. All are of great historic value.

Besides the Life-Saving Station, Fort Point also has an equally historic Coast Guard Lifeboat Station, built in 1919, on the same grounds. It has a lookout atop its roof and, at one time, lifeboats were housed on its first floor. Until recent years, a marine railway ran from here down to the beach so that 36-foot motor lifeboats could be launched from the boat bay. As late as 1990, the Coast Guard moored 44-foot motor lifeboats, 41-foot utility boats, and a 30-foot motor surfboat at the picturesque pier. Visitors can thus see both a U.S. Life-Saving Service Station and a U.S. Coast Guard Lifeboat Station on the same grounds. This is the only place on the entire Pacific Coast where you have this opportunity.

The Coast Guard decided during its 101st year of operations, in 1990, to abandon this facility because the heavy surge of rough seas damages their boats here. This, of course, was not a problem in the early days of the 36-foot motor lifeboats which could be winched ashore and stored in a marine railway in the boat room. Across the Golden Gate, a new Coast Guard rescue station has been built at East Fort Baker, a protected harbor just inside Lime Point. The issue now is—who preserves the historic Fort Point Coast Guard Station? The National Park Service, maritime historians and citizens groups want to see the historic station included in the Golden Gate National Recreation Area. It would fit perfectly as a unit of the Fort Point National Historic Site since the crews of the Fort Point Life-Saving Station had a long history of interacting with the Fort Point lighthouse keepers and their families as well as with the soldiers of the fort. Even the station's lookout tower was once located here. This would preserve the Fort Point Coast Guard Station for future generations and open it to all. The grounds are exceptionally beautiful and overlook the Golden Gate. Hopefully, the National Park Service will be able to save the unique and historic Fort Point Life-Saving and Lifeboat Station. It needs to be staffed and have its history presented to the public. The station buildings are rare public treasures. The opportunity is unique on the Pacific Coast. U.S. Coast Guard Station Fort Point's motto was "Second to None." It describes this historic place very well.

Original Fort Point Life-Saving Station building still stands and was most recently the officer-in-charge's residence, 1975. (R. Shanks)

Fort Point Coast Guard station is almost unique in the service for combining the buildings of the U.S. Life-Saving (at right) with those of its successor, the Coast Guard, at left. All three are historic, beautiful structures, 1975. (R. Shanks)

*Fort Point 44-foot motor lifeboat 44347 during man overboard drills
and towing drills off the station, December 2, 1989. (R. Shanks)*

*Fort Point Station logo was comprised of a life-ring combined with a
boat hook and an oar. It is a direct descendant of the U.S. Life-Saving
Service symbol, 1989. (L. Shanks)*

MILE ROCKS

At the entrance to San Francisco Bay once stood a magnificent wave swept sentinel, one of America's greatest engineering accomplishments. This was Mile Rocks lighthouse. For a full half-mile off San Francisco's Point Lobos, submerged or barely visible rocks extend into the Golden Gate. Farthest offshore are a pair of grim, black stones rising but 20 feet above the water. The larger of the two is only 40 feet long and 30 feet wide. Swift tidal currents and dense fog frequently surround them, thus increasing their threat to shipping.

Mariners and the U.S. Lighthouse Board were long aware of the danger. In November of 1889, the Board had a large bell buoy moored just off Mile Rocks. For a time, the buoy worked very well and provided an excellent signal. Then the full force of winter began to be felt. Northern California's heavy winter rains began their annual deluge and increased the strength of ebb tides. The buoy was soon reported missing, only to be reported on station a few hours later. This went on for weeks as the massive ebb current would drag the big buoy under. With slack water, the buoy would return, remaining on the surface during the weaker flood tides.

The lighthouse engineers tried a variety of technical innovations which had been successful in other exceptionally strong currents, but the currents at Mile Rocks were of almost unprecedented strength. In late 1890, the defeated engineers reported to the Board that Mile Rocks "must always be a menace to navigation as long as they exist." Mile Rocks were again unmarked.

To be sure, there were other lighthouses at the Golden Gate, but only Fort Point was on the south shore; and, although its big fog bell clanged faithfully, it was often inaudible at Mile Rocks. The peculiar configuration of the Golden Gate's shoreline deflected sound waves in such a way that "areas of inaudibility" were created. This meant that mariners entering such areas suddenly could no longer hear a fog signal. The Lighthouse Service was gravely concerned about this problem and a study was made to determine where such areas were located. It became clear that unless a light and, most particularly, a fog signal were erected on Mile Rocks, both Mile Rocks and the more distant Fort Point Ledge would remain dangerously unprotected.

One of America's great lighthouses, Mile Rocks was among the most spectacular wave-swept rock lighthouses in the world. (U.S. Coast Guard)

MILE ROCK LIGHT-HOUSE, SAN FRANCISCO HARBOR, CAL.   *Plate III*

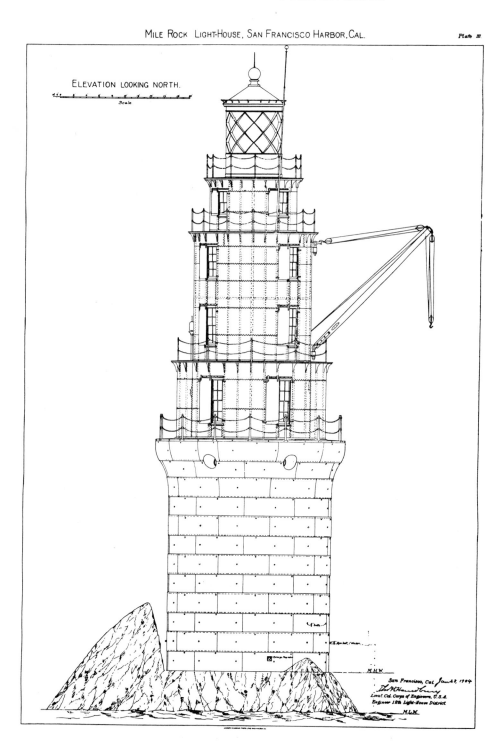

ELEVATION LOOKING NORTH.

On February 22, 1901, the liner *Rio de Janeiro* had cautiously entered the Gate in thick fog. Despite a careful watch and an experienced pilot, the passenger ship's position became confused. The lookout's warning came too late and the vessel struck Fort Point Ledge. Two hundred people were on board and the ship began sinking rapidly. Cries for help and a few quick distress calls sounded on the ship's whistle and then she was gone.

It was the worst shipwreck in San Francisco's history—the public and the Lighthouse Board reacted strongly. The Board had logged many complaints about Fort Point's fog bell and recommended that a powerful compressed air trumpet be placed there. Regarding the Rocks themselves, the Board said, "An efficient signal should be heard considerably seaward to give warning of the approach of Fort Point Shoal. The recent disaster of the steamer *Rio de Janeiro* on this reef, involving the loss of over 100 lives, might not have occurred if an efficient signal had been in operation here."

Congress responded and appropriated funds. Early in 1904, the 12th Lighthouse District's engineer, Lt. Colonel Thomas H. Handbury, had his plans for a light and fog signal returned from Washington, D.C., with full approval.

The contract for construction was awarded to James A. McMahon. McMahon rounded up a crew of skilled workmen and set out on a schooner to show them the construction site. Arriving at the wave-washed rock, barely protruding above the water, the reaction was uniform. The workmen refused to risk their lives on the tiny, seaswept rock.

McMahon was now without a crew, but he had an idea that another type of man, although less skilled in construction, might be better suited to the work at hand. He went down to San Francisco's waterfront, the Embarcadero, and rounded up a crew of deep-water sailors. They began work in September 1904.

The sailors were agile, hardy, and virtually fearless workers. The lighthouse site was to be on the larger of the two Mile Rocks. It was steep, slippery, and barnacle-encrusted. The barnacles were sharp, cutting, and often led to infection. Getting on the rock meant creeping up close in a small boat, steadying it on the rise of a wave, making a risky leap onto the rock, and then trying to keep from being swept off. Even with skilled sailors on the job, men frequently found themselves struggling in the water.

Original plans for Mile Rocks lighthouse, a great American engineering feat. Miles Rocks was generally considered one of the greatest sea swept rock lighthouses in the nation. (National Park Service)

MILE ROCK LIGHT-HOUSE, SAN FRANCISCO HARBOR, CAL.

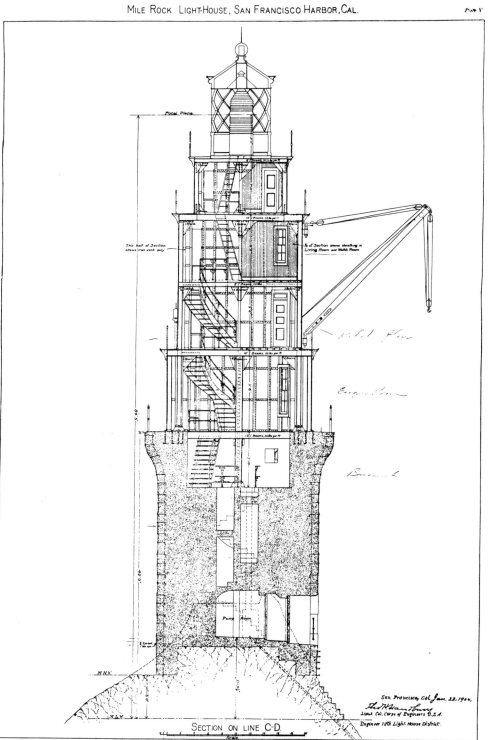

SECTION ON LINE C-D.

The gasoline schooner *Rio Rey* was anchored nearby to serve as living quarters and supply ship. The strong currents and high winds tore the 79-foot long schooner from her moorings. Finally, the ship had to be moored in a more distant, but protected, anchorage in the Bay.

Work was delayed by bad weather and often only a few hours of work could be done in a day. Eventually, however, the rock was blasted off and leveled, and soon the tower's base began to rise. The most difficult job had been leveling the rock, but landing the big $3/4$" steel plates was a close second. The plates were necessary to keep the cement dry and gave the caisson the appearance of being constructed in courses. In a sense, this was the case. A layer of steel plating was erected and then the concrete poured behind it. Concrete walls four feet thick were thus clad with steel plating. Near the base of the caisson was an entrance fitted with an oak door four inches thick and mounted in bronze.

As the cylinder grew in height, it became possible to rig a boom on each side of the caisson. From each boom dangled a Jacob's ladder. Work was now no longer limited to low tide and calm weather. On rough days, when the little 98-ton *Rio Rey* would arrive for a day's work, she would heave to near a spar buoy and put a whaleboat off to secure a line to the buoy. After securing the ship, the boat would return

Sailors from San Francisco's Embarcadero at work on Mile Rocks lighthouse during the hazardous early stages of construction. (U.S. Army, Presidio of San Francisco)

and take the workmen to the rock. Often the boat was near capsizing as she made the 300-yard trip to the lighthouse. Waves slashed at the rock and as the whaleboat was rowed under the Jacob's ladder, there was only a moment to spring from the rising boat to the rope ladder. The whaleboat was under the command of William O'Keefe, and there was no cooler helmsman on the California coast. O'Keefe had distinguished himself in the Spanish-American War by routinely doing such things as tossing unexploded live enemy shells overboard after they had landed on board his ship.

When workmen lost their footing on the tower, the usual routine was to toss them a life ring. If the man hadn't been swept too far away, he was hauled back to the rock and taken to the *Rio Rey* for fresh clothes. Otherwise, the whaleboat would chase after him, racing the swift current. In any case, the victim was soon aboard the gasoline schooner, putting on dry clothes. In a few minutes he would be back on the rock, usually to be greeted by the good-natured laughter of the other sailors.

The spirited sailors were equal to the job and the sentinel began to take shape. The completed base was 40 feet high. It contained a

By June 1905, work was progressing well on the upper portions of Mile Rocks lighthouse. (National Archives)

staircase, a cistern, and fuel tanks. Atop the caisson, a steel tower was erected. The white tower consisted of three tiers of decreasing diameters topped by a black lantern room. During most of its history, the caisson was also painted black.

There was not enough room for the large quantities of coal and water required by steam fog signals so a compressed air whistle, powered by 20-horsepower oil engines, was installed on the tower's first level. On the next tier above there was an office, kitchen and day room. In later years, a television set, radio, and radio-telephone were installed. This level had a second story and up the curving stairs were two bedrooms and a bathroom for the four-man crew. The smallest tier, just below the lantern room, was used for storage. At the very top of the 85-foot sentinel was the lantern room with its third order lens.

The exterior of the tower had a lifeboat mounted at the first level. Booms and catwalks with Jacob's ladders were mounted on opposite sides of the structure, at slightly different heights. The completed beacon was a grand sight and stood as one of the two greatest lighthouses in California's history. Despite its proximity to San Francisco, Mile Rocks

Inside the light tower. The officer-in-charge of Mile Rocks lighthouse pours himself a cup of coffee. Note the curving arrangement of the kitchen appliances, 1964. (Treasure Island Museum)

Mile Rocks lighthouse on a calm day. San Francisco's shore seemed close but keepers were as stranded as if The City had been far away. The smaller of the two Mile Rocks is visible to the right of the lighthouse. (U.S. Coast Guard)

was also one of the most isolated lighthouses in America. Too small to allow families, the men had to adapt to the same lonely life as at St. George Reef.[1]

Life on the rock station appealed to some, although there were others who called it "Devil's Island." Lyman Woodruff liked it enough to serve there 18 years. Woodruff was up to almost anything Mile Rocks could offer, and only once during his tenure was he unable to "swing aboard" the Jacob's ladder. While it was not a place to satisfy the polo player or golfer, Mile Rocks had its pastimes. Woodruff owned a fine six-inch telescope and became a knowledgeable amateur astronomer on his long night watches. Reading, athletic equipment, a radio, correspondence courses, musical instruments, and the like, filled idle hours. Housekeeping—as well as lighthouse keeping—took time, too, since the crew did their own shopping (while on liberty), cooking, cleaning, washing, and so on. A perpetual pot of coffee bubbled in the galley. A dedicated Italian-American boatman actually delivered supplies as needed for some years.

The most difficult adjustment was to the fog signal. There was no escape from its ear-splitting blast. The confinement, too, could bother some of the men, for although Mile Rocks was very unusual in having four balconies, the total space available to the crew was even less than at St. George Reef. The balconies and catwalks could be dangerous on windy days and, despite high chain railings, keepers were known to have been blown off.

Besides the terror of a keeper in the water, there were cases of sailors, fishermen, and recreational boaters being swept out to sea. The crew kept a sharp eye out for people helpless in the water, and the Lighthouse Service records mention rescues where the wickies were quite literally

---

[1]St. George Reef lighthouse, off Crescent City, California, is an isolated rock light station similar to Mile Rocks and is one of the most remarkable structures in America. Minot's Ledge in Massachusetts and Tillamook Rock in Oregon have been cited as the greatest lighthouses in the United States. Actually, St. George Reef Light is taller, larger, cost more to build, took longer to complete, and has proved more dangerous to its keepers than either Minot's or Tillamook. It was probably the greatest engineering achievement of the U.S. Lighthouse Service. It is described in detail in *Lighthouses and Lifeboats on the Redwood Coast.* It is also a lighthouse desperately in need of being incorporated into the nearby Redwood National Park. Currently, no responsible government agency is properly caring for this masterpiece, perhaps the greatest lighthouse in America.

A Mile Rocks light keeper begins the dangerous climb up the Jacob's ladder to the boom, C. 1950. (U.S. Coast Guard)

The Jacob's ladder has been drawn up as an arriving keeper nears the end of his perilous climb. Two Coast Guardsmen assist from the catwalk while a third crewman (on the balcony) secures the ladder. (U.S. Coast Guard)

The complex and dangerous operation of supplying water and fuel to Mile Rocks lighthouse requires a calm day. Note buoy tender moored in background while a launch brings fuel lines in under the catwalk. (U.S. Coast Guard)

the last hope of those being washed out to sea. In 1919, for example, Keeper W.H. Hicks had been praised by the Lighthouse Service for saving three men from drowning when their canoe capsized off the light.

With swift currents, breaking seas, high winds and numerous rocks, what anyone was doing off Mile Rocks in a canoe is a mystery. Occasionally, even less seaworthy craft would be found near the lighthouse. San Francisco teenagers had an understandable fascination for the romantic, isolated beacon and a few decided to pay a visit. Several teenagers built small "surfing rafts" and then shoved off from near San Francisco's Point Lobos just before slack water. They actually paddled out to the lighthouse and asked to come aboard. The friendly keepers lowered the Jacob's ladder and Mile Rocks had visitors. The stay was a short one, however, because the young people had to get back ashore before the tidal currents could gain strength and send them off toward the Farallon Islands.

Mile Rocks was always a "stag station", too small for families to be allowed. This resulted in some major adjustments since so many, probably most, keepers were family men. Some hated the life and transferred off at the first opportunity. Some developed private ways of feeling close to their wives. One keeper's wife would walk the family dog out to Land's End evenings and with a flashlight signal her husband a greeting that she was thinking of him and all was well.

Another keeper accepted duty on Mile Rocks for the sake of his wife. Very ill, she needed treatment in a major San Francisco hospital. The only way he could get a station quickly near the City was to go to Mile Rocks. This he did despite the hardships and his beloved wife was able to get the care she needed.

Most wives led lives completely apart from those of the Mile Rocks crew. Unlike most light stations where everyone lived in close proximity and interacted daily, at Mile Rocks, keepers' families might live far away from San Francisco. Peggy Mayeau, for example, lived with her parents in the Napa Valley while her husband Earl was stationed on Mile Rocks.

Some keepers used their tour of duty very creatively. William Miller came to Mile Rocks in the 1960s. He couldn't have had better preparation for life on a tiny rock. He'd previously served at the notoriously isolated Alaskan light stations as well as the most treacherous of them all, California's St. George Reef. Mile Rocks, St. George Reef, and the Alaskan light stations were about the toughest tour of lighthouse duty imaginable. If he had done a stint at Oregon's Tillamook Rock, he would have just about seen them all.

Anyway, William Miller actually liked duty on Mile Rocks. During his tour, the Coast Guard gave the men one week off for every two weeks served. He purchased a small ranch outside of Fresno for the Miller family and began developing it. Mile Rocks gave him 122 days a year off to work on the ranch and he had a good start toward a retirement business.

Keeper Miller and his fellow wickies knew they would be one of the light station's last crews since automation was approaching. They felt a pride in their work. They liked the frequent week-long liberties, a chance to do a job they saw as important, a certain self-controlled independence, the camaraderie, and one of the world's most beautiful views.

But Mile Rocks had its harsh side, even in the 1960s with television, radio, and regular reliefs. The fog signal's blast could never be escaped, monotony and loneliness sometimes occurred, quarters were cramped, and there was a certain risk every time you got on or off the place. Assistant Keeper Bob Schoener observed, "Sometimes the lights on the shore look a little distant, but you get used to it. And sometimes the weather acts up. Every now and then the waves get to shaking the tower and you wonder if you'll still be here in the morning. But you always are." The well-built tower, despite much shaking and swaying over the years, never failed her crews. But other actions were to fail the lighthouse.

In the 1960s, a group within the Coast Guard began developing plans to automate Mile Rocks. Plans called for removing the upper two tiers and the lantern room, and erecting a helicopter landing pad on the lowest tier. The effect would be to destroy the old seagirt tower's beauty and reduce it to a squatty caisson. San Francisco Supervisor William Blake led an outraged public in efforts to save one of California's engineering masterpieces. The Conference of California Historical Societies joined the protest. However, the group of modification advocates within the Coast Guard was committed to its plan. They argued that removing the tower would reduce maintenance costs and allow helicopters to service the facility.

The tragic and unnecessary dismantling operation began in 1965. A submarine cable was laid, which allowed the light station to be controlled from Point Bonita. Helicopters were used to speed the work. A new reflecting light was installed and the fog signal relocated. The helicopter landing pad was completed. In August 1966, the light was unmanned and converted to automatic operation. The conversion took many months and cost over $110,000.

Americans were left only with their memories of the Mile Rocks tower, but many demanded that future Coast Guard alterations be subject to public hearings and that historical significance be taken into account. Fortunately, the Coast Guard has taken important steps in this direction, and many of its personnel feel that the Mile Rocks dismantling was a tragic mistake.

The stub of the old tower remained, retaining some historic interest. Just as in the old days, the motor lifeboat from the Fort Point

During 1945, Mile Rocks had the unusual feature of both a whistle and a horn in use as fog signals. (U.S. Coast Guard)

Coast Guard Station made the run to the sentinel to service the equipment there. Thus, the ancient landing was again re-enacted. Those fortunate enough to witness the scene watched the 44-foot motor lifeboat maneuver under and parallel with the Jacob's ladder, maintaining its position by using its engines and rudder. Most motor lifeboat coxswains preferred to attempt the operation at flood tide, since the eastward flow of water made it easier to keep the boat under the east catwalk.

One of the crew stood on the bow to aid the men going up the ladder. In rough weather, that crewman had to be strapped to the railing. Those embarking were put on at the peak of a swell, so that the boat would fall away as the Coast Guardsman climbed the ladder, thus minimizing the possibility of the boat knocking the man off the ladder. At the top of the ladder, the man made his way along the catwalk to the tower, climbed a second ladder on the structure's side and then passed through a door into the tower. Leaving the tower was considered more dangerous than arriving since the boat was usually moving more than the ladder and lowering oneself could be tricky.

Mile Rocks lighthouse's office and watchroom with typewriter, pinups, ship's chair, and the weather and fog signal recording equipment, C. 1945. (Treasure Island Museum)

Kitchen portion of Mile Rocks light's combination kitchen, living room, office and watch room. (Treasure Island Museum)

Mile Rocks assistant keeper relaxes with his guitar, 1964. (Treasure Island Museum)

By 1964, Mile Rocks light had a large television set, new typewriter and a cheery kitchen. (Treasure Island Museum)

Mile Rocks farewell. The silent moment alone when leaving an offshore lighthouse or lightship, 1945. (Treasure Island Museum)

At least twice in the 1970s men were knocked off the ladder as the motor lifeboat was suddenly thrust upward by immense swells. Both times the Coast Guardsmen were rescued, although one suffered injuries. Automation was a mixed blessing since equipment failures sometimes occurred during the foulest of weather and landings had to be made while 15 to 25-foot high swells were sweeping the rocks.

Small equipment would be carried aboard by hand as described above. Heavier equipment was sometimes brought in by helicopter. The biggest operation was refueling.

Lighthouse Commissioner George Putnam's words, written in 1935, are still true today, "Even on fair days this light is difficult of access for the lighthouse tenders." Only a very calm day was chosen for refueling. In this operation, the motor lifeboat landed a crew of aids to navigation personnel at the light. The buoy tender anchored close by. On the light tower, one man stationed himself on the catwalk while another opened the door at the tower base. A line with a monkey's fist (a ball shaped knot with a weight inside it to facilitate throwing the rope) was thrown from the tender to the catwalk. The opposite end of the line was attached to the fuel hoses. The man on the catwalk drew the line in and soon the fuel hose reached him. He passed it down to the door below and the second Coast Guardsman connected it to the fuel tanks. Pumping then began and generally took an hour. Thus, despite automation, helicopters, and unmanning, two of the oldest and most dangerous tasks still continued to be enacted at Mile Rocks: landing and refueling.

In the northwest corner of San Francisco, in Lincoln Park, there is a magnificent view of the harbor entrance and Mile Rocks lighthouse. El Camino del Mar Street ends at Point Lobos at a parking area adjacent to the memorial of the cruiser *U.S.S. San Francisco*. From this parking lot, you can gain insight into the role lighthouses have played in San Francisco history. Not only can Mile Rocks be seen, but on the distant north shore, Point Bonita lighthouse as well. Just below the parking lot rim on the north side is the rectangular foundation that was once the base of the Coast Guard's Golden Gate Park Life-Saving Station's lookout tower. Here, surfmen scanned the Gate watching for shipwrecks.

The Coast Guard still faces amazing rescue challenges off Mile Rocks. In the early 1980s, Fort Point Lifeboat Station received a call for assistance during a tremendous storm. The crew responded, as usual, going out to the rescue in their 44-foot motor lifeboat under even the worst conditions. The motor lifeboat headed for Mile Rocks under the guidance of a highly respected and skilled coxswain, the one who pilots and commands a motor lifeboat. Sea conditions beyond the Golden Gate were the worst in years. But the coxswain and crew bravely entered the immense seas ahead. Waves 20 to 30-feet high were encountered. As they neared the distress scene, conditions worsened and the waves became even larger. Suddenly, a wave reported by the coxswain to be 50-feet high struck the 44-foot motor lifeboat, violently capsizing it. It was an extremely dangerous scene, especially with jagged rocks about. But the skilled coxswain righted the motor lifeboat and kept on going to the rescue.

Facing huge seas and overcoming terrifying odds in a professional manner was nothing new for the Coast Guard. But what was new was that the brave coxswain was a woman. The Coast Guard has become the leader in providing opportunities for women in a seagoing service and its policies are paying off. I have never been to Fort Point Lifeboat Station without hearing at least one of its male crewmen praise the competence and bravery of the women serving aboard the motor lifeboats there.

According to Jim Delgado in his "Shipwrecks of the Golden Gate", over 360 vessels have been lost inside San Francisco Bay or at its approaches. At low tide, you can see the remains of several vessels here. The triple expansion steam engine of the oil tanker *Lyman A. Stewart*, sunk in 1922 is here and adjacent to it, another oil tanker's bones may be seen. This is the *Frank H. Buck*, lost in 1937, after being rammed by the liner *President Coolidge*. The *Buck's* stern post and triple expansion engine can be seen as well. West of the parking area at Point Lobos are

Mile Rocks as it appears today, with a helicopter landing pad replacing the light tower. In the background, the Golden Gate Bridge stretches from Lime Point (at left) to Fort Point on the right. The lighthouse base has been painted with horizontal stripes in recent years. (U.S. Coast Guard)

the remains of the freighter *Ohioan*, that ran on the rocks in 1936. Her boilers are still pounded by the surf and torn pieces of the steel hull remain wedged in the rocks on shore. There are others, such as the *Coos Bay*, which struck the rocks to the east toward China Beach in 1927, seen today only as bits of battered steel. The *Coos Bay's* life-ring still hangs on the wall of the Fort Point Coast Guard Station. The life-rings and name boards of many other lost vessels are there, including the *Munleon, Richfield, Hartwood, Arrow, Albion River, Sea Maid,* and *Puerto Rican.*

One of the worst shipwrecks off Mile Rocks cannot be seen. On August 25, 1950, the big Navy hospital ship *Benevolence* collided with the freighter *Mary Luckenbach* in thick fog two miles off the light. The hospital ship sank in just 15 minutes. The Coast Guard 36-foot motor lifeboat from Fort Point Lifeboat Station was the first on the scene, picking up over 50 survivors and transporting them to the *Mary Luckenbach*, which remained afloat. One commercial fisherman saved dozens of lives as he repeatedly pulled struggling survivors on board his boat. He permanently ruined his back in the process and

The San Francisco Lightship *marked the entrance to San Francisco Bay while semi-permanently moored several miles off the Golden Gate. These small red ships served as floating lighthouses complete with light, fog signal and radio beacon. This is light vessel number 100, later number 523, during the last year of lightship operation in California, 1971. (U.S. Coast Guard)*

ended his career at sea, one of the real heroes of the Golden Gate. Together, the commercial fishermen and the Coast Guard saved 407 lives that terrible night. When the commercial fishing boats came into Fisherman's Wharf, they were loaded with human beings instead of salmon and crab. Tragically, 23 souls were lost when the *Benevolence* went down. To this day, charts show an unnamed wreck off Mile Rocks. It is the hulk of the *Benevolence.*

The National Park Service has a visitor's center below the Cliff House at the end of Point Lobos Avenue which offers help and information. The Land's End and Point Lobos area is rich in maritime history and certainly worth visiting. The Mile Rocks lens is currently located at Cabrillo National Monument, Point Loma, San Diego.

Lime Point's appearance was the most distinctive of all the West Coast's fog signal stations. At left is the two-story dwelling and at right is the fog signal building. Notice the twin steam powered fog whistles on each side of the smoke stack, C. 1908. (U.S. Coast Guard)

LIME POINT

The Pacific Ocean is the largest geographical feature in the world, bigger than both the Atlantic Ocean and the Indian Ocean combined. Its winds blow from the northwest, having traveled from Asia, down the coast of Canada, and beyond the Pacific Northwest to California. They create the great waves that give Washington, Oregon, and Northern California claim to the heaviest surf in America. To the south, the sheltered waters of San Francisco Bay offer protection from the pounding breakers, although the Bay can offer no protection from the Pacific's fog. From Cape Mendocino to Point Sur, the Pacific gives birth to heavy fog. In all the hundreds of miles of this coastline, there is but a single place where the fog and wind can penetrate the Coast Range mountains and enter the Great Central Valley. That place is San Francisco Bay. Commonly, the fog is preceded by winds which slam through the Golden Gate across San Pablo Bay and shriek through Carquinez Strait at thirty or forty knots. Soon the fog follows.

The light keepers could see the great, gray mass coming. It moved through the Golden Gate like a giant wave. The fog soon piled up against the Gate's north portal, Lime Point. It climbed the point, up 500 feet, and then, like a tidal wave, swept down the headland's lee side.

Below, at the foot of the towering headland, a little reef-like projection of rocks, just 20 feet wide, extends out nearly 100 feet into the Bay. Here, in 1883, a fog signal station, with big, duplicate, 12-inch steam whistles, was established.

It was a two-keeper family station, with a single-story fog signal building and a two-story residence. Both were made of brick and were strung out along the reef. Other than the white walls and red roofs, there were no visual aids to navigation. Lime Point and five sister stations (located at Angel Island, Humboldt Bay, Point Montara, Shelter Cove, and Año Nuevo Island) were designed not to show a light but to combat California's greatest hazard to navigation—fog.

By September 1883, all was in readiness, including the boiler shed, coal house, and the 1500-foot long tramway connecting the station to the wharf on Lime Point Cove. The fog signal station's two keepers each began standing two alternate six-hour shifts a day, giving continuous 24-hour service. There was a woodshed, but cord wood was used less than coal. Some years, over 150,000 pounds of coal would be shoveled into the fire box. Water came from a spring by way of a pipe to a 20,000-gallon tank. The first year, a landslide came roaring down the point and damaged the brand-new tank. It would not be the last time the station was hit.

By the 1890s, cattle grazing had so increased that the spring was becoming contaminated. This was satisfactory for the boilers but not for the keepers, so a fence was built to protect the water supply. While the keepers were busy worrying about their water, the Lighthouse Service began the process of equipping the fog signal stations with lights.

At Año Nuevo, a tiny, six-sided, wooden light tower had already been added, and it was decided that Lime Point, Angel Island, and Point Montara should all be equipped with 300-millimeter lens lanterns. The makeshift method of converting the fog signal stations to light stations resulted in some of the strangest light stations in America. Angel Island's lantern was attached to the bell house and Point Montara's lantern was simply mounted on a post. Lime Point's acetylene light was placed on the wall of the fog signal building, just 19 feet above the water. Oil houses were also built; and then, on November 26, 1900, all three lens lanterns were lighted. With the lighting of the lamps that night, California suddenly had three "new" lighthouses.

That same year, another landslide hit Lime Point, damaging the trail to the station. Five years later, there was a very large landslide and tons of rock fell but, amazingly, nothing was damaged. In 1906, the San Francisco earthquake struck, and the shock completely wrecked the big water tank. The station fared quite well compared to the damage the quake did elsewhere, but it was the worst disaster since the 1900 landslide had carried away the trestle supporting the trail. The station had been temporarily stranded, and some claimed that even when passable, the Lime Point trail was worse than Point Bonita's, a dubious honor at best.

Meanwhile, the station was the scene of experiments using crude petroleum as a replacement for coal to power the fog signal. Begun in 1903, the tests were aimed at finding a substitute for the heavy, bulky, and expensive coal that the lighthouse tenders were hauling up and down the coast. Oil finally did replace coal at Lime Point and was burned as late as 1932, when electrically-powered compressed air equipment was installed.

Watches at the entrance to San Francisco Bay required constant alertness. Lime Point had a particularly good view of the Golden Gate. The wickies were expected to sound five or six short whistle blasts, followed by a prolonged blast, to alert the Fort Point life-saving crews whenever a vessel was in distress. Lest the reader doubt the effectiveness of this method of communication between stations on opposite sides of the Golden Gate, it should be noted that the San Francisco *Chronicle* wrote of Lime Point in 1890, "It is this fog signal station which plays so important a part in disturbing the slumbers of

Sailor's view of Lime Point Fog Signal Station at the north entrance of the Golden Gate. The hill in the background now helps support the Golden Gate Bridge, C. 1900. (Laverne Dornberger)

new arrivals in the San Francisco neighborhoods of Harbor View and North Beach."

The Army appreciated the strategic location more than the newcomers appreciated the whistle. About 1910, a giant searchlight was mounted atop a flat roofed, rectangular structure next to the fog signal building. The great searchlight was a companion to the two at Point Bonita and was encased in a similar galvanized iron house. Occasionally used in locating lost vessels by the military, it was bigger, taller, and brighter than the little lens lantern. Lime Point was overshadowed for the first time.

In 1923, the Lighthouse Service decided to mark Point Diablo. Located midway between Lime Point and Point Bonita, Point Diablo rises abruptly from the north shore of the Golden Gate in the Marin Headlands. Mariners have little warning when approaching this area as the water is quite deep, then suddenly they face a 200-foot high cliff. The Lighthouse Service called Point Diablo, Spanish for Devil Point, "A dangerous menace to vessels entering San Francisco Bay in foggy weather."

A small white building with a red peaked roof was built at Point Diablo 50-feet above mean water to house two lens lanterns and a 12-inch electric siren. A stairway was constructed to give access up from the water to the little secondary light and fog signal. A telephone and an electric line was run the mile and a half across the cliffs to Lime Point. This allowed the Lime Point keepers both

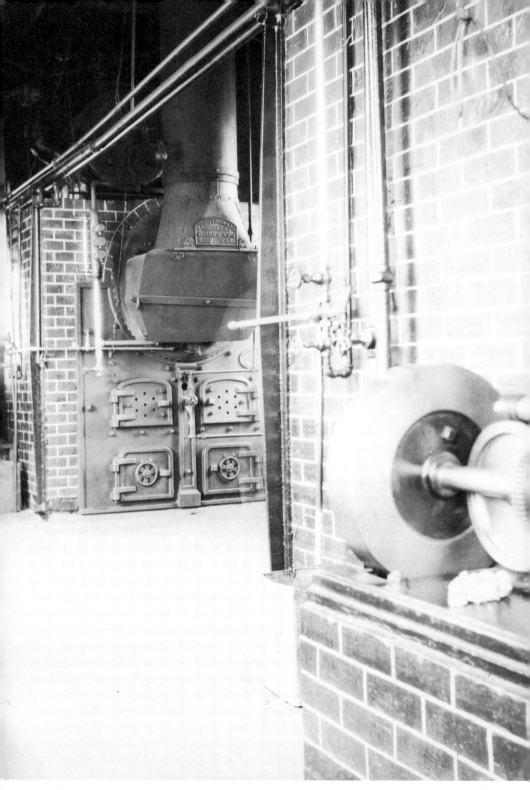

Interior of the Lime Point fog signal building showing the powerful steam fog whistle equipment. (U.S. Coast Guard)

Under Coast Guard operation, Lime Point was enlarged into a rather elaborate light station. The north pillar of the Golden Gate Bridge can be seen in the left background. The freighter India Bear *rammed the station just aft of the three story building. (U.S. Coast Guard)*

to "listen-in" on special telephones to make certain the siren was operating and to communicate between stations. The lens lantern and siren both could be controlled from Lime Point. "The station is visited," the Lighthouse Service explained, "once a week by the keepers of Lime Point light for the purpose of cleaning and oiling the apparatus." This was an early step toward automation of navigational aids, not radically different from current practices at automated light stations today.

During the 1930s, Lime Point was still staffed with Lighthouse Service personnel, old veterans with 17 to 26 years of light keeping behind them. Minor lights at Point Diablo and Yellow Bluff (near Sausalito) were both controlled electrically from Lime Point. Lookout duty was still important and—although the Army searchlight was eventually removed—there were still frequent marine disasters at the Gate. Two telephones were installed with lines to District headquarters, lifeboat stations, and Coast Guard and Navy radio stations.

In 1937, the 740-foot high Golden Gate Bridge was completed, its massive north tower just a stone's throw from the lighthouse. Neighboring Fort Point light was obscured by the south tower of the bridge and was closed down. However, despite again being overshadowed, Lime Point retained its strategic position and continued as an active light station.

The Coast Guard years began. Lime Point was taller now, a third story having been added to the residence. There were additions elsewhere too—the dwelling was now longer and had an entire new wing on the Bay side, there were other frame outbuildings, and the trail had become a road giving good access to schools and stores in Sausalito.

The bridge provided a convenient link to San Francisco, but it also provided a hazard harking back to the old days of the rock slides. Tourists delighted in dropping beer bottles and other trash off the bridge. A direct hit on a keeper's head would have been fatal but, fortunately, they always missed. From then on, Coast Guardsmen kept one eye on the light and the other on the bridge.

Lime Point was a popular station despite dangers from above. Ever since the residence had been expanded to create modern, six-room apartments, families enjoyed living there. It was a fisherman's dream, with striped bass running right under the lee of the station. Keepers would often catch their limit in under a half hour. Sometimes there was a surprise catch, such as a 65-pound skate.

There were other surprises too. On a dark night just a week before Christmas in 1959, the lighthouse had a visitor. The two keepers were shocked to suddenly find themselves looking down the barrel of a gun. The stunned Coast Guardsmen were ordered to hand over their cash. The bandit then left, firing two shots into the night to encourage the men to continue their vigilant watch rather than follow him down the dark road from the station. It may have been the only "lighthouse robbery" in history.

Beer bottles and bandits made the keepers nervous, but paint made them angry. Painting was a big enough chore on any windswept point, but Lime Point had a special problem. The crew, now boosted to three men, would just finish painting the station a gleaming white and the families would have their newly washed clothes out on the line to dry when the painters on the Golden Gate Bridge would begin working above. Despite its name, the bridge is painted orange, and soon Lime Point would find that its buildings and laundry had orange accents.

There were curious aspects too. Sausalito had become an artist colony, and Lime Point was a favorite subject. One day, Coast Guardsman James Roberts watched an artist spend the entire day scrutinizing the lighthouse, painting it with unusual care. Curious, Roberts asked to see the results late that afternoon. The masterpiece bore no resemblance to the squat fog signal station but featured a tall

Lime Point light keeper Nieves Saldate inspects his heavily damaged light station after the freighter India Bear *crashed through the wall, 1960. (U.S. Coast Guard)*

tower of the type common on the Atlantic seaboard. Roberts returned to the station and remarked philosophically, "The ways of artists are strange indeed."

On June 3, 1960, there was an event which embodied a much wider range of emotions. It was customary to start the fog horn whenever either Mile Rocks or Alcatraz became obscured. Now, with the summer fog blowing through the Gate, both were invisible and the horn was blaring and the light flashing. Officer-in-charge Nieves Saldate was on watch. The light was flashing its appropriate blink every five seconds and the big air horns blasted away twice a minute.

The calm routine was suddenly broken. For a split second, the building shook. Then a wall exploded. Saldate thought that the Golden Gate Bridge was crashing down on top of him. The culprit was big but not as large as the bridge. It was the Pacific Far East Line's freighter *India Bear*, and she had plowed into the lighthouse. The ship's pilot had realized she was over 200 yards off course when the lighthouse

The freighter India Bear *after her June 1960 ramming of Lime Point Light Station. The large hole in her bow can be seen as she is moored in an Alameda shipyard for repairs. The* India Bear *was owned by Pacific Far East Lines, an American shipping company based in San Francisco. (U.S. Coast Guard)*

suddenly loomed up. The *India Bear* went into full emergency astern, but it was too late. The vessel smashed through a plank walkway used for checking the tides and continued on to crash right through the station's bathroom, not stopping until she was well against the reef. The air pipes connecting the fog horns to the air compressor had been severed but, fortunately, the dwelling, a few feet to the left, was spared. When Keeper Saldate picked his way through the rubble, he must have been grateful that the bathroom was not in use when the *India Bear* came calling.

Actually, Lime Point had fared better than the *India Bear*. The light station suffered only $7500 worth of damages, while back at Todd Shipyard in Alameda, repairs to the ship amounted to $60,000. There was a huge hole in the freighter's bow which had to be repaired before the *India Bear* sailed by Lime Point again.

Poor acoustics and strong winds were blamed for obscuring the fog horn's blasts, and the swift tidal current was blamed for moving the vessel off course. There was some comment in the press about faulty radar equipment, but Pacific Far East Line maintained that the equipment was operating correctly.

A little over a year later, in July 1961, Lime Point was automated, and the residents, two families and a bachelor, left for other duty. The dwelling, despite its wonderful view, was removed and only the fog signal building remained. The little station continued to operate, now floodlighted for greater visibility.

Today, Lime Point is still on the light lists. The station is closed to the public, but a road leads to Lime Point from the East Fort Baker portion of Golden Gate National Recreation Area's Marin Headlands. The building has suffered some vandalism; and, although thousands pass above it on the bridge, Lime Point sits neglected and almost forgotten. Since Año Nuevo and Point Montara were eventually converted to light stations (complete with tower) and Angel Island and Shelter Cove fog signal stations have been destroyed, Lime Point is the only unaltered California fog signal station still in existence.[1] There is a need to preserve the structure, open up the fishing area, and protect the aids to navigation equipment still in use. It is a perfect spot for a Sunday afternoon. You can still catch those fish and watch the ships go by.

Tentative plans reportedly call for a joint effort between the National Park Service and the U.S. Lighthouse Society to open a fog signal museum in the historic structure. Lime Point is the last good example of a West Coast fog signal station and would be very appropriate for a museum. Perhaps a lens lantern and twin steam fog whistles can again be seen and heard at old Lime Point. A picture of the *India Bear* would be most appropriate on the bathroom wall.

---

[1]The last manned fog signal station in the nation was Manana Island Fog Signal Station off Monhegan, Maine. It was unmanned and converted to automatic operation in 1988.

Angel Island light station is seen as the two-story dwelling it became in later years. The bell house stands in front of the dwelling. (U.S. Coast Guard)

ANGEL ISLAND and POINT BLUNT

On a summer's morning in 1775, Juan Manuel de Ayala became the first European navigator to sail into San Francisco Bay. He was also the first European to leave the Bay. While he waited off the entrance for his men to search for a good anchorage, the tide changed. One of the Bay's notoriously strong ebb tides promptly washed Ayala and his ship, the *San Carlos*, back out to sea.

Returning to the Bay, Ayala found a fine mooring in the cove of an island. He named the island in honor of the Virgin Mary, Isla de Nuestra Senora de Los Angeles. Since this translates "Island of Our Lady of the Angels", it is not surprising that the name was eventually shortened to Angel Island. The little cove now bears its first European visitor's name, Ayala Cove.

From the very first, Angel Island's Ayala Cove drew small craft. While the *San Carlos* lay at anchor, large numbers of Coast Miwok and Ohlone Indians paddled over in their tule reed canoes. The native Americans warmly welcomed the Spaniards. In a month, Ayala left, ramming a rock near Lime Point on the way out. Many other mariners followed Ayala into San Francisco Bay. No small number of them managed to crash into various rocks. Angel Island attracted its share of these shipwrecks.

Angel Island saw more marine traffic pass by than any other place on San Francisco Bay except the Golden Gate, yet it was not until 1886 that a manned fog bell was established at the island's Point Knox. The bell was struck by clockwork machinery powered by a weight, rewound every few hours by the attendant. The station was operated by one keeper living in a square frame house with a red roof. The single-story dwelling, with its porch and outbuildings, was adjacent, but not connected, to the bell house. A long, wooden stairway was built down the sloping bluff to the well maintained residence with its fancy shingles and handsome trim. The station stood atop a massive rock, and huge boulders covered the beach below—truly a stern and rock-bound shore.

In November 1900, a light was added. It was a red lens lantern of the fifth order which showed a fixed light. When not in use during the day, the lens was drawn by a pulley inside the bell house. Each night, the lens was moved outside to shine without roof or cover. This system made Angel Island one of the most modest light stations in America. Still, the gleaming brass lens lantern attached to the bell house was both effective and picturesque.

Although Angel Island light and fog signal station had been built at Point Knox, mariners made repeated requests that a fog signal be added at the island's Quarry Point. They made their case by pointing out numerous wrecks. The ferry steamer *Contra Costa* ran ashore on the nearby Tiburon Peninsula. The ship *E.B. Sutton*, under tow from Port Costa, ran ashore at Quarry Point. The ship *Eleanor Margaret*, bound for Port Costa, ran ashore at Bluff Point, on Raccoon Straits. The *Maulsden* had missed the island but grounded nearby on Southampton Shoal.

Great numbers of ships passing the island were under tow. As was the custom in the early days of steam, sailing vessels were towed in and out of San Francisco Bay by steam tugs. Enormous grain wharves were located at Port Costa, Mare Island, and on the Sacramento and San Joaquin rivers. The heavy use of San Pablo and upper San Francisco bays by these grain ships was probably the major factor behind demands that Angel Island's navigational aids be upgraded. The immediate answer was to add the lens lantern at Point Knox, but the Lighthouse Board concurred with the mariners and asked Congress for a modern compressed air siren.

An early view, showing Angel Island lighthouse as a single story structure nestled among the rocks of Point Knox. (U.S. Coast Guard)

Angel Island's first keeper was John Ross. The Scotsman had emigrated to the United States, became a naturalized citizen, and served in the U.S. Navy. Eventually, Ross became an officer in the Lighthouse Service and was assigned to the new lighthouse tender *Shubrick*, a most distinguished ship. She was the first American lighthouse tender to be powered by steam, the first tender on the Pacific Coast, and the first tender to be completely built by the U.S. Lighthouse Board.

The *Shubrick* was desperately needed on the Pacific Coast, and immediately upon completion in 1857, she left Philadelphia bound for San Francisco. Ross was never to forget that voyage. Leaving Rio de Janeiro, yellow fever broke out among the crew. After passing through the Straits of Magellan, the Pacific greeted the 140-foot long ship with fierce headwinds and heavy seas. The coal supply ran so low that the crew was forced to rip out her beautiful interior wood paneling to keep the boiler fires going and her side wheel paddles turning. The furniture was being burned when the ship finally reached Valdiva Bay, Chile, where the crew rowed ashore and spent days chopping wood for fuel. Then it was on to a coaling station at Valparaiso, Chile, for more fuel. The *Shubrick* arrived in San Francisco on May 27, 1858; she would serve as the sole West Coast lighthouse tender until the *Manzanita* arrived in 1880.

While Ross remained to serve aboard the *Shubrick*, her salon steward soon departed. What conversations he and Ross may have had during the few peaceful moments of the trip are lost in time, but the steward undoubtedly would have been a most interesting conversationalist, for he was none other than economist Henry George, the famous advocate of land taxation.

In any case, John Ross was to experience an exciting life aboard the *Shubrick*. In the coming years, he would participate in many stirring adventures. In 1861, because of the Civil War, the *Shubrick* became a revenue cutter and enforced U.S. laws all along the western American shore. After the Civil War ended, the *Shubrick* was off to Alaska as the flagship of a six-vessel flotilla exploring Russian territory. During this period, her master, Captain C.M. Scammon, conducted studies of the grey whale and eventually became the world's most noted authority on the subject. Scammon's Lagoon in Baja California, Mexico, world-famous locale where grey whales bear their young, was named in his honor.

The black hulled little steamer had many exciting times on the West Coast. She saved the *Sierra Nevada*, after that vessel ran aground at Fort Point in 1862. With renewed lighthouse construction in 1867, the *Shubrick* was given the task of bringing materials to build Cape Mendocino light. About 13 miles south of Punta Gorda, she struck a rock. With water pouring in through a gaping hole, her captain made a desperate run to beach her at Big Flat. He succeeded and the *Shubrick* was later refloated. Dangerous waters were no stranger to the *Shubrick*. She had been placing buoys in poorly charted waters for years, going where no other ship dared travel.

In 1872, Ross was on board the *Shubrick* as she crossed the Columbia River bar towing a barge. The treacherous bar snapped the towline and the huge hawser recoiled across the *Shubrick's* deck. The line cut John Ross down, smashing his leg so severely that it had to be amputated. His seagoing career ended and he became a keeper in the Lighthouse Service. He served at both Yerba Buena and Fort Point lights. In 1886, he came to Angel Island to operate the fog bell. For 16 years, Ross faithfully tended the bell, accompanied by his wife and two children.

When the old veteran finally retired in 1902, he and his family remained close to the sea. The Lighthouse Service had for some years maintained a lamp house at Fort Point to store and maintain lighting paraphernalia. The facility was eventually closed when the stores were transferred to Yerba Buena Depot. The abandoned lamp house then became the Ross retirement home.

Mrs. Juliet Fish Nichols assumed the position of Angel Island lighthouse keeper in 1902. Born in China in 1858, she was the daughter of an Army physician, Dr. Melancthon Fish. Life began tragically for the youngster since her mother died giving birth to her, probably with her father as the attending physician. Named in honor of her deceased mother, Juliet and her family eventually returned to California and settled in Oakland. Dr. Fish returned to civilian life and became a respected member of the Bay Area medical community. He had remarried, taking his sister-in-law, Emily Maitland, as his wife. The family became socially prominent in the East Bay and Juliet's life improved dramatically after her early hardships.

In 1888, at age 30, Juliet married a naval officer, Commander Henry Nichols. Commander Nichols worked for some years on the Coast and Geodetic Survey and later became Superintendent of the 12th Lighthouse District which comprised the California coast. While her husband was serving as Lighthouse Service District Superintendent, Juliet's father died.

Commander Nichols sought to care for his now widowed step-mother-in-law, Emily Maitland Fish, and appointed her keeper of Point Pinos Lighthouse in Pacific Grove, California. Mrs. Fish served admirably there and helped gain some acceptance for women as light-house keepers in the service.

When the Spanish-American War broke out in 1898, Commander Nichols, Juliet's husband, was sent to the Philippines as captain of the warship *Monadnock*. While serving under Commodore Perry during the Battle of Manila Bay, the intense tropical heat overcame Commander

Nichols and he died of heat prostration. Thus, Juliet tragically lost her husband.

There was, at this time, an accepted practice of periodically allowing a Lighthouse Service officer's wife or daughter to become keepers of lighthouses upon his death. This privilege was also, occasionally, extended to the wives and daughters of light keepers as well. Given the extreme sex and racial discrimination of the period, few jobs were open to women or minority people. There is little doubt it was due to her connections with the Lighthouse Service that the now widowed Juliet Nichols was offered the position as keeper at Angel Island Lighthouse.

There was an unwritten Victorian rule that women lighthouse keepers, at least in California, were never assigned to stations except where it was a one-person station or if the only other keeper was a male relative, nearly always either a husband or father. In the latter case, the woman was almost always expected to be the assistant keeper and the man the head keeper. Although the Lighthouse Service was much more open to hiring women than the vast majority of employers of the time, even here a woman's opportunities were strictly limited and never included rising above the position of keeper at a small lighthouse. For

Angel Island was originally built as a fog signal station. Juliet Nichols lived here, her fog bell on the opposite side of the dwelling just out of the photo, C. 1910. (U.S. Coast Guard)

minority people, even when they might be the spouse or children of a light keeper, the Lighthouse Service was even more vicious in its discrimination. It was the U.S. Coast Guard, not the Lighthouse Service, that ultimately opened light keeping positions to minority people. This resulted in many lighthouse keepers by the mid-twentieth century being Asian Americans, Black Americans, Hispanic Americans, and American Indians. For this, the Coast Guard deserves great praise.

By the discriminatory standards of 1902, Juliet Fish Nichols was fortunate indeed to obtain a light keeping position. Reporting to her new post at Angel Island Light Station in September 1902, she soon realized the great danger that Angel Island represented during heavy fog. Keeping the lens lantern burning was not too difficult, but problems with the fog bell and its mechanical striking mechanism would prove to be a real ordeal. In thick weather, that fog bell had to work and work right if mariners were to avoid Angel Island's rock bound cliffs. Because of the strong mechanical vibration they produced, fog bells had a habit of breaking down just when you needed them most. If that happened, both the mariner at sea and the keeper on shore had to resort to desperate action.

Juliet Nichols' greatest test came during the summer when the San Francisco Bay fog is so often at its worst. Sunday, July 1, 1906, was a hot, clear day and sea conditions were calm. The coastwise steamers *City of Topeka, Capac*, and the new steam schooner *Sea Foam* were making good progress toward the Golden Gate. The trans-Pacific liner *Mongolia* was also rushing toward San Francisco. All were expecting to reach port the next day.

But, on the 2nd of July, fog began developing, first forming over 20 miles offshore near the Farallon Islands and soon spreading into the Bay. Juliet Nichols saw it as light fog at first, but it rapidly became dense and misty.

Stopped by the dangerous foggy conditions, the incoming coastal steamers anchored outside the Golden Gate. The *Mongolia*, with hundreds of passengers on board, dropped anchor right at the harbor entrance, off Fort Point lighthouse. The ships were to remain stranded offshore for up to 17 hours.

Juliet Nichols realized that these and other mariners were at the harbor entrance trying to reach safety. Angel Island was one of the Bay's worst hazards to navigation and the fog bell was vital to maritime safety. She quickly tried to activate the mechanical striking mechanism so the warning sound of the Angel Island fog bell would ring across the waters. But the cranky machinery refused to operate and Angel Island became a silent fog-shrouded menace. Mrs. Nichols took her responsibilities very seriously and was a resourceful and intelligent keeper. She grabbed a common nail hammer and carefully began pounding on the fog bell, giving the warning signal of Angel Island Light Station.

The Angel Island bell house. This is the fog bell Juliet Nichols pounded for over twenty hours. Note lens lantern beside the bell. (U.S. Coast Guard)

During a brief clear period, Keeper Nichols rushed off emergency telegrams to the Lighthouse Service requesting help from both the Lighthouse Inspector and the Lighthouse Engineer. She also quickly placed a fresh lamp in the lens lantern to keep the Angel Island light burning. But, in thick weather, a light might do little good as a warning and it was the fog bell that concerned her the most.

So, it was back to her post, pounding the huge bell whenever fog approached. On July 3rd, Mr. Burt of the Lighthouse Engineer's office arrived and by late morning had the bell striking apparatus repaired. It was none too soon, for at 7 p.m. the fog returned to the island, thicker than before. Many ships had by now made it into San Francisco Bay but others were continually arriving. Mercifully, the mechanism worked that night during the recurring thick weather.

Then, on the 4th of July, the fog returned yet again and at about the same time, seven in the evening. An hour later the fog bell striking "machinery went to pieces—the great tension bar broken in two." Juliet Nichols again grabbed her nail hammer and returned to the platform in front of the bell house. There she began striking the huge bell, its clanging undoubtedly nearly deafening. Her arm must have begun to throb with the pain of ceaselessly pounding the bell hour-after-hour.

Juliet Nichols stayed at her exhausting task, fearing that to stop for more than the briefest moment might allow a ship to wreck on the rocks. Ten hours passed, then fifteen, and finally, over twenty hours had gone by.

When the fog finally thinned about 8 a.m. on the 5th, Keeper Nichols could see "landmarks just visible" in the distance. Juliet Nichols then penned in the station log book, "July 4th and 5th, '06. Bell struck by hand with a nail hammer. Bell struck by hand 20 hours and 35 minutes." Her agonizing hours of pounding the fog bell had paid off. No vessel wrecked on Angel Island's shores. And Juliet Nichols' ordeal had established herself as one of America's great lighthouse keepers.

With a temporary lull in the weather, workmen sent by the Lighthouse Service Engineer arrived and replaced the broken great tension bar, restoring the mechanical bell striker to operation. This accomplished, Keeper Nichols put her arm to use again. She sat down and wrote an accident report on the bell striker and completed required monthly and quarterly reports and mailed them off.

She must have been pleased when late that month she received a letter of commendation from the Lighthouse Board in Washington, D.C., praising her dedication. It was a well earned honor from the Lighthouse Service's highest governing board. The next day she wrote a gracious acknowledgement letter. Then, in her log book, she wrote, "Distant threatening fog."

Juliet Nichols' career centered on her battle with fog. Her log book writings include such entries as, "Dense fog all night . . . bell struck continously for 16 hours." She might record fog for 80 hours straight as summer sea fog rolled in the Golden Gate or winter tule fog arose in the marshlands.

The mechanical striking mechanism bell continued to be a serious problem. From 1908 through 1914, the fog bell apparatus broke down seven more times; each time, the log book includes the notation, "Bell struck by hand." The causes varied—a hammer spring broke, the tension bar broke again, and even the rope attached to the clockwork weight snapped. Telegrams requesting help were dispatched and then the trusty nail hammer taken up again until either the fog lifted or help arrived.

Just before she retired in 1914, Lighthouse Commissioner George Putnam singled Mrs. Nichols out for praise in an article in *National Geographic* magazine. On November 19, 1914, Juliet Nichols retired from the Lighthouse Service. It was fitting that her weather report that day read, "Clear."

Upon retirement, Juliet Nichols moved to the Oakland hills with a good view of the Golden Gate's fog and of Angel Island. Through the Gate stretched the Pacific for thousands of miles to Asia, the place of her birth. Keeper Nichols was 88 years old when she died in 1947.

The most important change at Angel Island that occurred after Juliet Nichols retired was the construction of the Point Stuart light in 1915. This was a secondary light tended by the keepers at Angel Island. Point Stuart was a tiny white cottage with a lens lantern mounted on its red roof. Like Angel Island Light at Point Knox, it was reached by a respectable walk and long stairs. Perhaps it was this beacon's creation that led Angel Island to become a two-keeper station.

With two keepers assigned to the station, the single-story dwelling lighthouse was eventually deemed too small. It was expanded to two stories, apparently by a novel method: the house appeared to have been lifted up and a new story built beneath it. An enclosed porch was added, but otherwise there were few changes. It was as if, like a suddenly maturing adolescent, the residence had just grown up.

A series of men followed Juliet Nichols at Angel Island light. Peter Admiral was her immediate replacement. Frank Schou was head keeper by the late 1920s when Irving Conklin was appointed as assistant keeper. Young Conklin arrived by Army ferryboat and landed at West Garrison, a military post midway between Point Knox and Point Stuart on the island's west side. The light station had no real landing, just a stairway down to a little skiff used locally if needed. So Conklin had to walk to the lighthouse once he reached Angel Island. Assistant Keeper Conklin quickly learned two things about Angel Island Light Station. The first would have made Juliet Nichols smile.

Frank Schou introduced Conklin to the fog bell. It took twenty minutes just to wind up the heavy weights so the clockwork drive would power the mechanical striker. The weights were so heavy, Schou said, "They weighed almost a ton." At any rate, it sure felt like a ton. The mechanism had compound pulleys to ease the winding but it was "still damn hard to wind up." The weights were hung beside the bell house and descended down toward the Bay as they unwound. Every two hours the thing needed rewinding. Nearly sixty years after serving at Angel Island, Irving Conklin passionately recalled the bell mechanism, "The bell was a dog! That damn bell! It was so hard to wind up."

Conklin did better with the poison oak. Many people are allergic to its skin irritating qualities, but Assistant Keeper Conklin was immune. He offered to dig out the poison oak bushes which had, with time, come to surround the light station. Head Keeper Schou was delighted by the offer since he was highly allergic to poison oak. So, the well intending new assistant went down to the work house behind and a bit below the lighthouse and got a pair of gloves. Of course, in the process of eradicating the toxic poison oak, the gloves became saturated with the plant's oils. Conklin didn't think much about this problem and put the gloves back for Schou's use. The next day Schou's wife called to say that

Angel Island light station is seen as the two-story dwelling it became in later years. The bell house stands in front of the dwelling. (U.S. Coast Guard)

her husband was in the Marine Hospital in San Francisco with a terrible case of poison oak. Conklin quietly burned the gloves.

Keeper Schou's wife and daughter Olga lived at the station. Olga suffered from tuberculosis and spent much time sitting in the sun on the lighthouse porch. Respiratory diseases were not uncommon problems among lighthouse keeping families. Their counterparts, the surfmen of the U.S. Life-Saving Service, also risked lung diseases as well. Damp climate, long hours of work, close living quarters, and distant medical care seemed to take its toll. At a few lights, such as Cape Mendocino in Humboldt County, ill health plagued the station for years. The Schous were no exception, and, later when stationed at Southampton Shoal light, Mrs. Schou and Olga would be forced to live ashore where medical treatment was available and the weather was less harsh.

Life on Angel Island continued through the Depression, World War II, and into the 1950s. The station got a truck and the trips to Point Stuart became easier. In 1952, radio beacon calibration facilities were transferred from Southampton Shoal lighthouse to Angel Island. This meant still another duty for the men and more cramped quarters in the aging structure. By the late fifties, the long stairs leading down to the light had become unstable and difficult to maintain.

The Coast Guard decided that modern facilities must be built at Point Blunt, on the island's prominent southeast tip. The proliferating aids to navigation meant that the station's truck was frequently seen bouncing along the road from one facility to another.

Point Blunt's completion in 1960 gave Angel Island the short-lived distinction of having three lights (Point Knox, Point Blunt, and Point Stuart) and three fog signals. However, Coast Guard personnel questioned the continuing need for the original Angel Island lighthouse at Point Knox. In 1963, the vacant lighthouse was burned down by the Coast Guard. It was a sad loss for Americans, particularly since the Point Knox station could have served as a monument to the dedicated women in the Lighthouse Service. Present day Coast Guard regulations would never have allowed such destruction.

Like its predecessor, Point Blunt did not feature a lighthouse in the traditional sense, yet it was an official Coast Guard Light Station. The light and fog horn were mounted on the roof of a small rectangular, flat roofed frame structure. A watch building of much the same design, but with picture windows, was built nearby. Ranch-style quarters for the four keepers and their families were also constructed. A landing and various support buildings completed the station. Calibration service for ship's radio direction finders was also provided.

One of those who manned Point Blunt was Trueman Cook. Cook was one of the last of the Pacific Coast's civilian lighthouse keepers. The Coast Guard had assumed light keeping responsibilities from the

Lighthouse Service in 1939. Gradually, Coast Guard enlisted men replaced their predecessors until only a handful remained in the 1960s.

Keeper Cook was one of the last of a fine tradition, and he and his wife were well adapted to their island life. They would regularly feed a buck deer who banged on their window with his nose when hungry. Cook was almost casual about the frequent aid he gave to Bay sailors who often stranded on the rocks and beaches of Angel Island. Those whom he could not help directly, he assisted by promptly telephoning for Coast Guard rescue craft.

A typical example of the aid mariners received from Angel Island's keepers occurred in March 1960. A six-room houseboat was under tow to Sausalito. Weather conditions on the Bay were terrible. Visibility was very low and the storm-tossed waters battered the boat. The houseboat began to break up under the pounding. The wooden craft went down so quickly that the two men on board were trapped inside. The houseboat

Angel Island lighthouse at Point Knox was originally built as a fog signal station, accounting for its unusual construction. The Lighthouse Service considered Angel Island to be one of the worst hazards to navigation on the Bay and strongly urged Congress to appropriate funds for the station. Once built, maintenance was no easy task, as the steep, zigzagging stairs down the cliff indicate. (U.S. Coast Guard)

settled on the shallow Bay bottom with only four inches of roof sticking up above the surface. Both sailors managed to swim out, however, one through a door and the other by a window. Once on the surface, they faced a new problem. The houseboat had broken up so badly that the men were surrounded by wave tossed shattered planks. The two sailors dodged flying planks and held on to the roof until the surf tore it off. Cut and bruised, they swam for Angel Island, where the lighthouse keepers saw them on the beach. The keepers climbed down the rocks and brought the men to the Point Blunt light station. After receiving medical care, hot baths, and dry clothing, they were taken to the mainland by an Army ferryboat.

Through the 1960s and into the 1970s, Point Blunt continued to be a busy manned light station. It lacked the classic appearance of its more conventional kin, but it was a full-fledged light station. The old fog bell was unused, but it still stood at Point Knox and showed hammer marks from Juliet Nichols' blows long ago. Shopping was often done in Tiburon by the light keeping families. An old-fashioned pushcart was kept at the wharf for use by the light keepers and other Angel Island residents. I lived in Tiburon in the late 1960s and remember seeing a grocery clerk from Mantegani's Market trundling the cart down to the wharf for a light keeper's wife. Toward evening you might see a keeper and his son tie up at one of the town's floating docks as they made a quick trip to the mainland for supplies. Tiburon was one of the last ports on the West Coast where you could still see such sights.

The light keepers' children had to cross Raccoon Straits to Tiburon each school day. A van drove around the island picking up both Coast Guard and State Park families' children. Since the Army had long since left the island, the military reservation had become a state park and this gave the Coast Guard personnel new neighbors. Often there would be as many as 15 school-age youngsters living on Angel Island. A "school boat" took them to Tiburon to catch waiting buses. In stormy weather, the ride in the school boat could get so rough that the kids would have to sit on the cabin floor. A boy fell overboard once but was pulled back on board unharmed. Once or twice a year, the Straits would get so choppy that it was unsafe to make the trip and Angel Island children got a school holiday. During the spring, the trip could take as long as 15 minutes because the fast moving channel could become clogged with debris from flooded rivers. Usually, however, the weather was fine and the trip an invigorating way to begin the day.

Point Blunt lighthouse had a significant and interesting place in Pacific Coast maritime history. It was the last manned California lighthouse ever built. Fittingly, it was a short distance and within sight of the West's first lighthouse on Alcatraz Island.

Early in 1976, Coast Guard friends alerted me that Point Blunt lighthouse would be automated and unmanned soon. Wanting to

Point Blunt lighthouse keeper Trueman Cook and his wife on Angel Island, C. 1960. (Nautical Research Center)

provide a historical record of the light as a manned station, I arranged to join a Coast Guard "log run" to Angel Island.

Our trip began at Coast Guard Base San Francisco on Yerba Buena Island, as the old Lighthouse Service Depot was now called. Departure was to be early Monday morning, March 1, 1976. Before dawn, a storm swept the area with wind, rain and hail. It didn't look promising as I drove toward the Oakland Bay Bridge to reach Yerba Buena Island.

Arriving at the Base, I parked near Coast Guard Group Headquarters. A sign warned that I was "parking at my own risk" since giant eucalyptus tree limbs were occasionally falling on the parking lot. After parking, I walked past an old fog bell on display and then into the Headquarters building. I climbed up circular stairs identical to those found in a lighthouse to the operations department. There, two officers quickly directed me to a 30-foot utility boat that was fueling on the floating dock below.

On the dock, it was wet and slippery, but the weather was clearing and the rain was about gone. I was soon chatting with the *Thirty's* three-man boat crew. (In the Coast Guard, vessels under 100-feet in length are commonly referred to by their length.) A variety of Coast Guard vessels were docked at Yerba Buena Island, or "YBI" as the Coasties most commonly called it. There were two buoy tenders, the *Blackhaw* and the *Red Birch*, black hulled workhorses of the aids to navigation people. There were the thirty- and forty-fuot utility boats so commonly used on more protected waters or on calm days at sea. (Their future was limited, even in 1976, for by then new 41-foot utility boats had arrived and were being tested to replaced the *30s* and *40s*.) Sleek 82-foot patrol boats were moored there, too. They were handsome craft descended from the rum runner chasing 75-foot patrol boats of the Prohibition Era, but notorious for rolling heavily in foul weather. (I remember once having breakfast aboard the 82-foot cutter *Point Barrow* while she was tied up at YBI in calm weather and she still rolled. It made the whole crew laugh that an *82* could roll under even the calmest conditions. On the East Coast, the crew of a sister ship, the *Point Bonita*, call the crew's bunking quarters the "Zero Gravity Chamber" because they get thrown around so much in heavy seas.)

Soon the little *Thirty* was fueled and the boat crew and I were joined by construction workers carrying a long pole in two pieces. This was to be used as Point Blunt's new radio beacon antenna for guiding vessels and also as an antenna for monitoring the equipment after automation. After another wait of ten or fifteen minutes, we shoved off for Point Blunt, only to be recalled to the dock to take on board more personnel. Electricians had arrived to begin work converting the station to automatic operation and they climbed aboard too. By now the boat was crammed with nearly a dozen men on board, with men sitting and standing among the antenna, tools, and materials to be used in the automation work.

Once we were underway, I spent the trip talking with the boat crew. The weather had improved and it became one of those glorious San Francisco Bay mornings when the air is clear and crisp with just a nip to the wind. Fort Point and Point Bonita to the west dazzled with striking clarity as we briskly moved through small bumpy waves sailors call a "light chop".

The *Thirty's* coxswain, a veteran of polar duty aboard an ice breaker, ran the boat at maximum speed despite its heavy load of men and equipment. As a veteran of many a "log run" to light stations or lightships, I've learned that Coast Guard small boat coxswains are unsurpassed worldwide in their skill. But I've also learned that between leaving the dock and arriving at the light station, Coast Guard small craft have only two speeds—stop and full speed ahead. There is something about roaring across the sea at top speed toward a remote lighthouse that makes everyone on board come alive. Many times I've had Coast Guardsmen turn to me at such moments and tell me they love the Coast Guard and what they are doing. I share that feeling completely.

During such runs you hear some of the best sea stories. Despite often having to shout above the engine roar, the talk almost always begins. The coxswain usually initiates it, but others soon join in. We've all got our experiences to share and I remember them well, whether we were bouncing across the Columbia River bar, on the bar at Coos Bay, Oregon, with storm warnings flying, off Boon Island, Maine's rock bound shore, or nearing treacherous St. George Reef, California. It has always been the same for me—at the reef lighthouses off Key West, Florida, on the way back from the lightship off Cape Disappointment, Washington, at Minots Ledge light in Massachusetts, or simply crossing San Francisco Bay to Angel Island.

The talk usually centers on small boats, especially motor lifeboats, or on light stations. Even if the lighthouses are automated, the adventures live on in the men and women who service them. They

Point Blunt lighthouse was a typical Angel Island structure: a small, frame building with a lens lantern and modest fog signal to aid the mariner. (U.S. Coast Guard)

Keeper Jim Demerin inspects the lens lantern and small fog horn atop Point Blunt lighthouse. Mr. Demerin followed the grand light keeping tradition of rescuing those in distress near his light station, March 1, 1976. (R. Shanks)

still have to land, they still have to climb the stairs, they still must go out in foul weather to relight them. And, yes, they still feel the old pride in the beacons and the boats.

On the Angel Island trip, we talked, of course, of small boats and big lighthouses. The talk today was of Mile Rocks light, a dangerous rock lighthouse. The Coast Guardsmen servicing the station had to jump from the bow of a 44-foot motor lifeboat onto a rope ladder to climb up the lighthouse catwalk. The motor lifeboat had suddenly and unexpectedly surged upward on a swell and bruised men found themselves struggling in the water. Twice recently, Coast Guardsmen had been knocked off the rope landing ladders.

The coxswain had also served aboard a buoy tender which supplied St. George Reef lighthouse prior to automation. Located along the California-Oregon border, maritime historian Jim Gibbs has called St. George Reef the "King of Pacific Coast lighthouses." It is one of the most dangerous lights in the nation with incredibly treacherous waters. There was a Coast Guard mooring buoy, a very large floating ball anchored off the reef. The buoy had to be replaced and this particular situation had required sending a diver down 90 feet to detach the old buoy and reattach a new one to the mooring chain. As ship's diver, the coxswain had done the task, a real challenge in such waters. The stories ended all too soon as we approached the landing at Point Blunt. About twenty minutes had elapsed since leaving Yerba Buena Island and the morning bathed Angel Island in warm California sun.

Point Blunt was a narrow, steep knob connected to Angel Island by a low neck of land. The Coast Guard pier was on the east side of the Point which protected it from the full force of the Golden Gate winds. Tide was low and the T-shaped pier was high above us as we circled around and tied up at the head of the pier. Officer-in-charge Jim Demerin was on the dock waiting for us, his big Coast Guard van parked at the edge of the wharf.

The wooden dock had a vertical, steel ladder which led up the side. It also had a gangplank which could be adjusted to the stage of the tide and size of vessel. The large antenna was landed on the gangplank, but we all used the ladder to come ashore. The Coast Guard van was soon filled with men and equipment, only the three-man boat crew remained at the landing. I will always remember that morning as Keeper Demerin drove us up the dirt road to the lighthouse.

The road led up the hill from the landing, the right fork going past the well-kept station grounds with its fine lawn and modern quarters (the left fork ran out to the lighthouse). The residence had the reputation as one of the most comfortable in the Coast Guard. The immaculate grounds complemented the dwelling, even to incorporating large white concrete letters spelling "U.S.C.G." into the landscaping. Sea lions barked from the rocks below, deer roamed the hills, and the view may well have been the best on the Bay.

Atop the knoll-like point were two small, flat roofed, wooden buildings. Farthest seaward was a rectangular lighthouse with an antique lens lantern and a pair of small compressed air fog horns mounted on the roof. The building was painted white with a bright red vertical stripe. Its simplicity and the presence of a lens lantern continued the Angel Island tradition of modest lighthouse architecture. Nearby, a fog bell was on display, a dwarf compared to the original bell that still may be seen at Point Knox. The watch room stood too, but later when automation came, it was renovated to serve as an automatic lighthouse. It became the last of Angel Island's tiny light structures.

In the 1970s, there were increasing numbers of pleasure craft off Angel Island and Coast Guardsmen maintained a careful watch at Point Blunt. During late 1975 and early 1976 alone, officer-in-charge Jim Demerin had spotted small craft in distress on five separate occasions, and called Coast Guard rescue boats to their assistance. He estimated that his two assistant keepers had each made as many calls during the same period. The Bay's sailors had valuable friends at Point Blunt.

The Point Blunt knoll protected a small beach from the full force of the Golden Gate's winds. The Coast Guard pier was located in this cove. Its main purpose was to serve as a landing when supplies were brought ashore from the Coast Guard base on Yerba Buena Island. The pier came in handy, too, when the Bay winds suddenly whip up to 35 knots and sailboats sought shelter there to wait out the blow.

A paved road led up the hill from the keepers' residence, passing a mundane concrete building which served as a paint locker, and continued out of the station grounds. It was a five minute drive to Point Stuart light, secondary responsibility of Angel Island light keepers since 1915. The original structure was still in use, a small white frame building with a peaked red roof and a surrounding balcony. A stairway led down the steep hillside from the road to the beacon. A causeway led directly off the stairway onto the roof of the light structure to where a lens lantern has been mounted. The lens lantern differed from those used elsewhere on Angel Island only because it had a double tier of prisms. Inside each tier was an elliptical light bulb, the lower one coming on automatically if the upper bulb burned out. Inside the light structure itself were several spare bulbs, high quality lens cleaning paper, and huge storage batteries to operate the light during power failures.

Point Stuart was yet another example of the distinctive simplicity of Angel Island's light structures. Even its ramp-like stairway was reminiscent of the way wickies reached the original light on Point Knox.

With lens lanterns still used at Point Blunt and Point Stuart, Angel Island represented an unusually prolonged and extensive use of lens lanterns as important navigational aids. The tradition of light keepers tending nearby minor aids (in addition to their lighthouse) was once commonplace on San Francisco Bay. Such things were now a part of the past, and when the Point Blunt crew drove the big, white Coast Guard van around the island to Point Stuart to maintain the lens lantern, it was to tend the last manned secondary light on the Bay.

Angel Island's lights were always simple, low-maintenance structures. The beacons at Point Knox and Point Stuart may have been architecturally unimpressive but they were forerunners of the simple, low-maintenance facilities eventually developed by the Coast Guard to avoid constructing the classic lighthouses built by the old Lighthouse Service. Point Blunt represented the latest stage in the centuries-old evolution of lighthouses from complex and costly structures to simpler navigational beacons. In this sense, Angel Island's sentinels played important roles in the development of the world's modern navigational aids.

Eventually, as a part of the automation progress, the Point Blunt Lighthouse was torn down by the Coast Guard. The nearly identical watch room building was converted to become the automated lighthouse. The lens lanterns were removed by civilian employees of the Buoy Depot at Yerba Buena Island and beautifully refurbished so that their brass gleamed. That was the last I ever saw of the lens lanterns. Hopefully, they can be located and exhibited in an appropriate museum.

Then 12th Coast Guard District's "Local Notice to Mariners" announced, "On 28 June 1976, Point Blunt Light . . . was automated and resident personnel are no longer in attendance." The State Park personnel missed the little lighthouse and regretted its destruction. The Bay sailors certainly lost valuable and dedicated Coast Guard friends who watched over them, no matter what the weather. Jim Demerin was one of the great California light keepers and he maintained the finest traditions of the profession to the very end.

Just as Juliet Nichols had demonstrated that a woman could be a great light keeper, so, too, had Jim Demerin, an Asian-American, proved it for minority people. Perhaps Angel Island's most important contribution was to disprove the Lighthouse Service's long outdated prejudices about who could be a great light keeper.

Important parts of the lighthouse heritage remain on Angel Island, now a state park easily reached by ferry from Tiburon. The historic old fog bell still stands at Point Knox on the site of Angel Island light station, a forgotten monument to Juliet Nichols. The automated light still flashes green out on Point Blunt, although Jim Demerin and his crew are not there to aid in a rescue. At the park headquarters on Ayala Cove, the lens from Southampton Shoal lighthouse may be seen.

There is a real need for the California State Department of Parks and Recreation to develop an interpretive overlook at Point Knox so visitors may see the historic fog bell and learn of the island's lighthouse heritage. The bell and its mounting need occasional maintenance as well. Hopefully, the bell can remain in its appropriate historic location. Angel Island's role in maritime history is rich and important, but it is little known by the general public. Juliet Nichols, Jim Demerin, Irving Conklin, and the other great light keepers deserve to be remembered on Angel Island.

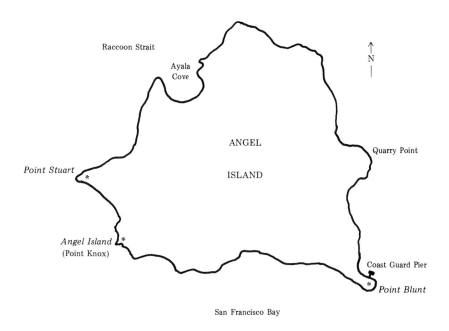

Map of Angel Island showing the location of Angel Island and Point Blunt light stations and the secondary light at Point Stuart.

East Brother lighthouse received loving care from its families. Note the potted plants and ornamental woodwork. Seven California lighthouses were built in basically this same architectural style; only three (East Brother, Point Fermin, and San Luis Obispo) stand unaltered today. The gleaming white foreground is the catch-basin for the cistern.

EAST BROTHER

The waters of the mighty Sierra Nevada Mountains rush down to the Great Central Valley forming over a dozen rivers. These are the tributaries of the Sacramento and the San Joaquin, which merge at the Delta and flow through Carquinez Strait into San Pablo Bay. These waters, in turn, move through a narrow strait formed by Point San Pedro and Point San Pablo and then enter San Francisco Bay. A pair of low, rounded rocks are just off each of these points and are known locally as The Sisters and The Brothers. Those off Point San Pablo, The Brothers, are at the edge of the shipping lanes which thread the strait. It was here, after discarding the idea of building a beacon on Point San Pablo, that the Lighthouse Board settled on the easterly of the two Brothers islands as the best site for a new light station.

East Brother lies a third of a mile off the Contra Costa shore and is one of those chunks of land that is too big to be called a rock and too small to be termed an island. At any rate, it was—despite the swift currents that surround it—a fine choice for a lighthouse. It was so good, in fact, that Assistant Lighthouse Engineer E.G. Molera had some innovative ideas for the proposed station's fog signal. The 1870s was a time of blowhole-powered fog whistles and fog cannons. Molera's ideas were as good, maybe better, than a number of strange noise making devices already in use along the coast.

Molera wanted to build a fog trumpet powered by the fantastic combination of a tide mill, wave ram, and windmill. The tide mill was basically a large pipe filled by high tide, which would pour water into a reservoir to be dug on the island. Apparently the water's weight would power a mill of some sort. The wave ram was another pipe with a trumpet-like mouth in which the pounding of waves would open a valve and the force of the water would compress air in a chamber. The windmill would, of course, add more storage water on windy days in the conventional manner.

Molera explained that the sound would be produced because "the air would be condensed by an apparatus moved by the water in the reservoir," thus providing an endless supply of compressed air to blow the fog trumpet. It was a fireless, fuelless, inexpensive wonder, which—instead of taking 45 minutes to fire and get up steam as a conventional whistle might require—could be started instantly. Eliminating coal fires could mean one or two keeper positions less per station. A giant sound board and two huge parabolic reflectors would direct the sound, with an "intensity . . . superior to any yet produced." Molera offered the U.S. Government free use of the plans if he were allowed to take patents in foreign countries.

Both West Brother and East Brother Islands can be seen in this 1930s photo of East Brother Light Station. From left to right, can be seen the lighthouse, the water house, the fog signal building and the landing. All except the water house stand today. (U.S. Lighthouse Society)

The idea of using wave action and tidal movements is one that tantalizes inventors to this day. Harnessing the energy of the ocean would be an unlimited source of power for an energy starved planet.

But Washington officials apparently did not encourage the creative assistant engineer, and East Brother was built with a conventional 12-inch steam whistle. Whether Molera's tide mill and wave ram would have worked is uncertain, but nearly a century later, some Canadian light stations were equipped with windmills which powered generators that reliably operated the light with the same low cost and ease of maintenance that Molera had envisioned. Similarly, many Coast Guard lighthouses, especially offshore ones, are today lighted using solar power. It was too bad that the Lighthouse Service brushed its dedicated young engineer aside, for East Brother might have achieved an important niche in lighthouse history.

As it was, greatness bypassed East Brother light station. Yet it was a beautiful frame structure with a square tower attached to the two-story California Victorian-style dwelling. (Lighthouses in this architectural style were also built at Ballast Point, Point Fermin, Point Hueneme, San Luis Obispo, Mare Island, and Table Bluff in California; at Point Adams, Oregon; and Hereford Inlet, New Jersey.) East Brother's flashing fourth order lens was displayed 37 feet above the ground in the three-story tower. The low, barren island was leveled and a concrete

catch basin and a cistern came to occupy a sizable chunk of ground at
the very center of the rock. The steam fog whistle was installed across
the concrete slab from the lighthouse, and beyond it there was the
landing with its derrick and engine house. A handsome, octagonal water
house, an oil house, coal house, and some tanks eventually completed
the station. East Brother was a compact and efficient light station.

On March 1, 1874, the light was first lit by T.L. Winship, Lighthouse
Service lampist, who was assisted by Samuel M. Ferrand, keeper, and
two assistant keepers. East Brother light would have three lighthouse
keepers for the ensuing six years, then be reduced to two wickies. The
facility was a family station and soon became popular with keepers and
their wives. April 9th that year, the fog signal was tested, and on May 1,
1874, the steam whistle began operation. Despite the tight quarters and
powerful fog whistle, keepers still happily transferred to East Brother
from harsher stations such as Point Arena or Point Reyes.

Still, East Brother was not an easy station. That first winter, a
violent gale hit, badly damaging the wharf and tramway that led
up to the fog signal building. The lighthouse log book records that
a strong northerly gale broke fences and that the foundation of the
coal house was even washed away. The first entry in the log book
tersely states, "Bad weather." The second entry? "A southeast gale."
Through the coming years, southeast and southwesterly gales would
not be rare.

To get the station fully operational, the "water boat" came out and
filled the cistern with over 44,000 gallons of water to be used for drinking
and for the steam fog signal. The lighthouse tender *Shubrick* then
arrived with ten tons of coal. With all that on the tiny island, the
Lighthouse Service was ready for action.

The first year or so was hard. There were inspections, painting,
and even waves breaking over the island during a southwest gale. In
one violent gale, the wharf and tramway that led up to the fog signal
building were damaged. One day an attempt was made to salvage a
buoy and on another occasion, the floating body of a drowned man was
picked up. As if this wasn't enough, on September 9, 1875, lighthouse
inspector A.J. Snell died on East Brother, undoubtedly during his
quarterly inspection. It took two days before the tender arrived to
remove his body.

Despite all, the inspection was successfully passed when a new
inspector, Silas Case, came aboard. With Assistant Keeper James
Rankin (later to become the heroic keeper of Fort Point light) on
board, it is no surprise things were going a bit better by 1878.
Still, during the early years, tragedy seemed to haunt the place. A
keeper's baby died.

In 1880, the wind blew so hard it snapped the flagstaff. That same
year, the tender *Manzanita* arrived with a new fourth order fixed lens

which was installed. Nearly 230 sacks of coal were also landed and all the empty sacks taken away to be refilled.

The Lighthouse Service provided transportation for its empty coal sacks, but not for East Brother keepers who wanted to go ashore. Keepers needed time off the island, certainly much more than a coal sack did. The lighthouse log periodically reports that keepers would go ashore to San Francisco or San Pablo "with a lady". When "with a lady", as luck would have it, that darn wind came up and the keepers return "was delayed by the wind." That was just as well, for when the wickie came back, it was brasswork or boatwork, neither of which could compete with a lady.

Up on the stormy Mendocino Coast at Point Arena light, Keeper George Koons had been writing in his "personal log book" about his desire to transfer to a less remote lighthouse. He'd been delighted when reassigned to East Brother on San Francisco Bay. But East Brother must have been a bit rougher than he'd expected, or perhaps it was too isolated. His stay as assistant keeper was a short one and the sloop *Magic* had come to carry his goods to his next assignment. Perhaps that would be more to his liking. It was Point Montara Fog Signal Station (later, a light station), a mainland facility with a bit better weather perhaps. After all, the fierce winds at East Brother had actually "moved the fence and wrecked it."

While Koons was at East Brother, Commander Charles McDougal had become lighthouse inspector and he had carefully gone over East Brother Light Station. His was a risky, difficult job, visiting isolated light stations by tender along 840 miles of California coastline.

Then, tragically, on April 2, 1881, the lighthouse tender *Manzanita* steamed by East Brother carrying Charles McDougal's body. He had drowned at one of the rough coastal stations, Cape Mendocino in Humboldt County, while trying to make a landing to inspect the light. Now he was making a last trip home to his wife and family at Mare Island up the Bay. His widow, Kate, would eventually become keeper of the next lighthouse north, Mare Island light.

Getting on and off East Brother Island could be quite tricky, but it was much easier than the offshore coastal lighthouses. Furthermore, pleasant communities were not far from The Brothers. During these early years, the keepers went ashore more often to the west in Marin County rather than the East Bay, commonly landing at San Rafael or Point San Quentin. San Rafael's Point San Pedro was popular because a ranch there sold the keepers butter, vegetables, and other items. They also went to China Camp, a major fishing village run by Chinese-Americans. The Chinese-Americans were the first commercial fishermen on San Francisco Bay and their graceful fishing boats, called junks, were common sights on the Bay. At China Camp in San Rafael, you could buy the delicious little bay shrimp the Chinese-Americans caught. It was a trek worth making.

East Brother light station covered virtually the entire island. The white egg-shaped object in the exact center of the island is the cistern. Note the tramway leading from the landing up to the fog signal building. (National Archives)

Sometimes the Chinese-American fishing families stopped by East Brother in their junks. The Chinese-American fishermen and the light keepers helped one another. Sometimes early San Francisco Bay lighthouse keepers would hitch a ride to San Francisco on one of the junks.

Usually the keepers took their own small boat ashore. A trip could be rough in a small boat on a bay with strong currents and high winds. July 14, 1882, Assistant Keeper Joseph Page left for San Quentin in the station boat. Shortly after noon, he capsized. Captain Charles Windsor, head keeper, hailed the steamer *Reform* which was passing the light at the time and sent her to the rescue. By the time the *Reform* got to Page he had been swept a quarter mile away and it wasn't until thirty minutes later that they got him back to the station dock. They saved the assistant keeper and his boat, but in frugal Lighthouse Service fashion, there was a plaintive note because the rudder, oars, mail, and groceries had all been lost.

Perhaps East Brother got to be too much for Joseph Page. He began going to Marin County via Point San Quentin and returning drunk. This was especially bad because the Marin shore was dangerous, especially off San Rafael. The tender *Manzanita* had come by and placed buoys marking a sunken wreck off The Sisters, the Brothers' counterpart islands off San Rafael. Then in 1882, a big four-masted ship went ashore about one-third the distance between San Rafael's Point San Pedro and the Marin Islands. This was, and is, foul ground which uncovers during low tides. Tugs arrived though, and pulled the big ship off San Rafael's mud flats.

Actually, many ships provided a pleasant diversion at East Brother. Steamers would blow their whistles often as they passed by in salute to the lighthouse and the keepers would ring the fog bell in return. Ships always seemed to bring a bit of excitement.

The scow schooner *Hector*, in 1884, out of San Rafael's Point San Pedro stone quarry, ran aground at West Brother, a stone's throw from the light. It was a bright moonlit night but somehow the *Hector* had run afoul of The Brothers. Assistant Keeper Albert Triplett went out in a small boat to see if she was alright. On a rising tide in the early hours of the morning, *Hector* floated free, off to deliver its cut stone.

The Bay was as rough on the light keepers as on the ships. One keeper returned in the evening only to discover that East Brother's light was not burning. His counterpart, it turned out, had capsized in the Bay and was no where near. Fortunately, the missing keeper was later found safe. During this period, yet another keeper capsized near the station, but was also saved.

Even landing supplies could be frustrating. With the tender tied up at the wharf unloading supplies, ten tons of coal in sacks were stacked on the dock. Suddenly, the wharf gave way and it all disappeared into the Bay waters. The frugal Lighthouse Service wasn't going to let all that coal remain at the bottom, however, and it managed to retrieve every last chunk of it.

The late summer was also irritating in 1887, from August through October, when there were days and days of heavy smoke. This was California's annual fire season when the Golden State typically experienced no rain. In those days, forest and range fires would burn for long periods and ashes fell across the land. At East Brother that year, it was so bad that all the buildings began turning black!

There were other difficulties—quarreling over bringing alcohol on board, a swamped boat, a schooner grounding, a fence blown down in a wind storm, and a keeper who couldn't return for three days because of high winds and a heavy chop.

Since 1888, a young Swedish-American, John Stenmark, had been serving aboard the lighthouse tender *Madroño*, longing for the days when he could become a lighthouse keeper and spend his days

At the center of East Brother Light Station was the cement catch basin and cistern for the water supply. Note the fancy stairway and platform atop the cistern. The fog signal building with its steam whistle is at right. (U.S. Coast Guard)

ashore with his wife. The *Madroño* and other tenders served the entire California coast supplying lighthouses and lightships, servicing buoys, and transferring personnel and their families. A handsome, well-maintained ship, the *Madroño* worked dangerous waters where other vessels seldom ventured. Lighthouse tenders had to service navigational aids established in waters where no ship was supposed to go, in order to warn mariners away from dangers there. It was in such treacherous waters that lighthouse (and, later, buoy) tenders routinely worked.

And so, this was where John Stenmark worked. One day the *Madroño* was anchored off southern California's Point Conception, a place fearful seamen often called "the Cape Horn of the Pacific" because of its high winds and huge waves.

It was customary at such places to anchor off, generally to the south of the point or island. In this case, the black hulled *Madroño* had rounded Point Conception and anchored off Cojo Cove about a mile and a half east of Point Conception. This was the usual Lighthouse Service landing point and only small boats could approach this dangerous area. A workboat was loaded with supplies, and Stenmark and his fellow tender crewmen began rowing ashore. Lighthouse inspector Thomas Perry was on board the workboat, too, coming ashore to inspect Point Conception Light Station.

It was rough, too rough, for the trip. Somewhere between ship and shore big waves capsized the workboat and everyone ended up in the sea. Under such conditions, supplies and oars became battering rams, and John Stenmark was hit in the head and cut by a big oar that swept by. The tender's boatmen clung to the capsized workboat, but the inspector was washed away. Stenmark went after him, grabbing the man just as he was about to sink beneath the water. The heroic Stenmark kept the inspector afloat until the *Madroño* could come alongside and pick them up.

As a reward for his bravery, Stenmark was given a position as assistant keeper at Año Nuevo Island lighthouse in San Mateo County. There, he rose to become head keeper. While on Año Nuevo he rescued several fishermen whose boats capsized nearby. Also, while there, his daughter, Annie, was born. In 1894, Stenmark transferred with his young family to East Brother.

The Stenmarks quickly took to the white, gingerbread buildings with their red roofs and green blinds. They even found that little West Brother was a good place to keep a goat. The station was only equipped with a small rowboat, but unlike most offshore light stations, anyone with a good pair of lungs could shout ashore for help. The possibility of aid set East Brother apart from places such as the Farallon Islands which were completely cut off from the outside world.

There was plenty of water-borne company, too, as river boats, hay scows, ferries, junks, naval vessels, and grain ships passed by bound for Mare Island, Port Costa, or the Delta. The night boats to Sacramento even had a custom involving the lighthouse. Upon leaving San Francisco, these passenger vessels were restricted by idiosyncrasies in county liquor laws from opening their bar until they passed Red Rock, about two miles south of the light. Thirsty passengers who were served before the ship got to The Brothers, traditionally toasted the beacon.

In spite of the frequent marine traffic, Stenmark had to fend for himself when each of his two sons were born. Both times he had to row all the way to San Quentin Prison on the distant Marin shore to get a doctor. As the children grew older, their education was provided by a teacher who would live on the island part of the year to tutor them.

More exciting than the arrival of the teacher, the San Francisco earthquake of April 18, 1906, shook the island vigorously. The lens was badly shaken and its prisms were loosened in their brass frames. Some prisms were cracked and all of the delicate glass chimneys for the lens' kerosene lamps were broken. The log book adds that ". . . doors opened of themselves and whole island rocked." Then, the next day, it adds that San Francisco was "burning fearfully". On the 20th, again, the log noted "San Francisco still burning tonight."

Perhaps the island's best remembered wreck occurred the following year. On June 13, 1907, at 2:30 in the morning, the steamer *Leader*, while under tow, hit the wharf, ruining it completely. Stenmark rushed to his nearly toppled landing and conversed excitedly with the crew. His exact words are not recorded, perhaps mercifully, but the sailors admitted being asleep when the tow struck.

Transportation both on land and sea was, however, improving. A road was built out to Point San Pablo from Richmond and access to town improved so that, after a few years, a live-in teacher was no longer needed. Along the road a new refinery had been built by the Standard Oil Company. One of their workers was Charles Morisette. The young refinery worker met Keeper Stenmark's daughter, Annie, now a lovely young woman. Soon, Charles was rowing out to the island courting Annie. Morisette was better at courting than rowing; and although he won Annie on his own, the Stenmarks had to give him rowing lessons. He could not have had better teachers, nor they, a more willing student. The Morisettes' subsequent marriage was a good one, lasting over a half-century.

After long years of service at East Brother, Stenmark passed away, reportedly dying on a boat trip to Antioch. He was mourned in California and in Sweden. He had represented both his countries well, serving as a seaman, rounding Cape Horn, piloting a schooner, wintering in Alaska, and eventually following with a distinguished career in the U.S. Lighthouse Service.

John P. Kofod took over East Brother from John Stenmark on a windy day in July 1914. Inspector Captain Harry Rhodes had come by two days earlier and, as he commonly did, had found plenty he wanted spruced up. Keeper Kofod had his work cut out for him and Captain Rhodes had the right man for the job.

John Kofod was a Lighthouse Service veteran. He'd already served at two notoriously windy, fog-bound coastal light stations, Point Reyes and Point Sur, and then had done a stint down the Bay at Yerba Buena. It's hard to imagine better preparation for serving at East Brother.

The tender *Madroño*, its black hull contrasting with its white superstructure, moved Kofod, his wife Metha, and family from Yerba Buena Island the few miles to East Brother. Kofod's grandson, Walter Fanning, went along on the *Madroño*, a day he would never forget. The *Madroño's* crew, as usual dressed in work clothes rather than uniforms, carried the keeper's furniture and belongings to the vessel. Everyone climbed aboard and it was off across blustery San Francisco Bay. The lighthouse tenders of that period usually could not tie up to the East Brother wharf because it was too hazardous so, upon arrival, the ship anchored off south of the wharf. The tender crew broke out a pulling boat, filled it with furniture and kids, and rowed over to the lighthouse wharf. Everything and everybody was landed safely, and John Kofod was the new keeper. Mr. Kofod assumed command on July 25, 1914, "a day of strong winds" at East Brother, the log book notes.

Walter Fanning recalls that era at East Brother as "a very quiet life with a very fixed routine." Keeper Kofod had a ship's clock that had to be wound every 24-hours. At 9 p.m. each evening Mr. Kofod would rewind it—and that was the signal and it was off to bed. The living quarter's lamps would be turned down and everybody would go to bed. The keepers didn't stand a formal watch at East Brother but would go and check the light and rewind the lens' clockwork drive at least once every three hours throughout the night. Linen curtains protected the lens by day from the sun and at dawn these would be drawn. When the linen curtains finally wore out and a new set was in place, the old linen curtains became the Kofods' dish towels.

The little room at the very bottom of the light tower became Metha Kofod's parlor. She had a player organ, a nice sofa and table, and interesting curios she'd collected. The most exciting event that ever happened at the light tower involved this parlor and the weights of the lens' clockwork drive. These weights were very heavy and hung below the lens' rotating mechanism. They descended a couple of stories down the light tower each night as they unwound, thus powering the rotation of the lens. One night, the family was stunned when the cable suddenly broke and the weights came crashing down through the parlor ceiling, blasting plaster all over the room and smashing the floor. Thankfully, no one was under the weight when it burst through the ceiling, and no one was hurt. (A similar incident occurred at Point Arena lighthouse in the tower during the 1970s.)

The wickies also had to keep a watch for fog. The boilers in the fog signal building were often warm and on cold days the Kofod grandchildren liked to go into there to feel the warmth. A little railroad track ran across the wharf and up into the fog signal building. This railway, powered by a steam winch, made hauling the sacks of coal ashore much easier. Each sack, when emptied, then had to be counted, bundled, and returned for reuse on the tender's next visit. A portion of the old railway track may be seen at the fog signal building to this day.

The keepers kept a sharp eye out for the Bay's frequent fog. If either Red Rock (south of today's Richmond-San Rafael Bridge) or The Sisters (off San Rafael) disappeared from view, the fog whistle had to be started. A fog bell still served as a back-up warning device to be used if the whistle failed.

The Kofods had brought their chickens along on the *Madroño* when they transferred from Yerba Buena Island. At East Brother, they found out fast that they had to have a good, solid board fence in the chicken yard or the birds would be blown away. They wanted to keep those chickens safe, since roast chicken was a family favorite. This was often supplemented by fish—rock cod, perch and bass—caught off the island. Since there was no refrigeration, much of the catch had to be salted for preservation. Fishing was done off the wharf or in the little flat-bottomed skiff that served as station boat.

Fresh water and garden soil were both in short supply at East Brother. There was the cistern, but the greedy boilers of the fog whistles consumed as much water as did domestic use. Keepers carried big tin cans of soil to the island for gardening and used "grey water" from baths and washing to water vegetables. During a drought, even the cistern ran dry, and the Lighthouse Service sent out the tender. The thrifty Lighthouse Service turned a problem into an opportunity. Captain Rhodes had the tender's hard working crew give the cistern a good cleaning before they pumped it full of fresh water. It was no wonder that every time a lighthouse tender passed the station, Keeper Kofod proudly dipped the flag in salute.

Sometimes the East Brother keepers helped the tender's crews in their responsibility for watching over minor navigational aids, even distant ones. For example, in emergencies, the East Brother assistant keeper might have to make the miles-long sail across San Pablo Bay to the Petaluma River to repair a "stake light", a common shallow water navigational aid consisting of a lantern mounted on a pole.

During the early years, East Brothers' ties had been to the Marin shore. But now, by John Kofod's time, the nearby Point Richmond shore had developed. A landing had been built directly across the narrow channel from the island and even a bus paused there to pick-up passengers. The arduous trips to Marin became less common now.

In 1918, the world was ravaged by a terrible influenza epidemic costing millions of lives. When the horrible disease struck the Bay Area, schools were closed, and the Kofod grandchildren fled to the island to safety. The isolation paid off and they survived the epidemic.

In December that same year, two of the Monticello Steamship Company's sleek steamers were operating in thick fog on the Vallejo-San Francisco ferryboat run. It was the morning commuter run, and the *Sehome*, Vallejo bound, was encountering increasingly thick fog after passing Angel Island and was now in the vicinity of Southampton Shoal. The company's San Francisco bound *General Frisbie* suddenly streaked out of the fog and, to the horror of those on board, rammed the *Sehome*, cutting a gash a dozen feet long in the *Sehome's* side and knocked over a boiler. The vessels held together and, miraculously, no one was killed.

Carefully, holding the ferries together to prevent sinking, the ships were maneuvered toward shallow water. Then, in the thick tule fog, a tug suddenly emerged from the grey mist and hit the precariously attached steamers. The *Sehome* went to the bottom, only her pilot house and boat deck showing. Everybody had been transferred to the *General Frisbie*, so again, in the second shipwreck, no one was lost. After that, everybody called it a day and left. Many were lucky to be alive.

Red Stack tug company went after the shattered *Sehome* a few days later. She'd gone adrift and was a hazard to navigation. Red Stack's tug started towing the *Sehome*, only to have her capsize and sink off San Rafael. Her pilot house and cabin were torn off in the capsizing. Soon after, Keeper Kofod looked out from East Brother and saw *Sehome's* deck house drifting by. He tried to salvage it with a block and tackle, but it was too heavy for his gear and his efforts failed. Kofod had to cut loose this big chunk of the ship and watch it float away. Eventually, the *Sehome* was salvaged and scrapped, another in a long line of ships lost on San Francisco Bay.

Christmas Day in 1921, California light keepers knew they had a real storm on their hands. Reports from various light stations were coming in of winds ranging from 60 to 90 miles per hour. Telephone wires and

California had over a dozen women lighthouse keepers. Here, "the Bell Lady" of East Brother, reportedly Mrs. John Stenmark, keeps a proud watch over the Bay. As fog approached the island, this bell was rung by hand until boilers could build up enough steam to blow the whistles. (Richmond City Museum, Stenmark Collection)

electric lines began falling at most of the state's light stations as the storm worsened and isolation set in. Then fences and outbuildings began to blow over, followed by roofs flying away and chimneys toppling. It was a real blow and the wind began kicking up some heavy seas as well. East Brother was particularly hard hit. The Lighthouse Service reported, "Heavy seas broke over the East Brother light station." The lantern room railing was blown away. Then the sea and wind combined forces to tear the "wharf house entirely loose" and smash it against the "bluff at the inner end of the wharf." It was almost as if East Brother light was going to end up like the *Sehome*.

During the twenties, a new crew came aboard at East Brother. In 1921, John Kofod returned to Yerba Buena Island, which was to be his last station. Willard Miller came on duty in 1922. He'd served at Los Angeles Harbor and Roe Island lighthouses after a career as a sailor and Navy man.

Miller had won the Congressional Medal of Honor while serving aboard the *Nashville* in the Spanish-American War. Keeper Miller was to serve at East Brother until 1942. He, too, saw some interesting times on The Brothers. The wickies salvaged the launch *Miss Pluto* in 1927, and in April 1930, witnessed a derrick barge wrecking the wharf (again). But the real shocker must have come in 1934 when the Lighthouse Service issued orders to close down the station as unneeded. Unexpectedly, East Brother went dark. Ship owners and other mariners immediately and strongly protested the action and, three days later, East Brother was relighted. The crew of the daily "Egg Boat" to Petaluma, the steamer *Gold*, which passed so close by East Brother often carrying its fragile cargo, need not have worried. The friendly beacon would still be there to guide them and countless other vessels for years to come.

Assistant Keeper Earl Snodgrass had come to East Brother a few years earlier after stints at the Farallon Islands and Table Bluff lights. He had worked aboard Cogshall Launch and Towboat Company up on Humboldt Bay, a major maritime outfit there. Snodgrass proved his dedication in 1942 when he rescued three men in a capsized sailboat off East Brother. A lighthouse man usually didn't get to be an East Brother keeper without plenty of experience and such experience was a recurrent blessing to Bay sailors.

By the thirties an electric cable had been laid across the channel from Richmond. There was also an old crank telephone which even worked—sometimes. However, the telephone was often out of order and the cable was occasionally torn up by ships dragging anchor. Then the keepers were right back to the isolated conditions of the nineteenth century.

Some things never changed. It was still risky taking a small boat across the cut to the mainland. With the great amounts of water pouring down from the mountains and valleys, ebb tides were particularly treacherous. It took everything two skilled oarsmen had to get across the channel when the tide was running. Once Assistant Keeper Earl Snodgrass tried it alone on a strong receding tide. Returning from a shopping trip, he approached the wharf and was swept against a pile. The boat capsized and everything went into the Bay. The keeper and his dog managed to fight to the surface and climb ashore; the groceries had no such luck.

Water *on* the island as well as that around it could also be a problem. Despite regular cleaning, it was almost impossible to keep the concrete catchment slab from being fouled by sea gull droppings. The drinking water was untreated and, reportedly, there was often a surprise in the bottom of a glass. The water could not have been too bad, however, as the cistern was the home of a legendary white frog that lived there for over five years.

Following decades saw other changes. The distinctive water house was supplemented by a more conventional tank, and the eucalyptus trees that Earl and Lilian Snodgrass had planted slowly struggled to reach a height of a couple of dozen feet. The Fresnel lens still cast its beams across the Bay, but the fog whistle had long since been replaced by an air horn.

Coast Guard control brought many more changes. There were typically three men assigned, the officer-in-charge and his family occupying the ground floor of the lighthouse, while two bachelors lived upstairs. The eucalyptus trees were taller now, and the water house had been converted to a storage building since new tanks had been built. The Coast Guard had given up on the old crank telephone and had provided a short-wave radio for communication. After 1946, water was brought out by the Navy, so the wickies no longer had to depend on rain water alone for their supply. The Coast Guard families shopped in Richmond and continued to cross the choppy strait in a small boat. However, they now had a power boat and thus the run of nearly a mile to the San Pablo yacht harbor was much safer than in the early days.

There were still dangers. In 1952, a tugboat hit the island. Its operators charged that the Coast Guard was negligent since they could not hear the diaphone fog horn. Fortunately, light stations were equipped with a recording device which automatically marked each operating period of the fog signal on a paper disk imprinted with the days of the week and hours of the day. The disk showed that the fog horn had indeed been operating when the tug rammed the island. The tug's crew probably did not hear the signal, since under certain conditions, "dead spots" occur in the air and powerful fog signals that can be heard for miles suddenly become inaudible.

Fire on the tiny rock was a greater danger. In April 1953, the Coast Guard substituted butane for fuel oil after a nearly disastrous blaze occurred in one of the oil stoves used for cooking. Quick action and good luck stopped the blaze and saved the station. Back in 1940, Keepers Willard Miller and Earl Snodgrass had a similar experience. Miller had accidentally knocked over an oil lamp in the boathouse during a late night watch. Kerosene was ignited and by the time a Coast Guard boat arrived to help, it was too late to save the boathouse, wharf and station boats. The remainder of the facility survived, miraculously.

During the 1960s, Coast Guardsmen continued to climb the antique mahogany stairway up to the tower. There were now four keepers assigned to the station, and they ran the lighthouse in two-man crews, alternating every 48 hours. They used the cistern but its water now came by Coast Guard buoy tender. All food was brought from shore, unlike the early days when the Stenmarks and their cohorts raised goats, pigs, rabbits, chickens, and vegetables on The Brothers. Some of the flowers were still there, and the white picket fence stood after ninety years.

In the late 1960s, Coast Guardsman Joseph Picotte was in charge of East Brother. He'd served previously at lonely Dry Tortugas lighthouse on Loggerhead Key about 75 miles off Key West, Florida.[1] East Brother was a definite change from tropical Dry Tortugas, one of the tallest lights in the country. But another change was in sight.

During 1968, officer-in-charge Joseph Picotte was notified that the station would be unmanned, the facility torn down, and an automatic light erected. Picotte looked at the antique log book, noting early entries signed by J.O. Stenmark. He located Stenmark's daughter, Annie Morisette, still living in Richmond, and together they went over the old book. Mrs. Morisette recalled such things as ringing a huge ship's bell as a warning while her father built up steam pressure to blow the old fog whistle. She was deeply saddened at the thought of the beacon's destruction.

In 1969, East Brother Lighthouse was unmanned and automated. The Coast Guard crews which rotated on and off the light were to be no more. Picotte was transferred to Yerba Buena Island to Coast Guard Group San Francisco's headquarters. Once every month or so Coast Guard electricians and other maintenance specialists would arrive in their 40-foot utility boats to service the automated lighthouse.

As was true of most lighthouses in the period from 1950 through the late-1970s, East Brother's future was in doubt. Automation suddenly

---

[1]In 1988, Dry Tortugas was still manned because of its remote nature and the advantages of having Coast Guard personnel present. In that year, Lisa and I joined the Dry Tortugas Coast Guard light keepers for an aids to navigation inspection of the other Florida Reef lights, including Sand Key, American Shoal and Sombrero Key. It was an amazing voyage. Some Coast Guard keepers actually climb portions of the exterior of the tall, intricate, Victorian iron skeleton reef lights to board them on their periodic visits.

left the Coast Guard with many historic buildings, a limited budget, and a real uncertainty as to what to do with them. I spent many hours in the 1970s behind the scenes talking with 12th District Coast Guard officials, urging that California's lighthouses be preserved. Previously, lighthouses and station buildings had often been torn down, burned, or left to the elements and vandals upon automation. A few had been sold to private parties, usually with disastrous results. In countless cases across America, lighthouses and other station buildings were razed, lantern rooms chopped off, lenses removed, and station buildings destroyed.

One of the earlier groups which came to the rescue was the Contra Costa Shoreline Parks Committee, under the leadership of Lucretia Edwards. This organization had the vision to save one of the last small family light stations on the coast. At the same time, the Coast Guard was changing as well. Coast Guard aids to navigation staff—Commander Dale Foster, Commander Joseph Blackett and Ollie DeGraaf—all saw the potential of our lighthouses, as did Admiral James Gracey and Rear Admiral Richard A. Bauman.

East Brother light station was placed on the National Register of

East Brother light station in 1968. Note how much of the island was covered by the concrete slab used to trap rainwater for the cistern in the island's center. Fog signal building and landing are at the right. (U.S. Coast Guard)

Historic Places. Under the untiring leadership of architect Tom Butt, an organization, East Brother Light Station, Inc., was formed to restore the facility and open it to the public. They spent long hours doing the hardest work imaginable, and I still remember Tom high up on the water tank precariously working on its badly weathered rungs. It was a grand day when John Kofod's grandson, Walter Fanning, got the old diaphone fog horn operating again. Local newspapers and television stations were very helpful in providing vital publicity.

By the early 1980s, the station was well on its way to complete restoration. East Brother was opened as a bed and breakfast inn, as well as for day use. Innkeepers were hired and they experienced many of the timeless adventures. Visitors were brought from Point San Pablo Yacht Harbor around the point and across the narrow channel to the lighthouse wharf in small craft. One innkeeper faced a stormy night laced with rain and choppy, four-foot seas. These were rather high seas to land at East Brother's tricky pier, but he did it anyway—on his sixth try—and brought his guests safely on board.

In February 1986, a volunteer at the light was on the preservation group's boat when it swamped in choppy seas. Others tossed him a life jacket which he grasped, but swift moving currents carried him away from East Brother. A distress call was sent out and the Golden Gate ferry *Sonoma* responded. The *Sonoma's* captain, Mick Beatie "just steamed straight for The Brothers." Fifteen minutes later, they found the volunteer, a mile south of the light. A Coast Guard boat met the ferry, took the man on board, and rushed him to Larkspur Landing on the Marin shore. There he was cared for and released. It was an incident that could have occurred a century before.[2]

Today, troublesome incidents at East Brother are rare indeed. Through the years the lighthouse has been wonderfully cared for. East Brother Light Station, Inc., has lived up to its lease from the Coast Guard quite well. Those who have spent the night there usually rave about the unforgettable experience on East Brother. For those wishing to visit, East Brother Light Station, Inc., may be contacted at 117 Park Place, Point Richmond, CA 94801. You'll have a chance to spend a night or a day at an authentic island light station and meet some of the dedicated people who work hard to preserve it. Guests can still fish, watch the ships go by, and—if you're lucky—at sunset, they'll even blow the diaphone fog horn for you. East Brother is once again a beautiful, magical place. I think John Kofod would be pleased.

---

[2]In 1988, one of the Golden Gate ferries also rescued a sailor off Alcatraz light. Pulling alongside the soggy mariner, the ferrymen faced the difficult task of getting down to the man and pulling him on board. As the crewmen struggled to reach down to rescue the mariner, the ship suddenly listed sharply and the rescue was accomplished with ease. The passengers had all rushed to the railing to watch the rescue and the ship had temporarily dipped down so that the railing neared the water.

Mare Island was one of the most attractive lighthouses on the Bay and Keeper Kate McDougal maintained the station with care. (U.S. Coast Guard)

MARE ISLAND

The need for a lighthouse at the southern end of Mare Island became apparent as early as the 1850s. The steamer *Napa City* was none too dependable when it made its frequent trips from San Francisco across San Pablo Bay to the new Naval Base at Mare Island opposite the city of Vallejo. The base's commandant, a young man named Farragut, had not yet won fame. Perhaps if he had, his requests for improved navigational aids might have resulted in a lighthouse instead of a lowly marker beacon. At any rate, when the *Napa City* managed to run aground off the island, the gallant Farragut sent a boat out and promptly rescued all the ladies on board. Five days later, the crew managed to free the ship and bring her in for repairs. The concerned Naval officer was David Farragut, destined to become Admiral Farragut, commander of Union Naval Forces in the American Civil War.

In 1873, Mare Island lighthouse was built on the island near the point where the Napa River enters Carquinez Strait. It was a combination Victorian tower and dwelling. The square tower spaciously accommodated the lantern room with its fourth order fixed white lens. The two-story, white, frame structure had tall chimneys, much ornamental woodwork, and porches on both stories. Railings for the porches and the lantern room balcony were beautifully done in the style of the period. Neat, white picket fences surrounded the station. A wooden stairway ran down the hillside to the wharf below. The wharf was shaped like a "T" with a red-roofed bell house and weight tower standing on one arm and a tide gauge on the other arm. Early writers described the point as picturesque and noted that the hills to the north provided a lovely dark background. The island was mostly grassland with scattered groves of wind-blown trees.

For most of the light's history, it was run by a woman, Mrs. Kate McDougal. Mrs. McDougal had close ties to Mare Island. Her husband, Commander Charles McDougal, was the son of the Naval Base's third commandant. Commander McDougal had chosen a career in the Lighthouse Service.

The story of Mare Island Lighthouse really begins over 200 miles up the California coast at Cape Mendocino Lighthouse on the Humboldt County shore. It was a challenging coastline to work, with high winds, heavy surf and countless offshore rocks. On a blustery day in 1881, the lighthouse tender *Manzanita* had managed to safely work her way in toward Cape Mendocino light station. She anchored just outside the breakers, probably off the beach to the south of the Cape. It was the quarterly visit by the lighthouse inspector whose job it was to thoroughly inspect the station and to bring the keepers their pay. At some stations, the tender could tie up along side a pier or at least have the protection of a bay or headland. But not at dangerous Cape Mendocino. For this was California's westernmost and most exposed headland, a place offering no protection from the open sea.

The lighthouse inspector on this trip was Commander Charles McDougal. Inspector McDougal strapped on his heavy money belt containing the gold coins used to pay keepers at the various lighthouses the *Manzanita* was to call on. The crew of the lighthouse tender lowered a boat and Commander McDougal began rowing ashore. The surf at Cape Mendocino is often extremely heavy and the crew of the *Manzanita* and the light keepers on the beach must have kept a close and apprehensive eye on his progress. Just as McDougal was passing through the surf, the breakers became unmanageable. The boat capsized and the heavy money belt helped drag the struggling inspector under. Commander McDougal drowned before the horrified eyes of his fellow Lighthouse Service personnel.

The Mare Island fog bell tended by Kate McDougal. On many a misty night, this bell guided mariners through Carquinez Strait. (U.S. Coast Guard)

Mare Island lighthouse as seen from the pier. Note the sentinel's ornamental woodwork. The curtains in the lantern room have been pulled to protect the lens from discoloration by the sun's rays. (U.S. Coast Guard)

The crew of the lighthouse tender *Manzanita* recovered Charles McDougal's body from the sea and began the long, sad trip home. Commander McDougal came from a well-known, distinguished military family with strong ties to Mare Island Naval Base at Vallejo. Word of the tragedy preceded the tender's arrival, and as she steamed up San Francisco Bay, the light keeper at East Brother Light Station logged her passing by, noting that the vessel carried Inspector McDougal's body. It was being carried home to Mare Island to his widow Kate.

Kate Coughay McDougal had lost her beloved Charlie. She was left with a pension of fifty dollars a month and four children to raise. There was but one appealing choice open to her now. Mare Island had a lighthouse and the present keeper was a woman, Mrs. Watson. She was interested in resigning her post. The job was offered to Kate McDougal.

The opening must have seemed a miracle in 1881 when sexual and racial discrimination were rampant. Being keeper of Mare Island Lighthouse was not only a secure, respected job, its location was adjacent to the Naval Base where relatives lived. She accepted the position and began her new career.

The loneliness seemed to bother her in the beginning but "she wasn't much of a complainer," her granddaughter Mary recalled, and Kate McDougal seemed to adjust well. Keeper Kate McDougal had a horse and buggy and could visit relatives and friends. The fact that the island was the site of a Naval Base reduced the isolation as well.

The Naval officers kept an eye on her and were very supportive. That first Christmas after Commander McDougal's death, his fellow officers decided they wanted to do something very worthwhile for Kate. Alexander Graham Bell had invented the telephone a few years previously and a relative of his was a Naval officer at Mare Island. He and some workmen put up poles and ran a telephone line from the Navy Yard out to the lighthouse. The project took longer than expected and the officers weren't able to wish Kate McDougal a Merry Christmas but they were able to wish her a Happy New Year by telephone.

In 1899, the Spanish-American War was on and Kate's son-in-law, a military man who had once been an English professor at the Naval Academy at Annapolis, sailed away to war. Her daughter returned to the lighthouse with a new baby and they were to remain there until 1917. The son-in-law was away on military assignments so much that this arrangement gave stability and continuity to the family.

The granddaughter was to grow up at Mare Island Lighthouse. As an adult many years later, that baby, Mary Gorgas Carlisle, fondly recalled life at the light. She remembered that early every morning Kate McDougal would climb the lighthouse stairs, put out the light, and bring the oil lamp down. The delicate lens would then be covered with yellow cloth curtains to protect it from the sun's rays.

The lamp would be polished, its glass lamp chimney cleaned, wicks trimmed, oil reservoirs filled, and brass polished. Then everything would be put away until sunset. That evening the lamp was again placed in the lens, shades raised, wicks lighted, and once again, Mare Island would guide ships passing in the night. Each night that lamp had to be changed once to insure a light lasting all night. It was the family custom that whoever went to bed last would climb the tower and put in a fresh lamp. Thus, the three women of the lighthouse—Kate, her daughter, and granddaughter—all shared the light keeping responsibilities.

During the day, Kate McDougal tended her garden and kept the station in good order. Keeper McDougal was fond of writing and kept a very meticulous log. She had a laborer, a common practice of the time, who would come in to do heavy maintenance work, move the oil cart, and care for the cows. A Chinese-American chef was employed and added much to the pleasure of life at the station. Kate's son-in-law was also present between military assignments. With all this help, Mary Gorgas Carlisle remembers her grandmother as having plenty of free time to enjoy her surroundings.

The 1906 San Francisco earthquake, however, caused excitement and may have thrown down the lighthouse's tall brick chimneys. This was widespread during the Great Quake. Early photos show the brick chimneys, while later pictures show metal stove pipes on the roof tops.

In 1910, however, Mare Island lighthouse was to face a great challenge. Carquinez Strait lighthouse was established across the mouth of the Napa River off the Vallejo shore. The new sentinel

Overview of Mare Island Light Station in 1904. At the upper right is the rain catch basin for the water system. Below is the lighthouse and on the pier is the fog bell house (at left) and the tide gauge (at right). (U.S. Navy, Mare Island Shipyard Historian)

was better located and made Mare Island light largely unnecessary. On July 1, 1917, Mare Island Light Station was discontinued.

The lighthouse was abandoned none too soon. Nine days later, the Navy Yard's ammunition depot exploded, wrecking 13 buildings. The old lighthouse survived the blast but was razed sometime after 1930. Only the building's foundation remains today.

When the lighthouse was closed, Kate McDougal went to live with Mary Carlisle's aunt and uncle. They had wanted her to give up light keeping for some time but Kate McDougal had stayed at her post until the end. Her transition was softened by the fact that the couple lived on Mare Island and her beloved beacon was close by. Her granddaughter, Mary, even got to return to the island to christen the destroyer *U.S.S. Taylor* when it was launched at Mare Island shipyard.

Kate McDougal lived to be 90. At the end of the island, an automatic fog bell was installed. It tolled once every ten seconds, its signal unchanged since the days when Kate McDougal tended the lighthouse. Of her grandmother and other women lighthouse keepers, Mary Gorgas Carlisle recalls that "they were great heroines." It is a well-deserved tribute.

Faded beauty. The abandoned Mare Island lighthouse. The lighthouse lens is gone, the pier removed, and the wind blows through the windowless old sentinel, September 1930. (U.S. Navy, Mare Island Shipyard Historian)

The Coast Guard maintains an important search and rescue station at Mare Island. Coast Guard Station Mare Island was founded June 1, 1975 primarily to respond to hundreds of distress calls received from recreational boaters on San Pablo Bay, Carquinez Strait and the Napa and Petaluma Rivers. From 1963 through 1973 the 82-foot patrol boat Point Chico *and smaller craft had handled rescue calls from moorings in the Benicia area, but after a time a station with shallow draft vessels adapted to the upper bays and rivers was obviously required. Thus, Mare Island Coast Guard Station was opened. Today two utility boats, one a 41-footer and the other a 21-footer, answer 300 to 350 distress calls a year from Mare Island.*

On the Sacramento-San Joaquin River Delta and its tributaries, Coast Guard Station Rio Vista uses 21 and 24-foot utility boats to respond to over 500 distress calls a year. An aids to navigation team based at Rio Vista also services lights and other aids on the rivers.

In the photo above, the Coast Guard ice breaker Burton Island *is shown moored at Mare Island Coast Guard Station. This was a most unusual sight, for ice breakers were rare on San Francisco Bay. This was a temporary mooring for the* Burton Island *after one of her voyages to Antarctica. (Treasure Island Museum)*

By 1909, Roe Island was a large and distinctive light station with a new dwelling and water house added at right. The fog bell can be seen at the end of the pier. (U.S. Coast Guard)

ROE ISLAND

Roe Island lighthouse was located 33 miles *inland* from the Pacific Coast. No California light station was ever constructed as far from the pounding breakers of the coast as this. Furthermore, the water flowing beneath its pile foundation was fresh, not salt water, and cattails and tules grew at its base rather than seaweed. The station was as far east as such dryland places as the Sacramento and Diablo valleys.

Roe Island light station stood at the east end of Suisun Bay, across the Sacramento River from Port Chicago. Roe Island was a low, marshy tract barely rising above the river. In 1889, property was deeded to the government by the Ryder family for a light station at the south end of the island.

By February 1891, the lighthouse was ready for operation. The island was low and easily flooded so that virtually the entire station had to be built on wooden piles. As a result, it was a compact station. The square 1 1/2 story frame lighthouse had a pleasant veranda on all sides. There was a dormer window on each of the roof's four sides, and at the apex there was a square balcony with a simple railing. Here, the lantern room was built, unusual in that its lower walls seem to have been made of wood rather than metal. Inside there was a small, fifth order lens which burned oil and showed a fixed white light of 2400 candle power. The station was cheerfully colorful with white walls, red roof, black lantern room, lead-colored (grey) trimmings, and green shades. The shades covered the lantern room windows during the day to protect the glass prisms in the lens from becoming discolored by the rays of the hot valley sun.

A T-shaped pier, fifty feet long, extended toward the Bay from the lighthouse's front door. One arm of the "T" held the bell house with its 800-pound iron bell, struck every ten seconds during fog. This light station had to contend not only with fog that originated at sea but also with the local "tule fog", a low-lying, dense fog that develops in valley bottoms and marshes. At the rear of the bell house a rather simple pole served as the weight tower.

On the pier's opposite arm were two small buildings that looked like outhouses. In fact, that was the function of the one nearest the dwelling. It was a better than average outhouse, however, since it had running water. A windmill was built beside the structure, and it pumped water up to a tank on the roof between the outhouse and the other structure, the oil house. The oil house held the station's oil supply for the lamps. Getting to either structure on a stormy night was sure to be a bracing experience for the keeper or his assistant.

An octagonal, wooden water house stood beside the dwelling. That, and a couple of sheds behind the lighthouse, completed the list of

Suisun Bay is often the windiest part of the Bay and the tules and willows bend in this 1907 photograph. The octagonal building is the water house, the duplicate structures on the pier by the windmill are the outhouse and the oil house, while the structure with the pole-like tower is the bell house. (U.S. Coast Guard)

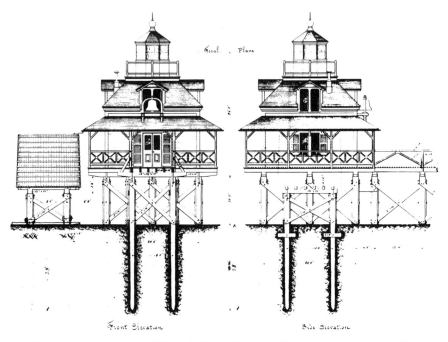

Original plans for Roe Island Lighthouse. The station was built on tall wooden piles to protect it from floods and extreme high tides. (National Archives)

Roe Island's launch at Yerba Buena Island Lighthouse Depot, probably in for repairs after the 1938 sinking in a storm at the lighthouse. (Treasure Island Museum)

Keeper Ted Pedersen began his career at cold Alaskan light stations and later served California's Año Nuevo Island and Roe Island lighthouses. He was officer-in-charge at Roe Island. Mr. Pedersen is shown here during his time in Alaska. (Wayne Piland)

Echo boards were interesting navigational aids the Lighthouse Service established on rivers in the foggy Delta of the Sacramento and San Joaquin Rivers. Vessels navigating in dense tule fog repeatedly blew their whistles and listened for an echo to help determine their position. This is New York Slough's East End echo board, a three winged echo board, on Winter Island near Rio Vista, CA. When vessels approached the board blowing their whistle in the fog, they could expect to hear the echo at about 200 yards from this board, thus warning them that Winter Island was ahead. A lens lantern atop the middle wing served as the light, 1953. (U.S. Coast Guard)

the station's earliest buildings. By the first decade of the twentieth century, however, much change had taken place. A second dwelling and another water house had been added beside the original ones. What caught the eye was that both structures were nearly identical to their older counterparts. The only obvious difference was that the new dwelling lacked a lantern room and had to be content with only a widow's walk.[1]

One of those who served at Roe Island was Ted Pedersen. Keeper Pedersen, lighthouse veteran Wayne Piland recalls, was an Alaskan. His father was a ship's officer on sailing vessels trading in Alaskan waters

---

[1]The Lighthouse Service used a very similar design for the Willamette River lighthouse, established in 1895, at the confluence of the Columbia and Willamette Rivers at Portland, Oregon. The structure looked almost identical to the newer section of Roe Island, even lacking a lantern room as well. It had a lens lantern and a fog bell. Willamette River Lighthouse was classified at various times during its career as a light station, a fog signal station, and as a range light. At least one of its keepers was a woman.

and his mother was a lovely Eskimo woman. After growing up in the North, Pedersen eventually joined the Lighthouse Service and served at some of the roughest, most isolated stations in North America. He eventually ended up in California at Año Nuevo Island and Roe Island lights. His wife, Elsa was a talented writer.

Roe Island light, Pederson found, could be reached only by boat. There was an excellent wharf, and the California Steam Navigation Company's riverboats would stop on call. The station also had a rowboat, which was kept tied to the pier. A marine railway and wooden sea wall were later built after a fair sized power boat was issued to the keepers.

The sentinel often experienced fine weather, but the storm of February 9, 1938, showed that it was not always an easy station. Violent gale winds whipped Roe Island, tearing the station launch from its moorings and throwing it against a bulkhead, sinking the vessel.

Roe Island light station after the Port Chicago explosion of 1944. The crumpled bell house is at right, blown halfway across the pier. Note the impact on the water house, the widow's walk, and the porch with the enclosed railing. (U.S. Coast Guard)

For decades, Roe Island served traffic bound up the Sacramento River. With the outbreak of World War II, a large share of the ships using the light were loaded with highly dangerous cargo. The lighthouse stood just 3000 yards north of the Port Chicago Naval Ammunition Depot on the opposite side of the river.

On the night of July 17, 1944, the lighthouse quietly performed its peaceful task of marking the channel. Across the strait, two merchant ships were being loaded with thousands of tons of ammunition. One, the *Quinault Victory*, was on her maiden voyage and Coast Guard boats patrolled this dangerous area for port security. In the segregated military of the forties, 250 black sailors, under the command of white naval officers, had been assigned the dangerous task of loading the ships. About 10 p.m., a trainload of ammunition arrived at the dock. Twenty minutes later, Roe Island felt one of the most horrendous explosions ever imagined.

A blinding flash literally filled the sky with flame. Other, less intense explosions followed. For a quarter of an hour, an odd, dull, orangish glow hung in the sky. When rescuers arrived, over 300 men, the ships, most of the train, and two Coast Guard boats were gone.

Lighthouse tender Locust *constructing a navigational light on the Delta upstream from Roe Island, on the San Joaquin River in the 1920s. (U.S. Coast Guard)*

Light House, Junction of Willamette & Columbia Rivers.

Willamette River Lighthouse at Portland, Oregon, was a near twin of the portion of Roe Island light station without the lantern room. Willamette River boasted a lens lantern and fog bell, and was officially classified as a light station by the Lighthouse Service during much of its career, C. 1908. (Author's collection)

When a rescue worker asked, "Where are the bodies?", a stunned survivor replied, "What bodies?" It was one of the worst disasters in California history.

Roe Island light station was badly damaged. The station looked as if some giant vandals had broken it up. The seaward water house wall was cracked from roof to foundation. The widow's walk was partially blown off. The bell house was knocked off its foundation and shoved halfway to the lighthouse. The huge sign warning of the "Cable Crossing" lost its entire center section and looked like an oversize picture frame. Debris was scattered for hundreds of feet beyond the station. Wayne Piland believes Ted Pedersen was still head keeper when the explosion occurred. The Pedersens later returned to Alaska.

Less than a year later, on May 5, 1945, Roe Island light station was officially discontinued. The blast, coupled with a poor location due to changing shipping channels, spelled its demise. Roe Island light had added another distinction to its long list of unusual characteristics: it was the only California lighthouse to be closed by war-related damage. It is unfortunate that it was not spared such a distinction.

After the tragic explosion, the Coast Guard declared Roe Island excess property and sold the station. A family purchased the lighthouse for a summer retreat. They used the lighthouse as a summer home for a number of years. Then, while they were away, the vacant lighthouse was struck by arsonists. Roe Island was burned to the ground.

Oakland grew out to surround the second Oakland Harbor lighthouse. Western Pacific Railroad cars can be seen alongside the lighthouse, while a ferry prepares to depart for San Francisco in the distance. (U.S. Coast Guard)

OAKLAND HARBOR

By the 1880s, Oakland had become a harbor of importance. Ships of every seafaring nation used the estuary known as San Antonio Creek and navigated its narrow channel as far as the foot of Broadway. As is true today, Oakland harbor was a place known for efficiency. Bids for the construction of a new lighthouse were opened in July 1889, and work commenced in September. By November, the structure was completed. It was a small structure, just a cottage actually, with a lantern room on top. The whole station sat on tall piles, and at low tide, the lighthouse appeared to be on stilts. The light was first exhibited January 27, 1890.

It was rather picturesque, standing 240 feet off the tip of the jetty, completely surrounded by water. When keepers rowed out to the station, they had a feeling of isolation, although they were located between two of the largest cities on the Pacific Coast.

Rowing was something the keepers at Oakland Harbor light did a lot of. Not just to go into town for supplies and mail, but also to tend the south jetty light across the Oakland Estuary and—at times—the red lens lantern a mile to the east. When the keepers were not rowing to the other lights, they had to tend a white, fixed, fifth order lens in the lighthouse and rewind the weight which powered the mechanical striker on the station's 3500-pound fog bell.

The fog bell was unforgettable. It hung less than a dozen feet on the other side of the wall from the bed of the keeper and his wife. Its presence was unmistakable in thick weather. Given the fact that the lighthouse "oscillated" in high winds, it must have been something to be there on a stormy night with the fog bell pounding and the station wavering in the wind.

As if that wasn't enough, the Southern Pacific Railroad's 294-foot long, side wheel paddle ferry *Newark* paid a visit to the lighthouse. The *Newark* was a big steamer with 42-foot diameter paddle wheels, some historians say they were the largest paddle wheels ever used on any ferryboat in the world. On the morning of December 1, 1890, Keeper Charles McCarthy and Assistant Hermann Engel were on duty. But it was Engel's wife, Freda, who first saw the ferryboat coming. The *Newark* rammed the already shaky beacon, smashing a pile and a platform brace. The ferry's captain cussed out the light keepers and backed off, even though the navigational aids were working and he'd done all the damage. The patient keepers filed a report and Assistant Keeper Engel soon took his vigilant bride and transferred to firmer ground at Point Bonita lighthouse on the mainland.

The fact that the sentinel stood on wooden stilts in 13 feet of water was shortly to lead to its downfall. The piles were becoming unstable by the early 1890s. To remedy this, stone was quarried on Yerba Buena Island at the Lighthouse Depot and transported by schooner to Oakland. The stone was placed around the piles to increase their stability, and the beacon gained a few more years of life. However, by 1903, the entire station was in danger of falling into San Francisco Bay. Teredos, underwater shipworms that work similar to termites, had been busily gnawing on the pile foundation.

A new station had to be built, and it had to be done utilizing a less appetizing means of support. The Lighthouse Service was more than equal to the task. Big, concrete-filled cylinders, four feet in diameter, were erected. In the center of each of the cylinders, three sturdy pine piles were driven clear through the cylinders and the muddy Bay bottom down to bedrock. On top of the cylinders, a decking of steel beams was erected. The steel beams were linked by concrete arches. This was as worm-proof a foundation as the lighthouse engineers could provide and it worked admirably. In fact, the teredos never again bothered Oakland Harbor light station. They did, however, turn their attentions elsewhere. As late as World War I, wharves and piers would suddenly and mysteriously give way and fall into the Bay. Sabotage by enemy agents was whispered along the waterfront; but careful inspection proved that teredos, not spies, were guilty.

The second Oakland Harbor lighthouse was sturdy above water as well as below. It was a white, two-story frame building with a red roof and green window blinds. Two porches, one serving each story, completely surrounded the almost square building. A short, square tower sat at the roof's very tip. The octagonal iron lantern room, painted black, held a French lens capable of casting a 44,000-candlepower beam. The bell, mounted on the side of the building, remained as the fog signal. The lower story contained storerooms, while the upper floor housed the keeper and his assistant.

After the new beacon began operation on July 11, 1903, the original lighthouse went dark and was declared a hazard to navigation. The following February, a "lighthouse auction" was held on the Alameda Mole. The local press claimed it was the first such auction in American history and termed it a "remarkable affair." The lucky bidder had 30 days to tear down the structure. He was required to remove everything, even the piles down as far as the rock.

The picturesque little sentinel had won the affection of Oaklanders, and the local press wrote:

> For many years this has been the guide of the night ferries, and during storm and fair weather, fog and moonlight, it has shone steadily and lighted the deep-sea liner in and the crawling bay scow schooner by. Some time ago a new light farther out was built . . . The passing of the old light will be a source of regret to all lovers of the Bay, as it has grown into

A rare photograph of the first Oakland Harbor lighthouse, a beacon much loved by Oaklanders until shipworms ultimately spelled its doom. (National Archives)

When constructed, the second Oakland Harbor lighthouse stood well offshore. (U.S. Coast Guard)

A keeper's wife stands beside the fog bell on the upper veranda of Oakland Harbor lighthouse. Note the fancy railing, columns, and nicely trimmed paint scheme of the Lighthouse Service era, C. 1920s. (U.S. Coast Coast)

the affections of the constant user of it. This harbor light was the one to which the Oaklander's eye always turned on the night ferry, and its merry gleam lighted many a happy party on yachting back to port.

The second beacon soon stood alone.

Eventually, the new light's setting began to change. The city grew out to engulf it. The Western Pacific Railroad quite literally built its ferry landing around the lighthouse. Ferryboats and trains soon puffed about the little beacon and keepers gained both a compensation and a distinction. The compensating factor was that they now could simply step off their porch onto the broad deck of the ferry slip and walk ashore. The rowboat remained but its use was much diminished. The distinction was that they became the only lighthouse in California with direct transcontinental train connections. It is not recorded how often, if ever, the wickies took advantage of their unparalleled transportation facilities, but the finest passenger trains of the day were but a few steps away.

Western Pacific Railroad's ferry slip with Oakland Harbor lighthouse at the tip of the upper pier, C. 1950s. (U.S. Coast Guard)

The ferryboats and ships, however, could cause trouble at the lighthouse. On April 30, 1914, Assistant Keeper Lambert R. Willard was on watch when a steamer with a big wake rushed by. A man in a small boat was capsized by the swell and was about to drown. Willard went to his rescue and pulled the man from the cold Bay waters.

On August 26, 1923, Keeper Charles H.A. Brooke was on watch at Oakland Harbor. A strong west wind was blowing and small craft were on the Bay, a combination that could mean trouble. Suddenly, Brooke saw a fisherman's skiff capsize near the north jetty while attempting to sail up San Antonio Creek to Oakland. Brooke went to the rescue and saved the fisherman from drowning. The keeper was later commended for his action in the "Lighthouse Service Bulletin".

But usually, life was rather pleasant at the Oakland Harbor light station. Noise was generally the keepers' only complaint, especially as Alameda Naval Air Station began to develop. Keepers seemed to be "rewarded" with duty at Oakland after years of hardship at isolated offshore stations such as St. George Reef or Mile Rocks. Both the electrification of the light and the substitution of compressed air diaphone fog horns for the bell made life easier for the wickies.

Gerhard Jaehne and Myron Edgington were typical of the station's keepers. Jaehne was born in Germany in 1885 and went to sea at 14, serving aboard sailing ships of many nationalities and rounding Cape Horn four times. As steam replaced sail, he "swallowed the anchor" and took up homesteading in Montana. He still looked to the sea; but now with a wife and children, he had reasons to stay ashore. Light keeping seemed an answer. After a stint at lonely St. George Reef, where no families were allowed, he was transferred to Point Reyes and spent the remainder of his career at family stations. By the 1940s, his children were grown, and he and Mrs. Jaehne were assigned Oakland Harbor as their last station.

Jaehne's assistant, Myron Edgington, had likewise, come to the station when he was well into his fifties. He had served some years in the Navy before entering the Lighthouse Service. He began his career at solitary Mile Rocks, was later transferred to Point Vicente, and finally ended up at Oakland Harbor.

The interior of Oakland Harbor lighthouse gleamed. Even the fog signal room, shown here, sparkled with approved Lighthouse Service dedication to cleanliness and polish. At the best kept lighthouses, the old timers say you could eat off the fog signal building's floor, it was so spotless. (U.S. Coast Guard)

Both Edgington and the Jaehnes were thoroughly adjusted to light keeping. Duties and accommodations were evenly divided. Each man daily stood 12-hour watches. Likewise, the upper story of the lighthouse was divided into two comfortable apartments. The station was immaculately kept, and Mrs. Jaehne was well-known for her fine cooking. Except for an occasional movie or shopping trip, they seldom went anywhere. Both men were deeply interested in their hobbies. Jaehne made pencil sketches and painted with oils and water colors. Edgington was devoted to the old seafaring pastime of macrame and made beautiful mats and tablecloths.

By the 1950s, Edgington had assumed command of the light station, assisted by two young Coast Guardsmen. A visiting hours schedule was set up, and on weekends and holiday afternoons, the public could tour the facility. Despite its proximity to Oakland (the fog signal could be heard downtown), the policy was apparently not too well publicized, and it was six years before a curious citizen arrived for a visit. The long-awaited visitor turned out to be a reporter for the Oakland *Tribune*, and soon, the little beacon became well known. Edgington spent his last years at the light guiding countless Oakland school children through the lighthouse.

As long as Edgington remained, the station continued to evidence the high standards of the old-time keepers. The brass and paint work glistened and the light operated flawlessly. When two Navy fliers plunged into the Bay not far from the light, Edgington organized his two assistants and led a heroic rescue attempt.

However, time was running out both for the veterans of the old Lighthouse Service and for Oakland Harbor light. In 1966, the old lens went dark after an automatic beacon was placed atop a big, upright tank in front of the station. Unfortunately, the lantern room was removed to be installed at the new Mark Abbott Memorial Lighthouse in Santa Cruz.

With automation, the Coast Guard no longer needed the old sentinel. The lighthouse was sold to a restaurant firm for the bargain price of one dollar. The restaurant people paid the Murphy-Pacific Corporation $22,144 to move the lighthouse six miles down the Oakland Estuary to Embarcadero Cove opposite Coast Guard Island. Using a gigantic crane and barges, the job was successfully completed.

Today, the lovely old structure is a restaurant called Quinn's Lighthouse. It is located at 1951 Embarcadero Street, Oakland, and makes a pleasant stop in one of the nicest sections of the East Bay waterfront. Hopefully, the owners can be motivated to reconstruct a historically accurate lantern room atop the sentinel's roof. It would add greatly to the lighthouse's integrity and beauty. The queen of Oakland Harbor deserves to look her best.

SOUTHAMPTON SHOAL

Southampton Shoal was not a lighthouse for deep water sailors. It was more the sentinel of tugboat skippers, yachtsmen, and river boat pilots. To be sure, the San Francisco Bay beacon served Navy ships bound for Mare Island, tankers from the "Long Wharf" at Richmond, and freighters bound for Carquinez Strait, but it was the Bay sailors who saw her daily and who miss her the most.

The lighthouse was built to mark two-mile long Southampton Shoal, which borders the east side of the ship channel between Berkeley and Marin County. Serious interest in a lighthouse here had begun about 1900. The Santa Fe Railroad was just beginning ferry service between Point Richmond and San Francisco, and the new ferry route passed close to the southeast edge of the shoal. The combination of frequent ferryboats and frequent fog made the shoal a dangerous place to leave inadequately marked, and the Lighthouse Board asked Congress for $30,000 to build a station. Hazards during foggy weather seemed to have been uppermost in the Board's mind, since they requested only a modest lens lantern for a light but wanted a hefty, 3000-pound fog bell for a fog signal.

Approval of the funds led to construction of one of the most distinctive West Coast lighthouses. Built two miles offshore atop eleven steel cylinders, it looked like a delightful Victorian home. Its two lower stories both had spacious verandas which led completely around the rectangular building. The third story had stylish gabled windows and a slightly peaked roof which culminated in a square tower, barely tall enough to provide space for its six windows but able to support the black lantern room.

Of course, the "House on the Bay", as it was soon dubbed, had some features setting it apart from its non-maritime sisters. At its top, instead of a widow's walk, there was a lantern room with a fifth order lens. (The lens was already a veteran when it arrived at Southampton Shoal, having been built in 1886.) Other distinctive light station features were the big water and fuel tanks and the davits holding the station boat. However, it was the big mechanically-struck fog bell booming across the Bay which made the visitor most aware that he was not in a genteel Berkeley or San Rafael home.

Southampton Shoal stood like a fine home well offshore in shallow Bay waters, although the lantern room and fog bell clearly marked the structure as a lighthouse. The supporting cylinders were thrown out of line by the 1906 earthquake, and some were never completely straightened (note the second cylinder from the left). (U.S. Coast Guard)

The light and fog bell began operation late in 1905. The early years were difficult ones at the two-man station. Soon after construction, the sandy bottom began eroding and threatened to undermine the cylinders supporting the station. A thousand tons of rock had to be dumped around the big, four-foot thick cylinders.

Then, in April 1906, the San Francisco earthquake battered the light, throwing the cylinders out of line eastward, away from the quake's epicenter in Marin County. The Lighthouse Service realigned as many caissons as they could and filled them with concrete, but for the remainder of its days, some were more than ten degrees from vertical. Again, more rock was added to stabilize the shaken beacon.

The early keepers had a miserable stay at Southampton Shoal, not only because their lighthouse had threatened to fall into the Bay twice in less than a year. The mid-Bay weather was cold and damp, and they frequently got wet taking the little station boat to Point Richmond for mail and supplies. By 1907, the Lighthouse Service inspector reported that the wickies were suffering from rheumatism and catarrh.

Considering the working conditions, the pay was not particularly generous. In 1909, the station's two keepers were each working 12 hours a day; Principal Keeper Thomas L. Winthar was receiving $62.50 a month and Assistant Keeper Frank Willer, $50 a month. They earned every penny of it.

Keeper's pay crept upward through the following years but always remained low. But tough economic conditions eventually made even light keeping wages look good. Young Ole Lunden could see hard times coming in 1929. Despite the beginning of the Depression, he had reason for optimism. His friend, Milford Johnson, was a lighthouse keeper on the Farallon Islands. When Milford came ashore wearing his handsome new Lighthouse Service uniform, Ole had been impressed. Lunden had decided he, too, wanted to be a light keeper and had applied to enter government service.

He eventually received a phone call from one of the secretaries at the Lighthouse Service office in San Francisco. She asked Ole if he "would accept an assistant keeper's job at Southampton Shoal?"

"Where the heck is that?" he blurted.

"It's on 11 cylinders out in the Bay off Point Richmond," the secretary answered.

"Do you think my wife would go out there and like it?"

"Well, we haven't had a woman there for a long time . . . so . . ."

This wasn't a very encouraging response, but Lunden was determined to give it a chance. He told his wife Bernice, "We'll give it a try. If you don't like it, we can always take the next boat in." Bernice had always figured that when they were married she would go wherever Ole went and Southampton Shoal was no exception. Besides, his previous job had been as a streetcar motorman and this sounded better than sitting home 10 or 11 hours a day

A classic San Francisco Bay scene. The scow schooner Tartar *ties up alongside Southampton Shoal lighthouse. Once common, scow schooners hauled hay, produce, and many other forms of cargo across the Bay and up such rivers as the Petaluma, Sacramento, and San Joaquin. (U.S. Coast Guard)*

waiting for her husband to return. The pay, however, out on Southampton Shoal hadn't improved much from 20 years earlier. It ranged from $90 to $105 a month, but that was much better than many Americans were to experience during the 1930s.

It wasn't long before the Lundens' bags were packed and "we went out there to Southampton." Southampton Shoal was a two-man station and the character of the head keeper would be a decisive factor in whether the Lundens would continue in the Service. They shouldn't have worried. The head keeper was Frank Schou, "And he was a prince. A gentleman of the first order. And we got along fine and dandy."

Schou's family preferred to live ashore in San Francisco, perhaps because of his daughter's health problems. At any rate, Keeper Schou warmly welcomed the young couple and soon began giving them a solid foundation in light keeping. The lighthouse living accommodations were divided in half, each side identical. Mr. Schou lived in one half of the lighthouse, the Lundens in the other—townhouse style. A rather democratic arrangement, considering many stations provided larger or more convenient quarters for the head keeper.

The Lundens were shown the layout of the station. On the very bottom of the lighthouse was the boiler room. Above it were the kitchens, living rooms, baths, and supply rooms. A major supply item was coal. Each keeper received four tons a year for personal use such as cooking and heating. The next floor up, where the gabled windows were, was the location of the bedrooms. Above this was the short tower and the lantern room with the lens.

The top of the lighthouse was crucial for more than might be thought. Its roof caught rain water for all domestic use, including drinking water. The wickies had to be very careful never to throw any garbage over the rail since it attracted large numbers of sea gulls. The gulls would then land on the roof and splatter the station with their droppings. The birds' presence on the roof would have decidedly negative effects on the quality of the drinking water. Bailing wire was placed all around the lantern room balcony to discourage bird landings and reduce their droppings. Bernice was advised to be careful what she

Southampton Shoal lighthouse guarding the shipping lanes, 1930s. (U.S. Lighthouse Society)

hung out to dry after washing since the sea gulls could make quick work
of clean clothes.

The Lundens' laundry was soon noticed by more than the sea gulls.
The Santa Fe Railroad's big tugboats passed by the light station frequently ferrying railroad cars across the Bay. When the tug crew saw
a woman's lingerie hanging on the lighthouse clothes line to dry, they
were stunned. They wondered what kind of a woman would live out
there. Ole recalled, "They made a close pass by the lighthouse to get a
good look at Bernice. She was the first woman they'd ever seen on this
offshore station."

The captains of the Santa Fe tugs, with their side-lashed barges
loaded with railroad freight cars, depended upon Southampton Shoal
light more than any other mariners. They frequently carried rail gon-
dola cars filled with scrap metal which made the vessel's compasses
unreliable. Because these huge tugs weren't equipped with radar (until
1951), they often had to navigate entirely by lighthouse lights and fog
signals. Leaving Third Street in San Francisco they would always try to
get a bearing on Southampton Shoal light as soon as possible. The San
Francisco fireboat's pilots often used Alcatraz light the same way, as a
primary bearing for navigation.

The Santa Fe tugs traveled from Richmond to both San Francisco
and Tiburon. At Tiburon, backing out of the ferry slip was very difficult. The tugs had to immediately enter the strong, confusing currents of
Raccoon Strait. As an example of what navigation was like, the tugboat
skippers would watch the sea gulls floating in the water to see which way
the current was going. Sometimes the currents were so confused that one
set of sea gulls would be going one way and ten feet away another set
would be moving the opposite direction. They sometimes had to wait
until the tug and attached barge were out in the stream to know what the
current was going to do to the vessel and her loaded barge. When Treasure Island was built by land fill and attached to Yerba Buena Island, it
changed the Bay currents and made navigation even more difficult.

The tugboat skippers and crews deeply appreciated the Southampton
Shoal light keepers. The tugs would come by close to the lighthouse and
talk with the keepers as they passed by. The tugboat men would occasionally pass by so close "you could swear they were going to take the
corner of the lighthouse off."

But the close passage often brought companionship and pleasure to
light keepers and tugboat men alike. The custom evolved of the tug's
crews throwing newspapers to the wickies as they passed by and, in return, the keepers tossed fresh fish to them. At Christmas, the tugboat
men all pulled in close by and wished the Lundens a Merry Christmas.

The keepers could, fortunately, get to the mainland fairly regularly.
On Tuesdays, one keeper could go ashore, and on Fridays it was the other man's turn. Bernice could go both times since she didn't have to watch

the station and she often went in twice a week. The keepers went ashore at Tiburon on the Marin County shore. To reach shore, Southampton Shoal was provided with two boats, neither prize winners. One was a dilapidated 28-foot double-ended power boat with a canopy. It was used to go to Tiburon to get groceries, mail, and to reach the keepers' automobiles, which were kept there.

The station's other boat was a skiff used primarily to row out and pick up drifting logs to supplement the coal supply for heating and cooking. There was far more driftwood on the Bay in those days, before the Army Corps of Engineers' vessels began sweeping the Bay of debris. Sawed into proper lengths, driftwood was a valued addition to the fuel supply. No matter which boat was to be used, Ole Lunden always tried to schedule his return to coincide with high tide. At Southampton Shoal, the keepers had to hook the vessel to davits and crank it up by hand onto the first deck level of the lighthouse. If you did this at high tide, you could save yourself eight or more feet of arduous lifting.

Southampton Shoal lighthouse's large concrete supports were tilted 11 degrees off center by the 1906 San Francisco earthquake. (U.S. Coast Guard)

Holidays were rotated between the keepers. Mr. Schou went home to his family in San Francisco at Christmas and the Lundens went to relatives in San Jose on New Year's Eve. It was a big day for the Lundens when Bernice's parents decided to visit the lighthouse. All went well until it was time to return ashore. As the two couples were heading back to Tiburon, at the very entrance of Raccoon Strait, the boat's engine died. The fast currents swept the boat into the path of the Montecello Steamship Company's ferry bound for Vallejo. The big ferry didn't seem to see them and came ahead bearing down on the hapless foursome. At the last moment, the ferry spotted them and avoided a collision. About that time, Ole Lunden and his father-in-law decided it was time to row, and row hard to get out of the shipping lane. They pulled toward Ayala Cove on Angel Island and finally reached the Immigration Station there. By then the foursome felt they must have looked like poor immigrants arriving from across the sea. The Immigration Service personnel gave the Lundens and Bernice's parents hot coffee and phoned Tiburon for assistance. Eventually, all reached Tiburon safely.

Just launching a boat at Southampton Shoal could be difficult. Launching the boat during a strong southeaster was almost impossible. The wind blew right at the corner of the lighthouse where the power boat hung on its davits. Under those conditions, if anyone tried to launch it, the boat would have been blown against the station's foundation cylinders and been broken to pieces by the waves. Sometimes when launching, the tide would run so fast that the wickies would steer north for Point San Quentin and end up far south at Angel Island's Raccoon Strait.

One previous keeper had a drinking problem and this made getting back to the light station problematical. When he had been ashore at Tiburon, the temptations had proven too great. Tiburon was a railroad town in those days, the site of the main repair shops of the Northwestern Pacific Railroad, and the bars on Main Street were well attended. The hard drinking keeper kept getting drunk when in port and ending up in hard fisted fights. When he was sober, he was a good wickie, but something had to be done to keep him out of bars. It was a matter of life and death. With alcohol impairing his judgement, the power boat would end up in the ferry lanes in danger of being rammed.

The Lighthouse Service District Superintendent Captain Harry Rhodes decided, therefore, to transfer him to the Farallon Islands. Farallon Islands Light Station, about 23 miles west of San Francisco, was the farthest offshore lighthouse in California. There was nothing on the islands but the light station and, best of all, certainly no bars. So the hard drinking wickie left Southampton Shoal for the Farallon Islands.

But the thirsty keeper managed to outwit even Captain Rhodes. He worked out a secret code with some of the crew at the Lighthouse Depot on Yerba Buena Island. When the order came in for "oranges," it meant more liquor was needed on the Farallons and the Depot men would send it out on the next tender in an orange crate. The hard drinking wickie was to find life difficult on the lonely, fogbound Farallons. Tragically, his wife contracted tuberculosis there and it infected the daughter of another keeper.

Life at Southampton Shoal was easier than on the Farallon Islands. At Southampton Shoal, you could "throw a line out the kitchen window and catch fish for dinner." Crabbing was quite good and marine life still plentiful in the Bay. Ole Lunden recalls how often porpoises played around the lighthouse. They were "just thick, like you could walk on them."

Besides going ashore, another major recurring problem at Southampton Shoal was the fog bell. The monster bell's striking mechanism often broke down due to the constant vibration produced every time the striking hammer hit the bell. It took a few minutes to rewind the clockwork drive weight that powered the bell timer and hammer. The timer was about two feet long and roughly three feet high. Its clockwork weight which powered the timer weighed about 50 pounds and was cranked up high and then allowed to unwind very slowly. As it unwound, the cog-like wheels on the timer turned. The rise and fall of the cog wheel caused a lever to raise and fall, timing the number and frequency of hammer strikes the bell would receive. The wickies could adjust the speed of the timer to change the bell signal by using its governor. The governor was of the same type used on many Fresnel lighthouse lenses and featured little metal balls which could be raised or lowered to determine the speed by which gears of either a fog bell timer or lighthouse lens turned.

Eventually, compressed air powered bell strikers were developed and these allowed the bell weights to be used solely as emergency backup striking power. Fog bells of either type were much easier to operate than steam powered fog signals, and thus, light stations with bells for fog signals generally only needed one or two keepers.

Both Head Keeper Schou and Assistant Keeper Lunden eventually transferred to other stations. They both went next to other San Francisco Bay island lights, Schou to Angel Island and Lunden to Yerba Buena. When Ole Lunden finally got a mainland station, it would be at Point Vicente in Los Angeles County.

Ole Lunden was replaced by Albert Joost from Yerba Buena Island. Joost had asked Lunden to trade places with him and the swap had been approved. It was to prove a tragic transfer for the Joosts.

Albert Joost served at two San Francisco Bay lights, East Brother and Yerba Buena. Southampton Shoal was his third island in the stream. His wife, an attractive and well-liked woman, adjusted nicely to lighthouse life despite having a deformed foot which left her partially crippled with one leg about four inches shorter than the other.

In 1936, just two days before Christmas, their happy island life was shattered. That day, the hardworking and dedicated husband-wife team

Two well known lighthouse couples who were distinguished guardians of the Golden Gate. At the bottom is Mrs. Albert Joost and Keeper John P. Kofod. At top is Mrs. Metha Kofod and Keeper Albert Joost. This photo was taken while all four served at Yerba Buena Island light station. Later, the Joosts transferred to Southampton Shoal lighthouse where Keeper Joost was tragically killed in a fire. Mrs. Joost was a true heroine of San Francisco Bay when she put out the fire and saved the lighthouse and then aided her fatally burned husband in reaching help at Angel Island. (Walter Fanning)

were alone at the lighthouse since the assistant keeper had gone ashore. Keeper Joost found it necessary to do some repair work on the station radio set. Mr. Joost set about repairing the radio set and its antenna, using a blowtorch to heat a soldering iron. But the blowtorch went out, discharging vaporized gas. Apparently Keeper Joost didn't realize what had happened or how much of the dangerous gas had escaped, for he relighted the blowtorch. It instantly exploded into flames, igniting both the keeper and the lighthouse!

Mrs. Joost rushed to his aid and was greeted by a horrible sight. Her husband's clothes were in flames and the lighthouse was on fire. They grabbed a fire extinguisher and together put out the flames which had enveloped Albert Joost's body. But Keeper Joost was horribly burned, the lighthouse afire, and his wife hampered by her deformed foot. Still, they managed to reached another fire extinguisher and put out the fire, saving the lighthouse.

The nearest medical help was on Angel Island, nearly two miles across the Bay. Mrs. Joost assisted her terribly burned husband down the lighthouse and into the station boat, trying to comfort him as they went. She helped her husband lower away the boat. It was now dusk and darkness was creeping across the Bay.

Somehow Keeper Joost managed to get to Angel Island. Some sources say his wife rowed him there, while others report that he went alone, insisting that his wife stand watch and light the beacon for the

The huge, 3000-pound Southampton Shoal fog bell was struck by a mechanically-operated hammer. The large head of the hammer swung through a hole in the lighthouse wall, giving the bell a mighty blow several times a minute during foggy weather. (U.S. Coast Guard)

evening. In either case, once at Angel Island, Albert Joost was rushed by a military boat to the Marine Hospital in San Francisco. His loving wife could not join him, putting her grief aside to keep the lighthouse lamps burning.

Night had now fallen and, alone, Mrs. Joost lighted Southampton Shoal's lamp and once again the beacon guided mariners across San Francisco Bay. It must have been terrible there in the empty lighthouse with the lingering stench of the fire, as she wondered what was happening to her husband.

Word reached the Lighthouse Service of the tragedy and later that night the lighthouse tender *Lupine* reached Southampton Shoal. On board was a relief keeper, finally allowing Mrs. Joost to leave her post of duty. The *Lupine* then took her on board and sped to San Francisco. Reaching the Marine Hospital, she found her husband alive but in critical condition. He must have been deeply proud of his wife, for she could

The clockwork bell-striking mechanism, shown here with the hammer at right, was powered by a weight. Keepers would wind up the weight, and as it descended, an attached cable would turn the striking mechanism to activate the hammer at set intervals. (U.S. Coast Guard)

tell him that Southampton Shoal light had not faltered. Neither had their love. Tragically, two days later, on Christmas Day, her husband died from his burns.

In 1939, the Coast Guard assumed control of the light, and diaphone horns atop the lantern room roof replaced the old bell. The number of keepers was eventually increased as well. A 24-hour watch continued to be maintained, and Bay sailors appreciated the presence of the lighthouse and its keepers.

Then, in 1960, the decision was made to remove the frame structure, leaving only the cylinders. Atop the cylinders, a concrete platform would be built with a small automatic tower with buoys. The station was unmanned, and the light doused. Civilian contractors sheared the building from its foundation cylinders. Two giant cranes lifted the entire lighthouse up and placed it on a barge to be towed to Tinsley Island on

A sad day for Bay sailors. Southampton Shoal lighthouse is removed from its historic home on the Bay in a misguided automation technique. Fortunately, the St. Francis Yacht Club of San Francisco saved the sentinel for future generations, July 5, 1966. (U.S. Coast Guard)

the San Joaquin River where it now serves as summer clubhouse for the St. Francis Yacht Club of San Francisco. Southampton Shoal's lens was placed on exhibit at Angel Island State Park.

Today, the caissons remain, some of the cylinders still tilted 11 degrees eastward as a result of the 1906 earthquake. The small robot light tower flashes, marking shoal water. A pleasant afternoon sail can be had by making Southampton Shoal the goal of a day on the Bay. Only cormorants and gulls will be there atop the cylinders, and they won't trade a fish for the morning paper.

Southampton Shoal lighthouse shortly after its move to Tinsley Island in the San Joaquin Delta. It is now owned by the St. Francis Yacht Club of San Francisco. (U.S. Coast Guard)

Handsome and distinctive, Carquinez Strait combined tower, dwelling, and fog signal building into a single, unique lighthouse structure. Twin fog sirens protrude from the roof. (U.S. Coast Guard)

CARQUINEZ STRAIT

In 1910, Carquinez Strait lighthouse was erected on the north side of the entrance to the strait near the city of Vallejo. Mare Island light, across the Napa River, had served as the area's principal navigational aid for years, but its location was not close enough to the strait to provide adequate aid to mariners. Thus, the second light station had to be established.

The light station was to be built off Carquinez Heights, at the south edge of Vallejo. The water was so shallow that an extremely long pier was built out to deep water so that the lighthouse tenders could service the station. Such a location also meant that the light would be close enough to Carquinez Strait to serve as a valuable guide to mariners.

Using a steam pile driver on a barge, Mercer and Fraser, general contractors from San Francisco, drove hundreds of wooden piles into the Bay bottom. The long pier was built first, and then, just short of the pier's end, a causeway was erected to provide access from the pier to the lighthouse. The sentinel was built upon a rectangular platform of piles where the muddy Bay waters would flow beneath the keeper's feet. A water tank was built at the point where the causeway and the pier met. At the tip of the pier, a little landing with a small shed was constructed.

For the lighthouse, engineers toyed with two basic construction plans. One called for a large dwelling and a separate lighthouse connected by an elevated walkway. The other plan, which was adopted, combined the light tower and fog signal building with the residence.

Carpenters swarmed over the platform, and soon the lighthouse began to take form. First the frame rose, then diagonal wood sheathing was added to cover the walls. Before this task was even completed, construction of the roof began. The attached fog signal building seemed to progress fastest, the light tower the slowest. The lantern room and fourth order lens were added last.

The exterior was finished in grand style. The horizontal arrangement of the siding gave the building something of the character of a beautiful line drawing. Of the ornamental woodwork, most impressive were the decorative columns that supported the massive front porch with its fine railing. The railing matched that of the lantern room balcony. The dwelling was two and one-half stories high, the light tower, three. From mean water level, the lighthouse was 40-feet high, but the distance from its actual base atop the piles to the top of the lantern was only about 30-feet. The cream-colored structure looked like a fine residence. However, the lantern room atop the square tower and the twin compressed air sirens protruding from the fog signal room roof clearly

Construction of Carquinez Strait Lighthouse in 1909. (U.S. Coast Guard)

Early photo of Carquinez Strait Light Station with the pier where lighthouse tenders would moor when bringing supplies. (U.S. Coast Guard)

marked the structure as a lighthouse. The fourth order lens was first shown on January 15, 1910.

The station would retain its classic appearance for decades to come, although eventually the pier would be extended and vertical mushroom trumpet fog signals and a lens lantern would be placed at the pier's end.

These "vertical mushroom trumpet fog signals" deserve special note. Basically, they consisted of a trumpet-shaped horn with its mouth pointed upward. Mounted atop the trumpet opening was a circular device called a cowl which deflected the sound horizontally in all directions. This characteristic made them popular on lightships where the goal was to have the sound go out across the sea in every direction. On lighthouses built ashore, the goal was to direct the sound seaward and so trumpets on sound signals were mounted horizontally and pointed out to sea. The idea was to maximize the sound out in a channel and minimize it back ashore at the light station.

Carquinez Strait was built well offshore at the end of an extremely long pier, allowing the use of lightship style fog horns. Lighthouse District Superintendent Harry Rhodes, a man of distinguished scientific achievement, took a keen interest in Carquinez Strait Light Station. For at least three years, he worked at perfecting Carquinez Strait's new vertical mushroom trumpet, experimenting with the cowl and its distance from the trumpet's mushroom top, with its compressed air system (it

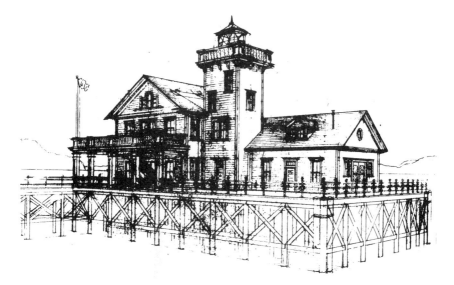

Original plans for Carquinez Strait Light Station. Several different plans were drawn before this one was adopted, 1907. (National Archives)

Much of San Francisco Bay consists of very shallow water. Thus, Carquinez Strait lighthouse had to be built at the end of an extremely long pier in order to be near the shipping lanes. (U.S. Coast Guard)

was over 900 feet from the station powerhouse to the trumpets) and the electrical system. The Lighthouse Service was interested and impressed enough to write up the project in its "Bulletin."

Significantly, these vertical mushroom trumpets were so successful that they were used on lightships through 1983 when one of the last two active American light vessels, *WLV 612*, the *Nantucket Lightship* (*ex-Blunts Reef Lightship*) was retired. You can still see vertical mushroom trumpet fog horns on some retired lightships now residing in maritime museums. Captain Rhodes and Carquinez Strait played a major role in their perfection.

Both the lighthouse and fog signal were of vital importance to mariners on windy Carquinez Strait. The sentinel was used by an endless line of ships. Besides the heavy Sacramento River traffic, there were ships out of the port of Vallejo and from the Mare Island Naval Shipyard. A fair portion of America's most famous Navy ships used Carquinez Strait light to find their way home for repairs during two world wars. The battleship *California*, launched at Mare Island in 1919, was one of a long line of ships that used Carquinez Strait light as their first guide post. Most commonly seen were the sleek, white steamers of the Monticello

The interior of Carquinez Strait lighthouse was tastefully furnished. The table in the background reminds one of the extensive record-keeping demanded by the Lighthouse Service as the book of invoices lies amid a pile of forms and papers. (U.S. Coast Guard)

Steamship Company which carried passengers from San Francisco to the wharf in Vallejo. Here, travelers connected with the electric cars of the San Francisco, Napa, and Calistoga Railway to reach the wine country of the Napa Valley.

For decades the sentinel played its peaceful role. However, times changed—just as the little stern wheeler *Zinfandel* no longer puffed down the Napa River loaded with wine, so too, the days of the beacon came to an end. Even the tender *Sequoia* no longer called, after tying up so many times alongside the long, narrow pier. The Coast Guard decided that Carquinez Strait light station must be modernized.

The original lighthouse was removed and the main light established at the end of the pier. In 1951, new family dwellings were built by the Coast Guard on the bluff overlooking the old light station. The new structure was flat-roofed and single story, consisting of four units. It was the antithesis of the beautiful original buildings.

Carquinez Strait light station's dwelling portion survives today. It serves as the magnificent centerpiece of Glen Cove Marina near Vallejo. October 1988. (R. Shanks)

Five keepers, one a veteran of the old Lighthouse Service, tended the station during its last years in the 1950s. It was considered "preferred duty", and many men sought an assignment there. Duties included six-hour shifts while maintaining a 24-hour watch, operating the light, and overseeing the automatic fog signal. The keepers used a 25-foot launch to make emergency repairs to aids to navigation on Suisun Bay.

The huge, 28-room residence, now painted white, was offered for sale in 1955. San Francisco building contractor Robert Hubert purchased it with the idea of making it the centerpiece of a charming small-craft marina. The price asked was low and included the old lens,

Lighthouse tender Lupine *upbound on the San Joaquin River to serve the Delta's navigational aids, C. 1920's. (U.S. Coast Guard)*

but moving the 150-ton edifice was problematical. Hubert hunted, but was unable to find anyone willing to move it. Finally, he decided to do it himself. He rented moving timbers—big 90-footers—the largest available. He hired a couple of barges and a cantilever crane. With his own construction crew, he began the operation.

The project almost cost Hubert his life. While preparing for the move, he fell from the old lighthouse dwelling, seriously injuring his chest. He spent a long time in the hospital, and the building remained in its original location.

Meanwhile, the Coast Guard closed the remaining Carquinez Strait Light Station facilities on June 3, 1960 and converted the site to automatic operation. The long pier, however, was allowed to remain.

So the historic structure languished, its future uncertain. Vandals broke in and destroyed the classic fourth order Fresnel lens, smashing the glass to pieces. It began to look as if Carquinez Strait Light Station might become totally lost.

Hubert clearly needed help. Three Asian-American businessmen—Ittsei Nakagawa of El Cerrito, Sokichi Satake of Concord, and Henry Kiyoi of Martinez—came to Hubert's rescue. The four men formed a partnership to develop the marina and preserve the lighthouse dwelling portion. Ittsei Nakagawa was designer of the project which they called Lighthouse Harbor.

Fortunately, they were successful and the beautiful Carquinez Strait Light Station dwelling today stands at the water's edge overlooking a pleasant harbor. Now called Glen Cove Marina, the historic structure is the centerpiece of the harbor. It is located east of Vallejo off Hwy. 780 at 2000 Glen Cove Drive and is currently operated by Western Waterways, Inc. There is public access to the marina and berthing facilities are offered for small craft. It makes a very pleasant stop along a most interesting and often busy shipping lane. There is a tiny gift shop in the harbor master's office.

It would be most appropriate if the lighthouse tower could be rebuilt at its appropriate place attached to the dwelling. To create a proper and exact restoration would not be especially difficult and would be a great service to the people of California and lighthouse lovers nationwide. Plans and fine photographs still exist and, as with any lighthouse restoration project, a historically accurate light tower, railing, and lantern room are essential. Perhaps the owners, local civic and historical groups, and other interested citizens of goodwill can bring this restoration project about. The Queen of Carquinez Strait deserves her crown.

Officer of the lighthouse tender Sequoia. *The officers and crews of the tenders came to know all the light stations well, C. 1920s. (U.S. Coast Guard)*

THE U.S. LIFE-SAVING SERVICE
IN CALIFORNIA

THE DEVELOPMENT OF THE COAST GUARD'S
SEARCH AND RESCUE
OPERATIONS ON THE CALIFORNIA COAST

The year was 1907. Fog had begun to drift in toward the northern California coast. The United States Life-Saving Service stations went into action as soon as the lookouts on watch sighted the approaching great, grey bank of summer fog. At San Francisco's Southside Life-Saving Station, located just west of Lake Merced, the north patrolman set out along Ocean Beach toward the wooden post set in the dunes seaward of Ulloa Street where he would meet his counterpart, the south patrolman from Golden Gate Park Station. There they would exchange brass "checks" (tokens) as proof that they had completed their assigned patrol. Meanwhile, Golden Gate Park's north patrolman was trudging uphill at the Cliff House, heading toward Point Lobos where Golden Gate Park Station maintained a lookout tower. The surfman on duty at the tower was scanning the edge of the rapidly closing fog through his telescope.[1]

To the northeast, Fort Point Station's lookout, at a tower located near the site of today's Golden Gate Bridge tollgate, had also seen the fog. He had already signaled his station to send a patrolman to the auxiliary boathouse at Baker Beach. Across the Golden Gate in Marin County, similar activities were taking place at Point Bonita Life-Saving Station. And so it was, northward up the coast of California at each facility: Point Reyes, Arena Cove, and Humboldt Bay. Small groups of dedicated men were alert to the possibility of ships in danger and were prepared to go to their aid, no matter how great the risk to themselves.

All were part of a highly competent and far-flung civilian service. Most of the U.S. Life-Saving Service's stations had crews of six to eight surfmen under the supervision of a keeper, the station's officer-in-charge. The keepers of the West Coast stations were under the administration of the 13th Life-Saving District's Superintendent, headquartered in San Francisco. The District Superintendent was accountable to the civilian service's national headquarters in Washington, D.C., presided over by the General Superintendent, Sumner I. Kimball. The Life-Saving Service was, in turn, a part of the U.S. Treasury Department.

---

[1]Portions of this chapter first appeared in a two-part article in the National Maritime Museum's *Sea Letter* magazine.

When conditions required that rescues be made from shore by breeches buoy, surfmen had to pull a heavy beach cart to the scene. Sometimes the crew hauled the cart for miles over hills and across soft sand—often fighting fierce head winds, rain, or hail. (U.S. Coast Guard)

Generally, life-saving stations were equipped with a lifeboat and surfboat, a life car, a line-throwing Lyle gun and faking box, a breeches buoy, a beach cart, lines, life preservers, Coston flares, medical kits, spare clothing for survivors, axes, shovels, lanterns, picks, and several dozen other pieces of equipment, all useful in rescuing seamen from ships in distress.

In addition to the keeper, there were usually eight surfmen at each station who worked six days a week and rotated duties. Typically, it took six to row the pulling boats (plus the keeper who handled the steering oar), leaving one man to stay ashore for lookout duty, and allowing the eighth his day off. At most California stations, patrols were operated only during the frequent summer fog, when the lookout's view was obscured, and during storms. Patrolling surfmen carried a lantern and Coston flares, which went off "like Roman candles" and were used for signaling ships to warn them off when they were too close inshore, or to let them know that their distress signals had been observed.

The station keeper, in addition to hiring personnel, submitting payrolls, and overseeing the men and equipment, had to lead most rescues personally. As if this were not enough, he had to provide lengthy, weekly reports that accounted for actions during rescues, listed every patrol, explained any damaged or lost equipment, justified any absences, and

Life cars were a very early rescue device of the Service. Metal-sheathed boats—life cars—were like small submarines that could pass through heavy surf. They were drawn between ships and shore much like a breeches buoy. At least Point Reyes and Humboldt Bay (and probably all the others as well) were equipped with life cars. (U.S. Coast Guard)

provided a myriad of other details for the District Superintendent's edification and enlightenment.

The year 1907 brought significant changes to the life-saving stations on the California Coast. After 29 years of gradually expanding West Coast operations, a new piece of equipment was introduced that was eventually to revolutionize rescue techniques. In that year, a new gasoline powered lifeboat arrived in San Francisco on the deck of a steamer. It was hailed locally as the first "power lifeboat" in the state, although in actual fact, Humboldt Bay Station may have received its lifeboat slightly earlier. The first motor lifeboat on the Pacific Coast had been introduced at the Cape Disappointment, Washington, station in 1905.

At any rate, when the men from the Fort Point station rowed over to the Union Ironworks to pick up the boat, "it was a day of great rejoicing" among the crew. Captain Cornelius Sullivan, a member of that crew, long remembered their elation as they towed the old pulling boat back to the station behind the new power craft. The back breaking hours of rowing would become a thing of the past. From these new motor lifeboats soon evolved the work horse of the U.S. Coast Guard's coastal life-saving operations, the self-righting and self-bailing 36-foot wooden motor lifeboat.

As 1907 drew to a close, northern California could boast a network of well-equipped life-saving stations, and the addition of the new powered res-

Golden Gate Park Station's surfmen and families pose with their beach cart and surfboat. (National Maritime Museum)

Beach Apparatus Drill at Golden Gate Park Station. The small cannon at the left is the Lyle gun, used to hurl a line from beach to ship so that a breeches buoy can be rigged. Each station had a drill pole to simulate a ship's mast. Surfmen became so proficient at rigging a breeches buoy to the drill pole that the entire operation could be done in less than three minutes. The Beach Apparatus Drill was practiced each week on Thursdays. (National Maritime Museum)

cue boat was yet another sign of progress in handling maritime disasters. It was not always so.

The United States Life-Saving Service began operations on the Atlantic Coast in 1871, and in 1878 extended its operations to California. The first station established in California was San Francisco's Golden Gate Park Station on Ocean Beach, which began operation on August 13, 1878. Its opening had been delayed since January, because no qualified man could be found who was willing to assume the rather awesome duties of the post at the low pay offered. A second station was opened a short time later on Humboldt Bay near Eureka, CA.

During the early days, the keepers of these two stations were the only front-line, paid Life-Saving Service personnel in California. The Pacific Coast District (comprised of California, Oregon, Washington, and Alaska) was by far the largest in the Service. It was also the most undermanned. By 1880, there were only six stations on the entire West Coast, four in the Pacific Northwest and two in California. Considering the length and danger of the district's coastline, six were few indeed—particularly when compared with the forty stations in New Jersey or with the 37 established in tiny District 3 (Rhode Island and Long Island).

Not only were the stations few in number, but initially, they were only manned by volunteer crews. When a shipwreck occurred, the keep-

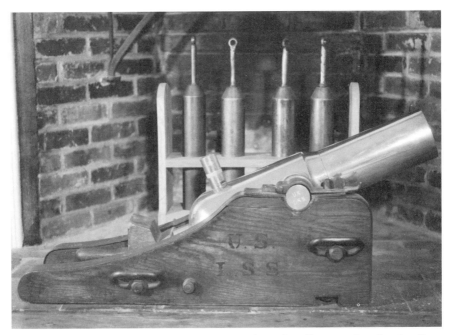

A U.S. Life-Saving Service Lyle gun and projectiles used to hurl a line from shore to ship in order to rig a breeches buoy. (Richard Boonisar)

er was expected to round up some volunteers and go to the rescue. Such a system resulted in delays in reaching the scene of the wreck and meant that the station's boats were often manned by inexperienced crews. When the schooner *Edward Parke* capsized on the Humboldt Bay bar, keeper Frederick Star had to obtain men from the crew of a ship docked near the life-saving station. The volunteers had difficulty in launching the heavy lifeboat, and when they finally arrived at the *Parke*, two seamen aboard the ship had already been swept away by the "fearful breakers".

In 1882, new funding allowed the stations to be fully manned during the winter season, although during the summer months only the keeper was employed. Such a policy showed that the East Coast based service had not yet learned to understand California weather patterns. San Francisco's heavy summer fog and strong onshore winds made winter only staffing completely inadequate at Bay Area stations.

Golden Gate Park Lifeboat Station's surfmen launching rescue boat on Ocean Beach in San Francisco. Before horses were issued, boat carriages and beach carts were pulled by hand, a backbreaking challenge. (National Maritime Museum)

Surfmen rowed lifeboats and surfboats offshore and purposely capsized and righted the boats. It was a dangerous feat, especially on rough days and often drew large crowds of onlookers. Humboldt Bay Life-Saving Station, pre-1915. (National Maritime Museum, Carl Christensen collection)

At times, however, Golden Gate Park station's keeper proved equal to his awesome responsibilities. When the Schooner *M. Mangles* stranded a few miles below Point Lobos in June 1882, the regular crew of the Golden Gate Park station had been paid off for the season and only the keeper remained on duty. After hiking down Ocean Beach, he arrived at the scene to find the *Mangles* eighty yards offshore and in danger of breaking up; and, no one on the beach to give him assistance. The keeper, alone and without equipment, dove into the surf and swam out to the ship. Once aboard, he ordered the schooner's yawl boat launched. Taking one crewman at a time, he rowed each ashore through the heavy surf, until all were saved. Two weeks later, the steamer *Escambia* sank, and again without help, the keeper spent the night searching the beach for survivors. He found four, including the ship's captain. The keeper took the men to the station, where he cared for them and clothed them from his own wardrobe.

The Golden Gate Park keeper had proved equal to the task on these two occasions, but his was the only life-saving station between Humboldt Bay and the Mexican border. The heavy traffic in and out of the Golden Gate demanded more than the services of one man. The next fiscal year (1883-84), funds were provided to staff both Golden Gate Park and Humboldt Bay stations with year-round crews. With the exception of the short-lived Bolinas Bay station, badly needed new stations for the approaches to San

A Life-Saving Service surfman on beach patrol burns a Coston flare to warn a ship away from a perilous beach. (Richard Boonisar)

Francisco Bay were not established until 1889, when Fort Point and Point Reyes Life-Saving Stations were built.

Working at Point Reyes proved to be one of the most dangerous assignments on the West Coast. During its first four years of operation, four of its crew were lost. Their tragic deaths well illustrate the hazards of a surfman's occupation. On December 12, 1890, the crew was dragging a boat up on Point Reyes Beach. A tremendous wave suddenly rushed in and overturned the heavy boat, fatally injuring two surfmen, Andrew Anderson and Fred Carstens. Then, less than three months later, another lifesaver, John Korpala, became ill with a fever, headache, and lung problems. He died March 3, 1891, in his room at the life-saving station. Undoubtedly, the exhausting work on cold, fogbound Point Reyes had contributed significantly to Surfman Korpala's illness. Two years later, on March 1, 1893, while the crew was training with the surfboat in the

Southside Life-Saving Station was one of two rescue facilities on San Francisco's Ocean Beach. Neat hedges were a common feature at life-saving stations and lighthouses. Large building is the main station, June 1923. (U.S. Coast Guard)

breakers, a huge wave struck again. The surfboat was violently turned over and George Larson was struck by the boat's wooden railing as she turned over, killing him instantly.[2]

The frustrations of trying to save lives without a crew took a toll of another kind up the coast at the Bolinas Bay Station. In the four years of its existence, the keeper had never had a regular crew, yet he was responsible for safety on dangerous Duxbury Reef. According to some historians, he had been driven to drink. Be that as it may, on April 15, 1885, the station caught fire. The local firemen, aware of the fact that the station contained ten pounds of gun powder for the Lyle gun, chose not to get too close to the rapidly burning building and the station was a total loss. Subsequent investigation showed the cause to be arson and the keeper the prime suspect. He was indicted and tried, later to be released after two juries failed to agree on his guilt. The station was not replaced until 1915. For the thirty intervening years, the crew of a ship stranded on Duxbury Reef could not expect prompt assistance there.

In addition to the ever-present danger, the job demanded the utmost in human strength and stamina. In the early years, the stations were not provided with horses for transport, and the surfmen were required to harness themselves to the heavy boat carriages and to the

[2]Surfman Larson's tombstone reads, "In Memory of George Larson, Surfman of the Point Reyes Life-Saving Station. Killed by the accidental capsizing of the surfboat while at practice drill. March 1, 1893. Aged 27 years. Died at his post of duty." His three fellow surfmen are buried beside him. The four graves are side by side on a tree covered little hill on wind blown Point Reyes. Coast Guardsmen and Park Rangers still care for the little cemetery.

Southside Life-Saving Station's boathouse opened onto San Francisco's Ocean Beach. Shifting sand dunes could be a problem here, 1923. (U.S. Coast Guard)

beach carts that carried the Lyle gun and other apparatus, and haul them to the scene of the wreck. Usually this was a journey of considerable distance over hills and sand and, often, it necessitated travelling over the high, rough terrain that lay in back of the beaches. An early report states:

> It is probable that to fully realize the heavy task involved, it would be necessary to actually see . . . seven surfmen harnessed to the loaded cart, violently tugging in oblique positions, almost inclined to the ground under the strain of the burden, as they toil toward the scene of a shipwreck.

The lack of horses meant slow progress and often an exhausted crew when they finally arrived at the wreck. The work was low-paid, even by the standards of the day, and there was no provision for disability or retirement. The work was not only hard and dangerous, but often damaging to a surfman's health. Understandably, there was a high turnover among the surfmen, and recruiting and retaining qualified personnel became a serious problem.

The job certainly didn't lack excitement, however. When the steam schooner *Mendocino* stranded on the Humboldt Bay bar in December 1888, the local life-saving crew went to the rescue. Rowing out through the waves breaking over the bar, the lifeboat was in continual danger of being swamped by the cresting water, while the troughs were so precipitous and deep that on several occasions the boat literally struck bottom. At one time or another, every oar was wrenched from the hands of the men, and four oars were actually broken. When they had completed their day's work, however, the surfmen had saved all on board but one.

A guardian of the Golden Gate. Surfman John Stoll stands watch at Southside Life-Saving Station on San Francisco's Ocean Beach scanning the Pacific for mariners in danger. (National Maritime Museum)

Sometimes the dedication shown and risks undertaken by the surfmen were unappreciated. In January 1890, a small fishing boat capsized in the dark shadow of Marin County's Point Bonita, with five men aboard. Darkness, and the fact that there was a strong southwester with rain and hail, made the accident invisible to the Life-Saving Service's lookouts on San Francisco's shore. The Point Bonita lighthouse keepers, however, saw the fishermen and soon lanterns glowed along the point, finally attracting the attention of a tug which carried the message to the City. While word spread throughout San Francisco, the fishermen continued to cling desperately to their boat's bow, the only portion still above water.

Golden Gate Park Station's north patrolman finally learned of the news at the Cliff House. He ran back to the station, giving the alarm. A Coston flare was burned to call in the South patrol, and the boat crew rolled out the surfboat on the boat carriage. Surf at Ocean Beach was too high to attempt a launching, and it was necessary to haul the boat overland to Baker Beach. The men took their positions on the boat carriage's drag ropes, and in the driving rain, began the long, uphill haul through the sand and mud. What was hard work under the best of conditions was made more difficult by a crew already short-handed

Surfmen on watch had plenty to see when the tanker **Frank H. Buck**
*went down in 1937. Golden Gate Park Lifeboat Station's lookout tower
at Land's End in San Francisco. The foundation of this building may
be seen just below the edge of the Point Lobos parking lot at the
overlook east of the memorial to the cruiser* **San Francisco**. *(National
Maritime Museum)*

through illness and by the absence of the south patrolman who took considerable time to catch up. At the Cliff House, the cart had to leave the
beach and traverse first the sand dunes to the east and then the muddy, chaparral covered hillsides to the north. A horse was borrowed but
fences and gates slowed progress, and eventually, a steep ravine forced
both horse and boat carriage to be abandoned. The boat then had to be
carried by hand through marshy springs, over rocks, and through brush
to reach the water.

When the crew reached Baker Beach, a strong ebb tide was running.

Once the surfboat was launched, it had to be worked well in toward Fort Point before the attempt could be made to cross the Golden Gate to the Marin shore. Four hours had elapsed since the patrolman had first heard the news at the Cliff House. When the surfmen finally arrived at the scene of the capsizing, nothing could be found. After a thorough search had been made, the defeated crew retraced their difficult route back to the station, arriving with the surfboat about 5 a.m. Although the men did not know it at the time, four of the fishing boat's crew had perished, the fifth being saved by a tug which had effected the rescue shortly before the arrival of the crew from the Life-Saving Station. It had been an exhausting, dangerous and frustrating night, and when the newspapers came out the next day, the Golden Gate Park crew was stunned to read the unfounded charges that it was their "utter inefficiency" that had accounted for the failure to save the four fishermen.

Any shortcomings of the Pacific Coast District of the United States Life-Saving Service could be traced directly to a lack of adequate funding by the Federal Government and to the fact that the Atlantic Coast and the Great Lakes had priority for new equipment and new stations. Horses had been supplied to some East Coast stations as early as 1885, and power lifeboats appeared "back East" several years before the first one was assigned to the West Coast. But considering the handicaps, California's surfmen did a very creditable job.

A major improvement in lifesaving protection at Ocean Beach occurred on March 2, 1894, when Southside Station was opened in San Francisco on a beautiful, tree-lined cove on Ocean Beach, at the outlet to the sea for Lake Merced. Ocean Beach had proved to be a particularly dangerous area, especially for the small Italian felucca fishing boats that frequently ventured too close to the breakers and were capsized or swamped in the surf. San Francisco's surfmen sometimes had to assist as many as four fishing boats at a time. The new station supplemented the coverage of Ocean Beach provided by Golden Gate Park Station, and was able to render more timely assistance to ships endangered by the rocky shores to the south.

Fort Point Station's principal responsibilities were the hazards presented by the approach and entrance to San Francisco Bay. The shoal waters of the bar and the Potato Patch were a constant danger. During the frequent summer fog or the gales of winter, the rocky headlands themselves formed dangerous, funnel-shaped walls along the approaches to the Golden Gate. Shipwrecks occurred with frightening frequency in Fort Point Station's jurisdiction, and weather conditions seemed to foretell one on the morning of January 3, 1895.

The wind had been rising alarmingly all morning and the lookouts from both Golden Gate Park and Fort Point's lookout towers kept a sharp watch on the water between the headlands and the Gate. They were particularly concerned with the wrecking schooner *Samson*,

Coston flares light up the night as surfmen gather on the beach in foul weather dress in this spectacular rescue scene. (Richard Boonisar)

which was spending the winter anchored off Point Bonita engaged in salvage operations.

Heavy rain and approaching darkness soon obscured the wrecking schooner. As the storm worsened to a gale, the *Samson* began to drag anchor. All efforts by her crew to prevent the schooner from being blown toward Point Bonita's towering cliffs failed, and those on board became increasingly alarmed at their situation. The wind reached 70 miles an hour and Point Bonita lighthouse keepers saw that the schooner was doomed—and, unless immediate assistance was forthcoming, the crew would share the ship's fate. The keepers repeatedly blew their fog signal in an effort to get the attention of the life-saving station patrols or lookouts, but the sound was lost in the noise of the wind and sea. About 1 a.m., the *Samson's* crew began burning torches, and they were seen by Fort Point's lookout. He burned a Coston flare in response and turned out the men at the station. The tug *Reliance* was called to Fort Point Life-Saving Station and she took the surfmen and their Lyle gun on board and the lifeboat in tow. Heading out into the waters of the Golden Gate, the little *Reliance* experienced extreme difficulty in making headway.

That the *Reliance* should have trouble was not surprising, for winds were so strong at Point Bonita that the lighthouse keepers "while mov-

Breeches buoy rescue at Punta Gorda. (National Maritime Museum)

ing about outside the buildings, were frequently compelled to crawl upon their hands and knees to avoid being blown over the cliff."

Meanwhile, the *Samson* continued to drag her anchor and drift toward the cliffs. The crew, in desperation, launched a yawl boat with two men aboard, which was immediately lost. The *Reliance*, meanwhile, had slowly continued to push into the seas, and as it approached the wrecking schooner, Keeper Hodgson of Fort Point Station surveyed the grim drama from the tug's bridge. Tremendous seas made any rescue attempt almost foolhardy, and the *Reliance's* captain so counseled Hodgson. But Hodgson had seen the *Samson* put over a second small boat which, if left unassisted, appeared certain to share the fate of the yawl boat. Under Hodgson's command, the surfmen set off from the tug in their pulling boat. The lifeboat struggled through huge seas, was nearly pitched upon the rocks, and ultimately lost four oars; but, when it returned, there were eight of the *Samson's* crew safely on board. Four men remained on the *Samson* when she hit the cliffs, but the lighthouse keepers were ready and three were saved.

With three San Francisco Bay stations now established, major wrecks increasingly came to mean coordinated action by the Bay Area's life-saving stations. On December 10, 1894, the schooner *William L. Beebe* broke her steering and drifted into heavy breakers at San Francisco's Ocean Beach. Golden Gate Park's lookout saw nine

The oiler of the steam schooner Tiverton *is rescued by breeches buoy. Chief Garner Churchill, Humboldt Bay Coast Guard Lifeboat Station's officer-in-charge, at left, directs the rescue. Humboldt Bay, 1933. (Wayne Piland)*

persons clinging to the rigging. He called out his own crew and then notified Southside and Fort Point. Southside brought out their Lyle gun and their breeches buoy; Golden Gate arrived with their surfboat; and Fort Point's crew set out aboard a tug. Thus, each station provided an alternate means of saving the crew in case other methods failed. Southside's breeches buoy was successful in bringing all nine survivors safely ashore; Golden Gate Park station provided the victims with shelter; and Fort Point's crew assisted by cleaning up the wreckage.

Tugs continued to be important in assisting the surfmen and sometimes more than one tug was needed. When the steamer *Olga* stranded two miles below San Francisco's Point Lobos, Golden Gate Park station called for tugs and then the surfmen rowed out to the stranded vessel. Three tugs soon arrived, along with Fort Point and Southside life-saving crews. The surfmen took soundings, ran lines to the tugs, and then—sizing up the situation—called for more tugs. Four more tugs arrived, along with 70 men to help jettison the cargo. With such massive assistance, the *Olga* was pulled free and towed to safety. The next day, it was off to Bolinas' Duxbury Reef for the same three life-saving crews. There, the steamer *Iaqua* was stranded. Despite a strong southwest wind, blinding rain squalls, and rough seas, all on board but one were saved. The next day, Fort Point's crew worked with tugs to save the ship as well. Coordinated rescues using several crews aided by tugs became a standard and highly successful rescue strategy.

In 1899 and 1903 respectively, two more stations, Point Bonita west of Sausalito in Marin County and Arena Cove at Point Arena in Mendocino County, had been added, strengthening the Life-Saving Service in California. These areas had been the scene of many wrecks and while Point Bonita and Point Arena both had fine lighthouses, the light keepers lacked both the equipment and the manpower necessary for full-scale rescue work. The light keepers had certainly tried to fill the gap, and Point Bonita wickie George D. Cobb had received the Life-Saving Service's silver medal for saving three lives in the late 1890s.

Despite the unhesitating help of lighthouse keepers, the burden of recurrent maritime accidents fell primarily upon the surfmen, and the hours on the job could be long indeed. September 3 and 4, 1904, were particularly long days for Southside's crew. The schooner *James A. Garfield*, carried by a strong tide toward San Francisco's breakers, stranded a quarter mile south of the station at 4:20 a.m.

Both the lookout and the patrol saw her, a tug was called and the surfboat launched. When the tug arrived, the surfmen rowed into the breakers with a line for the schooner. The *Garfield* was on the verge of destruction but, by using the surfmen's line, her crew was able to haul a hawser on board, enabling the tug to tow the schooner to safety. That same evening, at 6:30 p.m., the British ship *Drumburton* was reported fast aground 20 miles south of the station. Transporting their boat using a team of horses, the Southside crew spent all night hurrying to the *Drumburton*. All aboard the ship were saved, but the vessel became a total wreck.

It was a long trek back to their station, and when the Southside crew arrived home, they were to learn that the American steamer *Maggie* had stranded in thick fog west of Golden Gate Park station and that they were needed to assist that station and Point Bonita's surfmen in running lines to tugs attempting to haul the steamer afloat. *Maggie* was eventually towed to safety and Southside's crew went home for some rest. It would be just over a week before another major wreck would occur.

The surfmen were almost superhuman on land as well as at sea. The 1906 San Francisco Earthquake wrecked the Life-Saving Service storehouse in San Francisco, resulting in the loss of life-saving apparatus and other supplies stored within. Every life-saving station from Southside north to Arena Cove was damaged as chimneys fell, foundations cracked, and plastered walls ruptured. Fortunately, not a single member of the Service was killed or injured, and the crews of Point Bonita, Fort Point, Golden Gate Park, and Southside immediately went to work fighting the San Francisco fire, transporting supplies, aiding the homeless, and feeding the hungry.

At Golden Gate Park Station, Keeper Varney and his crew were human dynamos. They dug people out from under fallen brick, sheltered as many as 150 persons at a time at the station, fed and clothed hundreds more, acted as firemen and ambulance drivers, and hauled rations, supplies, and people, using the station team. Varney coordinated 15 horses with drivers and wagons borrowed to aid in the work. His station issued 30,000 rations to hungry citizens. Hundreds of people were fed at the crew's expense from the station mess, finally exhausting the station's supplies completely.

At Point Bonita, one of the light keepers' dwellings was badly shattered and the surfmen aided the family of Assistant Keeper Engel, who lived there. The Engel family was sheltered and fed in the life-saving station until an abandoned building could be converted to a temporary residence.

It was fitting that in 1907, the United States Life-Saving Service could reflect upon its accomplishments since 1871. Nationally, the Service had rescued over 121,000 people in more than 17,000 disasters. The Service had more than paid for itself economically as well as in human terms: nearly $200,000,000 worth of property had been saved, an incredible sum for the period.

The next year, the Service's *Annual Report* commented upon the public's attitude toward the Service. Increasingly, the surfmen were being called upon to assist in many difficulties which had little to do with shipwrecks. The crews found themselves frequently acting as physicians and nurses, often assuming the prerogatives of the police in apprehending suspects and recovering stolen property, becoming fire fighters, aiding imperiled swimmers, thwarting suicide attempts, and sheltering lost wayfarers. They had captured runaway boys, outlaws, runaway teams of horses, and lost pets. They had recovered lost horses, bicycles, buoys, loads of hay, automobiles, cows, hogs, bags of mail, fish nets, and even a balloon.

The geographical range of the Service's operations in California increased when the Fort Point crew took possession of their new power lifeboat in 1907. (The Coast Guard later used the term *motor* lifeboats for the same vessels.) The next year, the Life-Saving Service's *Annual Report* raved about the power lifeboats:

> They have more than doubled the scope of life-saving ser-
> vice at the stations where they are used, multiplying the
> opportunities for rendering assistance to distressed vessels

and persons because of the advantage their speed affords, and enabling the life-savers to reach scenes of disaster in good physical trim for the performance of their most difficult and perilous work.

An interesting and significant event occurred on November 18, 1907. The schooner *Lillebonne*, dismasted off Point Bonita, was aided by three craft rushing to her rescue. First to arrive was Point Bonita's pulling surfboat. A tug arrived next, but the third craft on the scene was Fort Point's new power lifeboat. The power lifeboat had arrived too late to help, as the tug had the *Lillebonne* in tow by then, but the motor lifeboat was used to tow the surfboat back to her station. It had not been an impressive start, being last to the rescue, but a new dimension had been added to life saving. It eventually reached nearly every station, altering the surfman's job and life style, just as the change from sail to steam had been revolutionizing the meaning of "sailor". Even though motor lifeboats were introduced by the Life-Saving Service, the surfmen are most remembered for their oar powered pulling boats. It was their successors, the Coast Guardsmen, who carved an image in the public's mind as rescuers in powerful, self-bailing and self-righting 36-foot motor lifeboats.

With the advent of power lifeboats, the U.S. Life-Saving Service began changing rapidly. In February 1908, the sloop *Edna* stranded on the Bay east of Fort Point Station. The power lifeboat was sent to the scene and unsuccessfully attempted to pull *Edna* free. The sloop's crew managed to free her at high tide and the power lifeboat then towed *Edna* to a safe anchorage. The power lifeboat was proving its worth, for the surfmen had been able to cope with a stranding without the aid of tugs. The use of gasoline powered boats was transforming rescue work, but it was also increasing the demands on surfmen. The *Annual Report* of 1909 speaks of a new type of boat: "gasoline powered pleasure boats", which had so frequently found themselves in trouble that by 1907 they amounted to 40 percent of all calls for assistance. This, too, was a change that became permanent; pleasure boats still comprise a significant percentage of Coast Guard search and rescue calls.

Despite the immediate success of motor lifeboats during the years just prior to the creation of the Coast Guard in 1915, the pulling surfboat still remained the most frequently used rescue boat. But the inroads were obvious already. The power lifeboat was virtually replacing the rowed lifeboat, and many of the pulling surfboats were being converted to power craft. By the 1930s, the pulling surfboat was reduced to an occasionally used adjunct of motor lifeboats. The pulling surfboat's twilight years saw it relegated to: (1) being towed by a motor lifeboat to remote locations where a landing from the sea was necessary, (2) entering the surf carrying a line from the power lifeboat, and (3) being taken by a truck and trailer to isolated beaches and launched.

Today, Coast Guard stations are no longer normally equipped with pulling surfboats.

The year 1909 saw an additional improvement in California life-saving facilities. The lighthouse keepers of the Farallon Islands were equipped with and trained to operate a Lyle gun and breeches buoy apparatus, and a small building was erected on Southeast Farallon Island to house the equipment. It was an unusual but wise step for the Life-Saving Service to train and equip Lighthouse Service personnel.

These years witnessed the first of many spectacular rescues where the Fort Point motor lifeboat raced to the San Francisco Bay bar to save small craft on the brink of drifting into the breakers. Under particularly adverse conditions, the power craft and its tow would put in at Point Bonita until weather conditions improved.

For long distance rescues, the old technique of having a larger vessel tow the lifeboat was used even with the power lifeboat. Such was the case when the revenue cutter *Snohomish* towed Fort Point's power lifeboat to Bolinas Point when the steamer *R.D. Inman* stranded there.

Despite the advent of power, long hours remained characteristic of the job. When the British steamer *Damara* stranded in 1910 off Fort Point, it was nine days before she was freed. The Fort Point crew spent the entire time on the scene, transferring wreckers and ship's crew between ship and shore by breeches buoy.

The last years before the creation of the Coast Guard saw the Life-Saving Service engaged in many classic and daring rescues. Among the most spectacular was the night in 1911 when the Point Bonita beach patrolman heard the whistle blasts of the steamer *Signal* as she lay among the breakers near San Francisco's Seal Rocks. There was a strong flood tide and a high sea running, and any rescue attempt was extremely risky. Despite the conditions, the Fort Point power lifeboat actually managed to maneuver alongside the vessel twice during the rescue operation, a daring feat among the high, rocky islets and massive waves.

By 1912, Point Bonita Life-Saving Station had also been equipped with a power lifeboat. It was used that year when an Oakland garbage barge, with eight men on board, was capsized by great seas and high winds a mile off the lighthouse. Speeding to the scene, the surfmen even hoisted their foresail to take advantage of the wind. Reaching the barge, they found a sea covered with wreckage and garbage. Conditions were so bad that the filthy, debris-filled waters were actually breaking over the

The drama of an actual rescue is vividly illustrated as the Bolinas Bay Coast Guard Station's crew struggles to reach the Yosemite *in 1926. Note their 36-foot motor lifeboat at left. The* Yosemite *was loaded with a cargo of dynamite and had struck Point Reyes. Placed in tow by the tug* Sea Ranger, *the* Yosemite *later sunk. (National Maritime Museum)*

Coast Guard to the rescue! Humboldt Bay Life-Saving Station's surfmen remove Navy sailors from the stranded cruiser U.S.S. Milwaukee *off Eureka's Samoa Beach in 1917. Coast Guardsmen also rescued the crew of a Navy submarine aground nearby. (Captain George Melanson)*

Interior of the Point Reyes Life-Saving Station boathouse. A life car hangs from the rafters and the crew stands alongside surfboats sitting on boat carriages, pre-1927. (Stella Hunt Soderberg photo, Jack Mason Museum)

lifeboat. The debris was so thick in one area that it was impossible for the lifeboat to remain amidst the wreckage. However, Surfman Johnson could see one of the barge's crew in the water and he plunged overboard and swam through the foul seas to save the sailor.

Also spectacular was the rescue of the crew of the steamer *Samoa* by Point Reyes' surfmen in 1913. Twenty-one men were brought ashore safely by breeches buoy despite fearsome breakers on Point Reyes Beach, one of the most violent beaches on the California coast. The breakers were throwing lumber about so violently that it was necessary for two surfmen to rush into the water as the breeches buoy neared shore and grab each sailor to protect him from flying timbers.

In 1913-14, the Bay's life-saving crews found they had an entirely new type of rescue on their hands. Adolph Sutro and others were testing their new "hydro-aeroplanes" and these had a tendency to turn over on landing or take-off. Fort Point's crew, in particular, began fishing pilots and planes from the Bay water, often only to have both back in the water a short time later.

The surfman's profession was a very dangerous one. This was the scene inside the boat room at Coquille River Life-Saving Station, Bandon, Oregon after the loss of three of its surfmen. Keeper Edward M. Nelson and surfmen Billy Green and Jimmie Sumner were lost April 12, 1892, during the capsizing of the surfboat by giant sneaker waves on the Coquille River bar. Point Reyes and Fort Point also suffered similar tragic loses. (Bandon Historical Society)

The 1914 *Annual Report of the Life-Saving Service* heartily approved a Senate bill combining the U.S. Life-Saving Service with the Revenue Cutter Service to form the modern Coast Guard. The report was justifiably proud that the Service could look back upon 43 years of existence during which its crews had saved over 150,000 lives and had annually saved property which exceeded the cost of maintaining the entire national system.

In 1915, the Life-Saving Service merged with the Revenue Cutter Service under a new name: The U.S. Coast Guard.

The humanitarian and financial benefits of the Life-Saving Service continued in the Coast Guard. The spirit and tradition of the Life-Saving Service lived on as well. Neither did the change in any way interrupt the daring rescues. The Coast Guard wasn't really new, but was a continuation of the Life-Saving Service, the Revenue Cutter

Point Reyes Life-Saving Station. The larger building housed the keeper and crew, the smaller building housed the surfboat and beach cart. Surfmen patrolled the beach for a mile on each side of the station. (National Maritime Museum)

Service, and ultimately also of the Lighthouse Service, all under a single new name. The rescue stations were manned by the same people operating the same stations with the same equipment. The traditions of valor remained.

The major change after 1915 was that the station keepers and surfmen were now under the command of Revenue Cutter service officers. The Life-Saving Service had operated with few officers above the level of officers-in-charge of local rescue stations. The Revenue Cutter Service, on the other hand, ran many ships and consequently had numerous officers in its ranks. Placing these officers in command above the Life-Station keepers was often unwelcome. Only the keeper and surfmen had detailed knowledge of local waters and the expertise in small boat handling required for efficient and safe rescue operations on bars and in the surf.

Thus, the lifeboat stations necessarily retained a fair degree of independence and appropriately continued their own traditions. But the first years of Coast Guard operation, through the mid-1920s, were very lean ones for everyone in the Coast Guard. Funding was inadequate and the results were devastating to the maritime community.

A good example occurred in late August 1920, when the steamer *Arakan* ran ashore in fog off Point Reyes Beach. The ship radioed for help, but the Coast Guard was unable to assist. According to historian Jack Mason, when the distress call went out to the Coast Guard, the

The historic Arena Cove Life-Saving Station in 1950. Largest building is the unique station built by the Life-Saving Service. Tall pole at left is the drill pole where the breeches buoy rescue was practiced. The round roofed quonset hut probably housed the Coast Guard's beach patrol during World War II. Lower building with open doors once housed the beach cart and other rescue equipment. (U.S. Coast Coast)

service was not prepared to assist. Point Reyes Lifeboat Station's motor lifeboat was in San Francisco for repairs, Bolinas Bay station had only a surfboat available, and Point Bonita's two motor lifeboats were in such poor condition that one had been out of service for a year. Point Bonita finally managed to get a motor lifeboat to the scene, but once there, "most of the time they were repairing the engine, not able to give any help." Point Reyes surfmen built a large fire on the beach, the traditional action to offer encouragement to the stranded mariners. Tugs from San Francisco finally arrived at Point Reyes and saved both the crew and the steamer. The Coast Guard was subject to painful and severe public criticism. The service admitted "an urgent need for better apparatus" and ordered an investigation.

Bolinas Bay Lifeboat Station's lookout tower. Surfmen stood watch here scanning the sea off Bolinas looking for mariners in distress. Although it looked much like a lighthouse, that was never its purpose and it was used only as lookout tower. Today the structure still stands but is imperiled by erosion, 1923. (U.S. Coast Guard)

A surfman's wedding. Newly wed surfman and his bride sit in the beach cart at Bolinas Bay Lifeboat Station. The beach cart normally was used to carry the Lyle gun and other rescue equipment to shipwrecks. Everyone including the station cook turned out for the wedding picture, 1934. (Howard Underhill)

The Bay Area lifeboats stations were eventually upgraded, most being equipped with reliable, high quality 36-foot motor lifeboats. The experiences at Point Reyes Lifeboat Station are representative of the type of rescues rendered by Bay Area Coast Guard stations during the period. In 1927, Point Reyes received a new lifeboat station as well being allotted two 36-foot motor lifeboats. Built on Drake's Bay, this was one of the finest new stations on the coast. The Coast Guardsmen were now ready for almost anything. And well they should be, for as Captain Charles Peterson of the steamer *Matsonia* put it, "Point Reyes is very dangerous. There is something there that draws ships in."

Thus, in 1929, the steam schooner *Hartwood*, carrying 26 persons and fully loaded, ran at full speed ahead onto Point Reyes rocks. An urgent distress call was broadcast and half of those on board managed to get

Bolinas Bay Coast Guard Lifeboat Station. Large building is the main station and to the right is the smaller structure which housed the beach cart and other rescue apparatus. The station's architectural style was a favorite of the newly formed Coast Guard around 1915, yet Bolinas Bay Lifeboat Station's historic building is but one of a few survivors across the nation, 1923. (U.S. Coast Guard)

Humboldt Bay Life-Saving Station was the second rescue station built in California. It has a lookout tower atop the roof and launchway for lifeboats, 1930. (Garner and Thora Churchill)

into the ship's one usable lifeboat. Point Reyes Lifeboat Station's Coast Guardsmen were prepared now. The Coast Guard motor lifeboat went out and quickly located the ship's lifeboat and rushed those on board to safety at the Drake's Bay lifeboat station. The Lyle gun and beach cart were then hauled up to the cliffs above the wreck. Captain Howard Underhill carefully aimed the Lyle gun, fired the little brass cannon, and its 18-pound projectile with attached rescue line soared over the wildly rocking *Hartwood*. Soon a breeches buoy was rigged and the surfmen began pulling the sailors ashore, one by one. But the *Hartwood* was rolling wildly in the huge swells. Every time the ship rolled, the breeches buoy line would alternately sag, then snap taut. This violent action could break the lifeline or even throw a person out of the breeches buoy and into the sea.

Point Reyes surfmen were experts with breeches buoy rescues and had earned service-wide acclaim "for one of the greatest rescues ever effected by breeches buoy" when they had saved the *Samoa's* crew in 1913. But increasing seas were now violently snapping the line to the *Hartwood* and after saving three men using this method, the Coast Guardsmen gave it up as too dangerous for those being brought ashore. The breeches buoy was kept rigged, however, in the hope that conditions would improve and its use could resume.

Trying another strategy, the surfmen brought their motor lifeboat alongside the heavily rolling *Hartwood* in an attempt to save the ten crewmen still on board. It was impossible to get close enough for the sailors to jump into the lifeboat, so a line was thrown to the crew. It was tied between ship and lifeboat and by hanging onto the line, the sailors began making their way across the waves to the bobbing motor lifeboat. The *Hartwood*, however, was in danger of breaking up at any moment, so Coast Guardsmen on shore resumed using the breeches buoy. By combining the two rescue techniques, all were saved. It was none too soon as the *Hartwood* went to pieces rapidly.

The next year, in 1930, the tanker *Richfield* was just off Chimney Rock near the Point Reyes Lifeboat Station when a massive wave knocked her onto the rocky outcroppings and ripped out her hull. The Coast Guard lookout had seen the wreck happen and the 36-foot motor lifeboat went to the rescue. The tanker's cargo of gasoline poured into the sea, creating the danger of a surface fire, but the Coast Guardsmen went in anyway and saved the *Richfield's* entire crew. The surfmen then tried to salvage the tanker, but the heavy seas pounded the damaged hull until she was a complete wreck.

During a winter night in 1931, the steamer *Munleon* left San Francisco bound for the Pacific Northwest. It was windy with rough seas as the steamer passed the *San Francisco Lightship* and changed course toward Point Reyes light. Beyond the lightship somehow *Munleon's* course became confused. A sudden area of fog was encountered. The mate, now piloting the ship, thought that he must by now be safely beyond Point Reyes' headlands. But things did not seem quite right and the mate and the quartermaster

Point Arguello Lifeboat Station in Santa Barbara County was the only classic, traditional-style lifeboat station built in southern California, C. 1940. (U.S. Coast Guard)

became concerned. It was too late. Point Reyes lighthouse loomed ahead in the fog. The captain, below deck, simultaneously felt his ship sliding over rocks. He ran to the wheelhouse only to see a cliff rising hundreds of feet above him. As the ship continued to move forward, he realized that the *Munleon* would slam into the headlands. The ship struck with a force that almost threw the off-duty crew from their bunks. Everyone was stunned. The captain looked up and saw Point Reyes lighthouse to the northwest shining "straight and clear." He grabbed the mate, who had been in command on the bridge, shouting, "There's Point Reyes! We haven't passed it! We're not even abeam of it!" But anger could never save a ship.

The *Munleon's* plight was not promising. A gale was blowing, it was dark and seas were formidable. The *Munleon* began filling with water quickly, settling between huge offshore rocks. There was time for a brief distress

Point Reyes Coast Guard Lifeboat Station about 1928. On the launchway can be seen at left the 36-foot class "H" motor lifeboat and at its right the pulling lifeboat, C. 1928. (Point Reyes National Seashore)

call before flooding silenced the radio. Now, only signal flares were left to call for help.

Fortunately, the *Munleon's* single distress call was heard. Point Reyes surfmen rushed out to the wreck in their 36-foot motor lifeboat and began the hazardous task of taking the crew off the ship. Working among large rocks in a gale was very dangerous and required experienced seamanship. As the veteran Coast Guardsmen say, it's almost always rough off Point Reyes light. But in three trips that night with only the lighthouse beams and a compass for guidance, the Coast Guardsmen saved all on board.

Point Reyes Lifeboat Station's heroic rescues of stranded steamers were typical of those performed by all California Coast Guard lifeboat stations during the period from 1915 through the 1950s. In 1960, however, a marine tragedy of a totally unexpected type occurred.

On the cold, rainy night of November 23, 1960, Point Reyes Lifeboat Station had answered a seemingly routine distress call.

The famous 36-motor lifeboat Number 36542 *in service on Bodega Bay in 1975. She was much beloved by her Coast Guard crews. She is the last old time Coast Guard motor lifeboat still operating on the Pacific Coast and is now owned by Point Reyes National Seashore. This is the lifeboat whose crew mysteriously disappeared off Point Reyes lighthouse in 1960. David Kissling (at right) is coxswain. (R. Shanks)*

Point Reyes claimed many a vessel. Lumber steamer Hartwood *on the rocks in 1929. (Howard Underhill)*

The 36-foot motor lifeboat assigned to respond to the call, *Number 36542*, was the station's pride. Built at Curtis Bay, Maryland, by the Coast Guard in 1953, *36542* had begun her career at Arena Cove Lifeboat Station and then had been transferred to Point Reyes. She was just the thing to handle a distress call on a stormy night. A disabled commercial fishing boat needed towing into Bodega Bay. The *Thirty-six* and her crewmen, Coxswain Mark Anthony Holmes and Engineman Hugh James McClements, responded to the distress call, successfully locating the fishing boat and completed the slow tow into Bodega Bay. After dropping off the fishing boat, the two man Coast Guard crew then headed *36542* out of the harbor. Seas were rough and piloting the open motor lifeboat in the rain and spray must have made the trip back toward Point Reyes seem long. Perhaps talk revolved around the coming day, which would be Thanksgiving. About three miles north of Point Reyes lighthouse, the *Thirty-six* radioed the lifeboat station to expect them to tie up in about an hour. Then nothing else was heard.

The motor lifeboat did not arrive as expected. The Coast Guardsmen at the Drake's Bay station became concerned. Enormous waves along the coast didn't ease their fears, but the *Thirty-six* had been designed to handle even the worst sea conditions. The *36542* was self-bailing, self-righting, with water-tight compartments and had

The tanker Richfield *was another victim of Point Reyes, sinking off Chimney Rock in 1930. (Howard Underhill)*

Steamer Munleon *rammed Point Reyes' rocks and sunk in 1931. (Howard Underhill)*

been built of cypress and oak, the best wood available. For all practical purposes, she was as close to an unsinkable boat as could be designed. Why hadn't she come home?

The next morning, Thanksgiving Day, she was found. The *Thirty-six* had run ashore on Point Reyes Beach between the lighthouse and the RCA communications station. The motor lifeboat was in fine condition, her engine was even running, although it was overheated from being out of the water. A careful inspection revealed that *36542* was completely seaworthy. Oddly, though, her tow rope was wrapped around the hull three times. Worst, her crew had disappeared.

A massive search began using Coast Guard patrol boats, planes and helicopters. Coast Guardsmen and volunteers hiked through miles of soft sand searching for the crew. Mounted posses covered the beaches and headlands of Marin and Sonoma counties. It was to no avail. By the end of the year, the bodies of the two lifeboatmen washed ashore.

What had happened? How could two skilled seamen be lost aboard a perfectly seaworthy boat? By February 1961, the *36542* had been repaired and returned to service at Point Reyes Lifeboat Station. She was such a fine vessel that she continued her career and later served well at Bodega Bay, Fort Point and Yerba Buena Island Coast Guard stations. Eventually, she became the last active Coast Guard 36-foot wooden motor lifeboat on the state's coast,

Bodega Bay Coast Guard Station with its lookout tower overlooking the Bodega Harbor entrance, 1985. (R. Shanks)

Bodega Bay Coast Guard's 44-foot motor lifeboat Number 44324 *operating on Bodega Bay in 1987 under coxswain Mark Galusha. This is the vessel which saved the most lives during the capsizing of the charterboat* Merry Jane *in 1986. Like the older 36-footers, the 44-footers are self-bailing, self-righting and feature water tight compartments. They are nearly unsinkable. (R. Shanks)*

outlasting all her California sisters. Only the 36-footer at Coast Guard Station Depoe Bay, Oregon, would remain in active Coast Guard duty longer.

So how could her crew mysteriously die at sea with such an exceptional boat in excellent operating condition? Her later crews wondered this, too. I sailed with her crew out of Bodega Bay Coast Guard station on *36542* in 1975. As we experienced the slow, heavy rolls of the *Thirty-six* near the harbor entrance, her crew shared their feelings. When she had been found, her tow line had been wrapped around her three times. This would indicate that she had capsized three times. It was common, as we were doing that very moment, to run thirty-six foot motor lifeboats without being strapped in. The night her crew was lost was dark, rainy, and rough.

Huge sneaker waves, sometimes 20 or 30 feet high occur along the Pacific Coast. They can appear when only moderately rough conditions are prevailing, and are always much larger than whatever size waves are predominant at the time. It is not uncommon for

Bodega Bay Lifeboat Station's officer-in-charge Scott Richardson stands in front of his station. Chief Warrant Officer Richardson is a third generation Coast Guardsman, 1989. (R. Shanks)

there to be several sneaker waves, often three, in immediate succession.[3]

The *Thirty-six's* crew thought they knew what had happened that terrible night off Point Reyes. In the darkness, three large freak waves could have hit the vessel by surprise. The waves would have been difficult to see coming; on dark nights sailors often only notice the enormous sneaker wave's white crest just before it hits. The massive waves could have hit the motor lifeboat broadside and capsized her, spilling her crew into the ocean. The *Thirty-six*, responding as she had been designed to do, would have righted herself and kept on going, moving swiftly out of reach of the Coast Guardsmen in the water. With their boat gone, the cold, rough seas and strong currents made reaching shore safely impossible.

It was one of the most ironic tragedies of the sea. A boat and crew who had saved so many lives lost theirs because their boat was so perfectly seaworthy. A lesser boat would have been broken up by immense waves and there might have been something to cling to, perhaps even something to climb onto. A *Thirty-six* was too well built to break up, too well designed to sink, and too well engineered to stop running.

Today *36542* is back at Point Reyes, the last operating 36-foot motor lifeboat on the Pacific Coast and apparently, but one of two operating *Thirty-sixes* in the country. She is now owned by the Point Reyes National Seashore and I can attest that she still handles beautifully. Coast Guard lifeboat men from San Francisco to Puget Sound still talk about her. Many hold her in deep affection for she is one of the last of a heroic breed. Bodega Bay Coast Guard Station's crew has taken a special interest in her and under the leadership of Chief Warrant Officer Scott Richardson has helped the Park Service restore the beloved old motor lifeboat.

The Point Reyes Lifeboat Station is being restored by the National Park Service to full operating condition, complete with operating marine railway. At scheduled times it should be possible once again to watch *36542* gliding down the Coast Guard launchway and into Drake's Bay. It is the last place on the entire Pacific Coast where you can see such a sight. The station, launchway, and motor lifeboat are national maritime treasures and have been nominated as National Historic Landmarks.

Besides Point Reyes, five other California lifeboat stations are of

---

[3]Jon Humboldt Gates book, *Night Crossings*, provides detailed accounts of huge sneaker waves on the Humboldt Bay bar drawn from Coast Guardsmen, bar pilots, and commercial fishermen. See also the author's *Lighthouses and Lifeboats on the Redwood Coast*, especially the chapter on Trinidad Head light station.

great historic significance.[4] Golden Gate National Recreation Area's Fort Point Coast Guard Station is the only location on the West Coast where both a complete U.S. Life-Saving Service Station and a Coast Guard Lifeboat Station may be seen together. The Fort Point Life-Saving Station was built the same year (1889) as Point Reyes' long gone Life-Saving Station and is a twin to that facility. It is the best surviving example of a life-saving station on the West Coast, being complete with station and boathouse. The Coast Guard lifeboat station, with its look-

[4]Golden Gate Park, Southside, and Point Bonita Life-Saving Stations were all discontinued and razed between 1946 and the early 1960s.

Bow of the Coast Guard cutter Taney *lifts completely out of the water in a huge swell estimated to be 75-feet in height from trough to crest. San Francisco bar, February 1960 storm. (National Maritime Museum)*

out atop the roof, is an unique and excellent example of early station architecture and is also very historic.

Humboldt Bay Coast Guard Lifeboat Station at the town of Samoa, across the harbor from Eureka, CA, represents the culmination of classic Coast Guard lifeboat station design and the pinnacle of lifeboat station architecture. It retains its launchway and has been called the most beautiful Coast Guard station in the country.

Bolinas Bay and Arena Cove Life-Saving Stations still stand, nearly completing a tragically short list of surviving rescue stations. Both are exceptionally fine examples of unique architectural styles and also deserve inclusion on the National Register of Historic Places. Bolinas Bay and Arena Cove both retain their lookout towers nearby and Arena Cove also boasts its boathouse and the building which held the beach cart and Lyle gun.

Point Arguello lifeboat station in Santa Barbara County survives after having had its boathouse torn down by Vandenburg Air Force Base. It is a 1930s style classic station, now used as a recreation building. It is lovely and historic, and deserves historic preservation. It is the only old style classic lifeboat station in southern California.

It is hoped that we can make the same progress in saving our historic life-saving and lifeboat stations as we have with our equally important lighthouses. It is the least we can do to honor those great surfmen who stood ready since 1878 to launch their boats under the worst conditions to save the lives of people they had never even met. The rescue stations and lighthouses symbolize the most altruistic and daring aspects of our maritime past. There is no richer maritime heritage in America.

It is important to emphasize that the heritage of our lifeboat stations is a living one. Coast Guard men and women stand watch this very moment still ready to go out in the worst weather and risk their lives to save those in distress at sea. They stand watch at Coast Guard stations on coasts of the Pacific and Atlantic Oceans, as well as on the Great Lakes.

California's Bodega Bay Lifeboat Station is one outstanding example. Located north of Point Reyes on the Doran Beach sand spit at the entrance to the busy commercial fishing port of Bodega Bay, this lifeboat station is the direct descent of Point Reyes' historic lifeboat station. It was created in the 1960s when the Coast Guard moved its search and rescue operations from Point Reyes to Bodega Bay. The Bodega Bay Lifeboat Station is a modern flat-roofed building but it retains much of the feel of the older, classic stations. The station building includes a watch tower for scanning the harbor entrance, a radio room where distress calls are received, two offices, a day room, recreation room, galley, and sleeping quarters for those on duty. Two 44-foot motor lifeboats, a 30-foot motor surfboat, a high powered inflatable boat, and the 82-foot patrol boat *Point Chico* are stationed here. The *Forty-fours* and the *Point Chico* are the heart of the Bodega Bay search and rescue operations.

The station's files contain many newspaper accounts documenting the role it plays in the waters from Point Reyes north to the Sonoma-Mendocino County line at Gualala. In the files, articles and bold headlines hint of the stories, "Dramatic Bodega Rescue", "One missing, one saved in Bodega Bay shipwreck", "Dramatic Rescues on the Coast". The newspapers remind us that the legacy of the Life-Saving Service lives here. Surfmen (and women) still go to sea in the rescue boats and face the sea's eternal dangers.

One such case occurred on the afternoon of February 8, 1986. The 65-foot charter boat *Merry Jane* was returning from a sports fishing trip. It had been a two-hour run through long, westerly swells as she headed in from the fishing grounds at Cordell Bank. As the *Merry Jane* was approaching the harbor entrance, she passed between Bodega Head and Bodega Rock, a commonly used passage but one which becomes dangerous in heavy weather. Sea conditions appeared safe enough to use this shortcut into Bodega Bay.

But a large storm had raged far out in the central North Pacific Ocean for the previous five days. This storm was never closer than 1500 to 2000 miles from Bodega Bay. But the Pacific Ocean is the world's largest body of water and waves can travel for thousands of miles unhindered. It is the Pacific Ocean which has produced both the largest storm waves and the largest seismic waves known to man.

As the *Merry Jane* approached Bodega Head, her captain radioed a preceding vessel that was making the passage and learned that sea conditions were good. He could also see that there was a wide area through the channel free of any breakers. The *Merry Jane*, with 51 people on board, entered the channel.

The charter boat only had one warning as she headed through the passage, a swell broke off the vessel's starboard side toward Bodega Rock. A breaking swell is a sailor's warning sign. When swells begin to break, the vessel is in danger, especially on bars and narrow passages.

Soon after the breaking swell was seen, a huge wave struck the charter boat from her port side. The stern and then the entire vessel rose sharply upward. The mighty wave overpowered the *Merry Jane* and turned her broadside. The vessel heeled 90-degrees starboard, literally turning on her side! People began tumbling into the sea. Some fell off the deck and others were swept from the flying bridge. Fourteen people were suddenly struggling in the water. Then a second massive wave struck. More people were washed overboard. The desperate captain turned the vessel to face the waves, struggling to avoid another near capsizing. The *Merry Jane* hit another substantial breaking wave head on. Someone else was carried off the foredeck by that wave. Nineteen people were now in the water. Not one was wearing a life jacket. A deck hand rushed to the ship's radio and broadcast a distress call. Huge waves, breaking surf and 19 people in the water without life jackets—it was a nightmare come true.

Coast Guard Station Bodega Bay heard the call and instantly responded. Forty-four foot motor lifeboat *Number 44324* was underway in moments under the command of coxswain John Walsh. It sped past a commercial fishing vessel, *Sea Dog III*, also rushing to scene. The captain of the *Merry Jane* was desperately trying to pull his passengers from the water. Floatation devices had been thrown overboard in an attempt to help those struggling in the water. The Coast Guard *Forty-four* and the *Sea Dog III* arrived in minutes and began pulling people from the water. But there were many people and time was running out.

Back at Bodega Bay Lifeboat Station, another highly skilled Coast Guard Coxswain, Dominic "Nick" Rice, grabbed a 16-foot motor utility boat and with a volunteer crew sped out to the scene. Going out to an area with huge waves in a 16-foot boat was not standard procedure but Coxswain Rice had a plan. He carried a surfboard with him.

As the 16-foot Coast Guard boat passed beyond the harbor entrance jettys, Dominic Rice could see victims and debris in the water ahead. He could also see large waves breaking between Bodega Head and Bodega Rock. Ahead of him was a line of surf and inside the impassable breakers, the coxswain could see two survivors struggling, a man and a boy. But the 16-foot boat could not pass through the surf and the motor lifeboat, which could, was busy at the desperate task of saving other struggling people.

Coast Guardsman Rice turned the 16-footer over to one of his seamen and launched his surfboard. He began paddling through the surf, passing a body on the way. Rice reached the man who told him he could hold on a bit longer, so the coxswain went to save the boy. Dominic Rice pulled the youngster onto the surfboard and carefully brought him back through the pounding surf to the safety of the 16-footer. The Coast Guardsman then repeated his heroic trip and saved the man, again using the surfboard.

A third Coast Guard vessel, the 30-foot motor surfboat, had now arrived and aided the search. With incredible efficiency the Coast Guard 44-foot motor lifeboat crew had saved five people from the water and recovered four bodies.

The *Merry Jane* had picked up two survivors and had 30 passengers plus her crew safely on board. The *Sea Dog III* also had one survivor on board, plus a drowned person. Many of those on all three vessels needed prompt medical attention and it was decided to get them to the Bodega Bay station immediately. With the motor surfboat now on scene, the 44-foot motor lifeboat, the 16-footer, the *Merry Jane*, and the *Sea Dog III* all headed in to the Coast Guard Station.

Medical assistance had been called and soon survivors, emergency medical personnel, the news media, and relatives and friends of those on board all converged on the Bodega Bay Lifeboat Station. It was an extremely hectic and emotional situation, and for some, a heartbreaking and difficult time.

Coast Guard and Sheriff's Department helicopters began arriving offshore but could find no survivors. Coast Guard men and women then began searching the beaches for possible survivors. The motor lifeboat and motor surfboat crews refused to give up, hunting until after midnight. But no additional survivors were found. A total of 19 people from the *Merry Jane* had ended up in the water and ten were saved. The nine tragic deaths marked this as one of the area's worst shipwrecks in recent years. The brave Bodega Bay crew was widely praised. The heroic coxswain, Dominic Rice, with his tiny boat and surfboard, received the Coast Guard lifesaving medal for his efforts. All the Coast Guard and commercial fishing personnel had acted with valor.

And so, as we conclude this book, it is important to remember that we have been speaking of maritime history and heritage. But we also have been speaking of the present and of the future. Most of the lighthouses will once again guide mariners tonight. And the lifeboat station crews will stand by their radios and in the lookout towers. The ancient motto of the surfman, "You have to go out, but you don't have to come in", is still remembered. The motor lifeboats and motor surfboats are ready. The heritage and valor continues.

Humboldt Bay Coast Guard rescue craft off lifeboat station. Left to right: 82-foot patrol boat Point Winslow, *44-foot motor lifeboat Number 44396, and a 30-foot motor surfboat, 1988. (U.S. Coast Guard–Paul Powers)*

The last officer-in-charge of Fort Point Lifeboat Station was Senior Chief Richard "Rick" Dixon, at right. He is being congratulated by the Commandant of the 13th Coast Guard District upon receiving a life-saving medal for extreme valor on the Tillamook Bay bar, in Oregon in 1978. When Fort Point station was decommissioned March 23, 1990 it was the last Coast Guard station on the Pacific Coast still using the original buildings of the U.S. Life-Saving Service. (U.S. Coast Guard)

Last active lighthouse tender in America is the proud Fir. *At this time she still serves several lighthouses and countless buoys from her home port on Lake Union at Seattle, Washington. Her preservation is of national importance, 1969. (U.S. Coast Guard)*

PRESERVATION OF LIGHT STATIONS AND LIFEBOAT STATIONS

The period from 1946 through the mid-1970s saw tragic destruction occur at many historic light stations and lifeboat stations. During the 1950s it was not uncommon for valuable and historic buildings to be torn down or burned to the ground. Well into the 1960s, lighthouses were decapitated by having their lantern rooms cut off. As late as the 1970s, keepers' residences, fog signal buildings, and other important light station structures were destroyed. Fresnel lenses were unnecessarily removed from lighthouse lantern rooms. Lifeboat station launchways and lookout towers were ripped out and even entire stations destroyed. Today, thanks to greatly increased public and governmental awareness of the vital importance of our American maritime heritage, care of our historic light and lifeboat stations has somewhat improved.

My wife Lisa and I have spent years visiting and revisiting lighthouses and lifeboat stations in all regions of the country, including the Pacific Coast, New England and the Middle Atlantic states, Chesapeake Bay, the South, and the Great Lakes. We have covered over 200 stations. From research and these trips some important lessons were learned.

WHO IS PRESERVING AMERICA'S LIGHT STATIONS AND LIFEBOAT STATIONS?

The two groups doing more to preserve America's treasured lighthouses and life-saving stations are the U.S. Coast Guard and the National Park Service. The Coast Guard maintains hundreds of lighthouses and the Park Service has about sixty in its jurisdiction. They spend more money, devote more hours, and have responsibility for more of our light and life-saving stations than anyone else in the nation. While both organizations have a few officials who are not supportive of our maritime treasures, the majority of staff in both the Coast Guard and the Park Service work hard and care deeply about America's lifeboat stations and light stations. These two organizations represent many of the best traditions of American government service.

I would like to cite two representative examples. In July 1989, we visited Craighill Lower Range Lighthouse, an attractive offshore caisson lighthouse on Chesapeake Bay. The crew of the Coast Guard buoy tender *Red Cedar* was working in the searing, humid heat restoring the historic sentinel. The conditions were so difficult that one crew member had passed out from heat exhaustion. Yet, the work went on and the enthusiasm and caring of the *Red Cedar's* officers and crew was

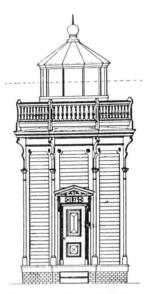

Original plans for Yerba Buena Island lighthouse. (Nautical Research Center)

impressive. Down Chesapeake Bay, the crew of the Coast Guard cutter *Morro Bay* was restoring Thomas Point light and the Kennebec aids to navigation team on vessel *55121* had just recently completed work on Newport News Middle Ground light. All are offshore lighthouses. We were with members of these crews and I can assure you that all this work was done under very difficult conditions, yet with a real sense that something of lasting value was being accomplished. Some Coast Guard units "adopt" a historic light or lifeboat station and spend many hours restoring and maintaining it. Without the Coast Guard, countless light stations, particularly those treasures offshore, would be lost. Most people in the Coast Guard do care about the Service's heritage.[1]

A second wonderful example involves several of the National Park Service's acclaimed coastal parks that have carefully preserved life-saving stations and recreated the famous beach apparatus drills of the early Coast Guard. Park Service staff in National Seashores at Cape Hatteras, NC; Cape Cod, MA; Fire Island, NY; Sleeping Bear Dunes,

---

[1]So why has there been criticism of the Coast Guard's care of our lighthouses? Unfortunately, there have been a few individuals periodically in charge of Coast Guard lighthouses who lacked understanding of historic preservation values. These few uncaring individuals have sometimes destroyed buildings, removed lenses, refused to approve maintenance, and not followed the Coast Guard's own goal of preserving the light stations (and lifeboat stations). They represent a tiny percent of the officers, but account for almost all of the preservation problems.

MI; as well as Gateway National Recreation Area, NY, all perform the time honored breeches buoy drill with complete accuracy using the Lyle gun to throw the rescue line and then rigging the breeches buoy. Many hours of hard work is involved in obtaining correct equipment and complete uniforms and in studying and practicing for the breeches buoy demonstration. Park visitors witnessing this popular program gain unequaled insight into early Coast Guard rescue work and our maritime heritage. Without the National Park Service, our early maritime rescue operations would never come alive again and our precious heritage would be lost. (Point Reyes National Seashore hopes to soon begin breeches buoy demonstrations.)

Two other groups of dedicated people need special mention. These are our magnificent local historical and preservation societies and our state parks. Many exceptionally good preservation projects have been carried out by these caring people. Examples in California include the California State Department of Parks and Recreation; East Brother, Inc.; Point Arena Lighthouse Keepers Association; Del Norte County Historical Society; City of Pacific Grove; Humboldt Bay Maritime Museum Association, and many others. They have their fine counterparts elsewhere in the state and across the nation. Many stations owe their continued preservation to the people of these important groups as well.

TRENDS IN LIGHTHOUSE AND
LIFEBOAT STATION PRESERVATION

First, there is the vastly increased number of preservation projects underway by local preservation and historical organizations and responsible government agencies. Second, there is usually the important realization that *all* the buildings at a station must be preserved in order to adequately understand the life that went on there. At one time it was thought sufficient just to preserve the lighthouse while neglecting all the other important station buildings. Mostly this has been overcome, although in Maine, I noticed many of their unique and historically important fog bell towers being allowed to decay. In most of the country the lighthouses and station buildings look much better than ten years ago. In Florida, however, the famous reef lighthouses off the Florida keys desperately need restoration work. Several Coast Guard people mentioned that their requests for funds for proper maintenance had not been heeded. The Florida reef lights (American Shoal, Fowey Rocks, Sand Key, Carysfort Reef, Alligator Reef, and Sombrero Key) are national treasures. Hopefully, the Coast Guard will soon budget the funds to carefully maintain these sentinels. There should eventually be a Reef Lights National Monument.

In California, two of our greatest lighthouses desperately need immediate preservation. Cape Mendocino in Humboldt County and St. George Reef in Del Norte County sit completely abandoned by the

"America's greatest lighthouse" and "King of Pacific Coast lighthouses" are but two of the superlatives maritime historians have applied to St. George Reef lighthouse. Located northwest of Crescent City, CA, this lighthouse has been declared excess property by the Coast Guard and desperately needs preservation. Hopefully, Redwood National Park will include St. George Reef lighthouse in its boundaries. It would be a national shame to lose what may be the Pacific Coast's most significant lighthouse and one of the greatest engineering triumphs in American history. (U.S. Coast Guard)

Coast Guard and cry out for help. This is especially ironic since St. George Reef light is probably the greatest lighthouse in America. This lighthouse has been transferred to the General Services Administration (GSA) as excess property. If it is not saved soon, it will be lost. Ideally, both lighthouses should be transferred to Redwood National Park. Maritime history is so closely intertwined with the history of the redwoods on the California north coast that this national park should include interpretation of St. George Reef, Cape Mendocino, and neighboring lights. In Cape Mendocino's case, the iron plate lighthouse may have to be relocated on higher ground on the light station property to prevent it from falling into the sea. It should also be refurbished by the Coast Guard and kept at Cape Mendocino. This needs careful planning and immediate attention. Cape Mendocino is an area that can rival Point Reyes National Seashore for historic and ecological importance. I can't begin to tell you the pain former light keepers and Coast Guardsmen feel seeing St. George Reef and Cape Mendocino being destroyed by neglect. Redwood National Park Superintendent Bill Ehorn has stated he would like to see St. George Reef lighthouse become a part of the Park. Residents of Del Norte County and the Board of Supervisors want to save the lighhouse and it is hoped they and the National Park Service will together succeed.

SOME SUGGESTIONS TO IMPROVE
OUR HISTORIC PRESERVATION WORK

Certainly the most obvious is the recent misguided pattern of removing classical Fresnel lenses from their rightful home in the lighthouses. There is no good reason for lens removal. Coast Guard automation methods have varied both over time and geographically. The best techniques involve simply automating the Fresnel lens. When a classic lens ends up in a museum, it's often a sign of failure and museum staff are forced to rescue a lens. One veteran lighthouse man colorfully put it this way, "Taking the lens out of a lighthouse is almost like killing a whale to display its bones."

Many museum people have accepted lenses simply because there was no one else willing and qualified to display them. In many cases, museum staff have made heroic efforts to save our Fresnel lenses. A number have expressed interest in seeing lenses returned to the lighthouse whenever possible. Unfortunately, this is not always possible. For example, Farallon Islands lighthouse lens has been preserved by the Treasure Island Museum in San Francisco because the Farallons light had its lantern room removed. Unless Farallons' lantern room was rebuilt, this would, of course, not be possible.

Unbelievably, lenses are still occasionally being removed from lighthouses even today.[2] This is rarely necessary. The best preservation projects place the classical lens in the lighthouse lantern room where it belongs. I am really proud that we have been able to do that at Point

---

[2]In the year 1989 alone two lighthouses in California faced lens removal threats. Point Cabrillo in Mendocino County almost had its lens removed by the Coast Guard to become an exhibit. Fortunately, Mendocino County historians led by John Sisto of the Point Arena Lighthouse Keepers Association strongly protested and the lighthouse was saved. Point Cabrillo's lens would remain in the tower. The Coast Guard graciously issued a formal apology. The officer who had made the decision was genuinely unaware of historic preservation values.

At Los Angeles Harbor lighthouse the results were far less fortunate. The lens was removed and given to a local maritime museum. Those who protested at Los

Cape Mendocino lighthouse and Sugar Loaf Rock. This rugged and historic site is a marine and ecological treasure crowned with a magnificent Pacific Coast style lighthouse. August 1989. (R. Shanks)

Bonita, Point Reyes, Point Arena, Pigeon Point, Point Cabrillo, Yerba Buena, Point Hueneme, Point Conception, Point Pinos, and many other California lighthouses. It would be wonderful to have all these lenses lighted. For example, I'd like to see Point Sur's lens restored to the lantern room. The Allen Knight Maritime Museum in Monterey helped preserve the Point Sur lens from destruction by vandals when that station was unmanned. Now, however, Point Sur Light Station is properly a part of the California State Park System and the lighthouse calls out to have its lens reinstalled. There are dozens of examples across America where lighthouse lenses need to be reinstalled in their rightful lantern room and used again. The harsh flash of a reflecting

Angeles Harbor were not only historic preservationists but the ship's pilots who guide the massive cargo vessels into the harbor. Regarding the new automated lens, Captain Jackson Pearson, Chief Pilot for the Port of Los Angeles said of the solar powered plastic lens, "It's not sufficient. We complained about it. It was difficult for ships to see." But tragically the Los Angeles Harbor lens was not reinstalled in the historic lighthouse. A classical Fresnel lens which had reliably guided mariners to safety for 75 years was needlessly removed. The beauty of its beams no longer shine from its lantern room. Instead, it would remain in the window of a kindly museum.

airway beacon is very different from the time honored, warm glow of a Fresnel lens. No lighthouse sight is more impressive then a lighted Fresnel lens in the light tower. Exhibits pale by comparison.

OTHER ISSUES REGARDING LIGHTHOUSE PRESERVATION

Two policies need addressing. First, in several cases, lighthouses have been relocated from their historic setting. In a few emergency situations this is justified, but we are seeing cases where lighthouses have been moved to become tourist attractions or even museum exhibits. A great deal of historic integrity and the very feel of a place is lost when a lighthouse is moved from its native setting. In California five lighthouses have suffered in this manner and Cape Mendocino is threatened with relocation.

Second, historic light stations and lifeboat stations need to be open to the public. Both have traditionally welcomed many generations of visitors. The American people paid for them and they deserve to be able to visit them. In California, the magnificent sentinels at Point Cabrillo, Yerba Buena, Alcatraz, Point Vicente, Point Conception, Point Hueneme, Trinidad Head, new Point Loma, Cape Mendocino, and several other fine light stations need to be opened to the public. Some of these could provide joint use for Coast Guard housing and allow visitors during certain hours to selected portions of the station, excluding the residences. If there are public easement problems such as at Point Conception and Cape Mendocino, these need to be overcome. The California Coastal Conservancy could play a vital part in saving these and other beautiful stations.

With the high cost of housing, historic light station residences and lifeboat stations are also sometimes well adapted to housing Coast Guard personnel desperate for affordable places to live. A carefully planned visitor policy can open the stations to the public, often provide housing for Coast Guard people, and offer protection to the historic structures by having on-site personnel. This policy has already begun at some Coast Guard stations and can be expanded. Private living quarters would be, of course, off limits to the public while lighthouses, fog signal buildings, lifeboat station boatrooms, lookout towers and the like could be opened for scheduled tours on selected days. If necessary, these tours could be by reservation only.

As another example, you have never really seen the famed Outer Banks of North Carolina unless you've been to the top of Currituck, Bodie Island, and Cape Hatteras lighthouses. While we were there, large numbers of frustrated visitors were disappointed at not being able to climb these magnificent sentinels. This is not good public relations for either the Coast Guard or the Park Service, and several members of both agencies urged me to comment on this issue. Currituck and Bodie Island lighthouses could easily be opened for tours. Cape Hatteras, the tallest lighthouse in the nation, will have to be secured from erosion problems. The Park Service seems to be carefully addressing that issue. They do, however, need support for their funding pleas. In fact, one of the best things we can do is strongly support Congressional funding for the Coast Guard and Park Service. Both organizations need and deserve our fullest support, as do local and state preservation projects.

THE LIFE-SAVING AND LIFEBOAT STATIONS

Generally, lifeboat station preservation and interpretation is about 20 years behind the lighthouses. It reminds me of the 1950s and 1960s. Historic, classic 1930s and early 1940s style Coast Guard lifeboat stations and their lookout towers, boathouses and marine railways are being modified, destroyed and abandoned. These older stations are real maritime treasures, rich in the heritage of the American coast. The lifeboat stations offer the same potential as the light stations. They

Humboldt Bay Lifeboat Station at Samoa near Eureka, CA, has been called the most beautiful lifeboat station in the country. It was built in 1937. It is a classic 1930s style Coast Guard rescue station with lookout tower atop its roof and marine railway for launching motor lifeboats. It is one of the maritime treasures of the California coast and may be toured by appointment. May 18, 1977. (R. Shanks)

are equally interesting and beautiful. Their past and present officers and crews have the same dedication, pride, and affection for these stations as did the lighthouse keepers. Yet their contributions have been inadequately recognized. No one ever saved more lives at sea that the U.S. Life-Saving Service and its successor, the Coast Guard.

Like the light stations, the classic, older lifeboat stations offer beautiful buildings, scenic locations, a rich history, and pride among those who served there. Older, abandoned stations offer the same adaptive use opportunities as do the light stations.

Fortunately, some of the historic lifeboat stations, such as Humboldt Bay remain active today. Many offer tours by appointment or at specified hours of the week. What needs to be done here is to preserve the architectural integrity of the lifeboat station's buildings and to offer public tours. A small museum at each station would be a source of pride and a respository of historic records. These stations and their vessels continue to make historic rescues yearly. A major appeal to serve in the Coast Guard is knowing you have a hand in making maritime history. Often, recent Coast Guard history is more difficult to research than that of a century ago because it is inadequately recorded. Because of this problem, some Coast Guard units, such as the 110-foot cutter *Sapelo* at Eureka, have recently established their own ship's historian from among the crew. This is an excellent step forward.

Currently, two problems at the historic lifeboat stations are the preservation of the marine railway and boathouses built for the 36-foot motor lifeboats and the preservation of the remaining lookout towers. Some of the stations also have their 36-foot motor lifeboats on display and these need to be cared for so that they don't disintegrate.

The East Coast and the Great Lakes still have large numbers of historic stations from the era of the U.S. Life-Saving Service. Unlike the Coast Guard lifeboat stations, many U.S. Life-Saving Service stations are in private hands. Restrictions need to be added to protect these historic buildings from modification should a new, uncaring owner obtain them. Hopefully, some can be acquired by purchase or through donations for public use and preservation.

THE *FIR*, LAST ACTIVE LIGHTHOUSE
TENDER IN THE NATION

The Coast Guard's lighthouse tender *Fir (WLM 212)* is currently serving lighthouses and buoys out of Seattle, Washington. Given the vital importance of lighthouse tenders to light stations and lightships, saving at least one tender is a nationally significant project. The *Fir* was designed and built by the Lighthouse Service and she was commissioned by the Coast Guard. Spanning both services, the *Fir* represents the culmination of lighthouse tender design and the foundation of the Coast Guard's buoy tender fleet. She was the last ship built with the Lighthouse Service's lighthouse logo on her bow. If ever there was a Coast Guard ship worthy of preservation, it is the *Fir*. She has served Washington, Oregon and California lighthouses and buoys for over half a century.

When I first stepped on board her, it was like being transported back in time to the days of the Lighthouse Service. Her bridge, companionways, hull design, wardroom, buoy deck, and countless other features are those of the golden era of the Lighthouse Service. You almost expected to meet the district lighthouse inspector on board or a light keeper bound for an offshore station. All those I've met who have served on her cherish this ship. I've met Coast Guard people from the Great Lakes to the Chesapeake Bay who long to serve on her. A viable historic preservation project needs to be worked out for her by the Coast Guard and historic preservation organizations prior to eventual decommissioning.

WRITERS AND RESEARCHERS ON WEST COAST LIGHTHOUSES AND LIFE-SAVING STATIONS

Saving the buildings and the vessels is one part of maritime historic preservation, but saving the social history is the other. The key to saving that aspect of history is original research. We have been very fortunate on the Pacific Coast in having a number of qualified, serious researchers working on Coast Guard history and producing original material. Only New England rivals the West Coast in the number of high quality books dealing with the subject.

Jim Gibbs provided the foundation for contemporary regional work with his excellent *Sentinels of the North Pacific* (1955). He deserves the honored title of father of Pacific Coast lighthouse writing and research. His was an important step by providing a thoughtful orientation to West Coast lights. He has followed this work with several other interesting books dealing with both lighthouses and shipwrecks. His autobiographical book, *Tillamook Light* (1979), is a classic and deals with his duty as assistant keeper of dangerous Tillamook Rock Light in Oregon. Mr. Gibbs is both a former lighthouse keeper and a professional journalist. He has been writing for nearly four decades.

Francis Ross Holland continued our development of Pacific Coast lighthouse knowledge with his work on Point Loma light (1968), and his *America's Lighthouses* (1972). Mr. Holland's chapter on the West Coast in this work is helpful in understanding early construction of our sentinels. Mr. Holland is a retired National Park Service historian.

My *Lighthouses of San Francisco Bay* (1976), *Lighthouses and Lifeboats on the Redwood Coast* (1978), and *Guardians of the Golden Gate* (1990), combined archival research with numerous in depth interviews with Lighthouse Service and Coast Guard friends. These books represented the first detailed accounts of California light stations. It was the memory and records of these wonderful veterans that enabled detailed accounts of California lighthouse and lifeboat station life. I was deeply honored when Coast Guard commandant Admiral James Gracey called the books Coast Guard "classics". I have a master's degree in sociology and have been trained by California lighthouse keepers since age eight. I am particularly fortunate to have received magnificent cooperation from the U.S. Coast Guard which has allowed me to experience most of the lighthouse and lifeboat activities I write about.

Ernest L. Osborne and Victor West's *Men of Action* (1981), concentrated on the U.S. Life-Saving Service in southern Oregon and represented the first book solely devoted to the U.S. Life-Saving Service on the Pacific Coast. Both men are respected local historians. Their work draws heavily on the authoritative *Annual Reports of the U.S. Life-Saving Service.*

Frank Perry offered excellent accounts of three California light stations with his *Lighthouse Point* (1982), a history of Santa Cruz Light Station, and with his books *East Brother* (1984) and *Pigeon Point* (1986). Mr. Perry's works are well researched and detailed. His *East Brother* is especially important because of his success in locating former light keepers and their relatives and including their experiences in his work.

Donald Graham made two outstanding contributions to West Coast lighthouse history with his *Keepers of the Light* (1985), and *Lights of the Inland Passage* (1986). Both books cover the lighthouses of British Columbia in a manner of the excellent tradition of first hand knowledge, careful research and fine detail. Mr. Graham is a Canadian lighthouse keeper with a master's degree in history.

Norma Engel wrote her very enjoyable *Three Beams of Light* (1986), which is the biography of her parents' experiences at Oakland Harbor, Point Bonita, and Ballast Point light stations. This was the first book on California light stations by a member of a U.S. Lighthouse Service family. She added much to our knowledge of these three sentinels and to her we are indebted.

Jon Humboldt Gates' *Night Crossings* (1986) provided fascinating and detailed coverage of five maritime accidents and rescues on the Humboldt Bay bar. Mr. Gates is the son of a Humboldt Bay bar pilot and a talented writer.

In 1988, Ross R. Aikin produced his *Kilauea Point Lighthouse,* the first detailed account of a Hawaiian light station. It was a welcome addition from that state.

It is noteworthy that several areas of the United States are in great need of detailed research. Oral histories need to be recorded now. Alaska is especially in need of good research, particularly while many Coast Guard keepers are available to share their stories. The South is equally in need of new books, although Love Dean's *Reef Lights* was a wonderful contribution to Florida's maritime history. A few fine books are in print, but Chesapeake Bay, Delaware Bay, and the Great Lakes need detailed coverage. U.S. Life-Saving Stations and U.S. Coast Guard lifeboat stations across the nation need detailed books. Ellice Gonzalez's *Storms, Ships and Surfmen* covers Fire Island, NY (1982), and Edouard Stackpole's *Life Saving Nantucket* (1972) covers Nantucket Island, MA. These are two fine examples of local histories on the Life-Saving Service. Many Coast Guard vessels warrant books and articles.

SOURCES OF INFORMATION
ON PRESERVATION PROJECTS

There are a number of very useful sources of information on lighthouse preservation projects. They can direct you to historic preservation projects in your area. These admirable organizations specialize in providing information on the local lighthouse preservation projects that are so vital. Some of the following even do a few preservation projects themselves, yet are also good sources of information on the large number of local and government restoration activities that are the heart of the preservation movement. I highly recommend the following:

The U.S. Lighthouse Society, Fifth Floor, 244 Kearny St., San Francisco, CA 94108, publishes an excellent magazine, *The Keepers Log*, well worth the price of membership alone. They have also undertaken the preservation and restoration of one of the West Coast's great vessels, *Relief Lightship, Number WLV 605*, a ship I had the pleasure of being on board when she was stationed on the Columbia River bar. Society founder and "Head Keep" Wayne Wheeler also hopes to preserve the lighthouse tender *Fir* when she is eventually decommissioned. Mr. Wheeler has announced plans to establish a fog signal museum at Lime Point Fog Signal Station. All three projects are highly commendable. The Society also sponsors tours, lectures and other interesting events.

The Nautical Research Center, 335 Vallejo St., Petaluma, CA 94952, (707) 763-8453, is a valuable research library under the direction of founder Colin MacKenzie. It is devoted primarily to lighthouses and related matters. While it covers the U.S., it is unique in being a very good source for hard-to-find information on foreign lighthouses and lightships. For example, I learned much about the fascinating lighthouses of Japan here. Open by appointment.

The Great Lakes Lighthouse Keepers Association, P.O. Box 580, Allen Park, MI 48101, is yet another good source of information on restoration activities. They publish a magazine, are restoring St. Helena, Michigan light station and work closely with many other lighthouse restoration groups. The idea of strong regional preservation groups is a sound one.

The Shore Village Museum, Maine's Lighthouse Museum, 104 Limerock St., Rockland, ME 04841, publishes an occasional newsletter full of unique and highly worthwhile information. Director Ken Black is a former lightship captain. Mr. Black is generous in sharing his expertise and information.

The Coast Guard Museum of the Northwest on Alaskan Way in Seattle, the Coast Guard Academy Museum in New London, CT, and the Treasure Island Museum off San Francisco all offer outstanding exhibits on lighthouses and lifeboat stations.

THE LIFE-SAVING SERVICE AND COAST GUARD LIFEBOAT STATIONS

There are stations which have been or are being converted to museums offering very worthwhile visitor opportunities. These are wonderful places not to be missed. It is an indication of how few life-saving and lifeboat stations have as yet been preserved for public use that we can list most of them here. Among them are: Point Reyes Lifeboat Station, Point Reyes National Seashore, Point Reyes, CA; Port Orford Lifeboat Station at Port Orford Heads Wayside State Park, Port Orford, OR; Coquille River Museum, Bandon, OR; Hull Life-Saving Museum, Hull, MA; Old Harbor Life-Saving Station at Race Point, Cape Cod National Seashore, MA; Mystic Seaport, Mystic, CT; Spermaceti Life-Saving Station Number 2 at Gateway National Recreational Area, Sandy Hook Unit, Highlands, NJ; Spermaceti Cove Life-Saving Station Number 1 at Twin Lights State Park, Highlands, NJ, on the grounds of Navesink Light Station; Life-Saving Station Museum, Ocean City, MD; Life-Saving Museum of Virginia, Virginia Beach, VA; Chicamacomico and Little Kinnakeet Life-Saving Stations at Cape Hatteras National Seashore, NC; Sleeping Bear Dunes National Lakeshore, Empire, MI; Gilbert's Bar House of Refuge, Hutchinson Island, Stuart, FL.

Point Reyes National Seashore has begun developing what may become the finest Coast Guard Lifeboat Station preservation project on the Pacific Coast. Point Reyes has a fully operable 36-foot motor lifeboat and boathouse complete with working launchway. Hopefully, Fort Point Coast Guard Lifeboat and Life-Saving Station in San Francisco's Golden Gate National Recreation Area will join this list. Many fascinating and historic active Coast Guard stations can be toured by appointment.

The author would appreciate hearing about other historic preservation projects and organizations involved with maritime rescue stations. He would also enjoy hearing from anyone who has served or lived at a California lighthouse or at any Pacific Coast lifeboat stations. He is grateful for information on these subjects and for the opportunity to make copy negatives of photographs. He may be reached at P.O. Box 355, Petaluma, CA 94953.

Coast Guard to the rescue! Life-ring in hand, a Coast Guardsman stands alert at the bow of a 30-foot utility boat, C. 1950s. (U.S. Coast Guard)

LANGUAGE OF THE LIGHT
KEEPER AND SURFMAN
A GLOSSARY

Airways Beacon—A rotating, reflecting light similar to those used at some airports.

Balcony—The projecting exterior walkway around a lantern room or watch room on a lighthouse. Nearly all lighthouses have one or two balconies. Sometimes called a gallery, but actually the gallery is the interior walkway inside a lantern room.

Ball—The chimney covering atop the lantern room roof.

Beach Cart—A cart used to carry the beach apparatus to a shipwreck. Beach apparatus included a Lyle gun, breeches buoy, lines, shovels, and the like.

Beach Patrol—Any patrol along the beach to search for wrecks or to warn vessels away from the shore by using flares. During World War II only, the term came to be applied specifically to military patrols aimed at preventing sabotage and landing by enemy agents.

Bell House—The frame structure housing the fog bell and clockwork bell-striking apparatus (timer). It generally had an attached tower (called the bell tower) which held the weight used to power the clockwork drive.

Breeches Buoy—A device used to carry people across impassable surf during evacuation from a shipwreck. It consists of a ring-shaped life preserver with a pair of oversized canvas pants attached to the ring. A line is shot from shore to ship and secured at both ends. The breeches buoy is then drawn across. The person to be rescued climbs into the life ring, putting his feet through the pants legs. He is then hauled ashore.

Buoy Tender—see lighthouse tender.

California Cottage lighthouse—A lighthouse with a dwelling surrounding the light tower. Major architectural style for California lighthouses built during the 1850s.

Diaphone Fog Horn—A fog signal consisting of a piston driven by compressed air.

Drop Tube or *Weight Trunk*—The hollow shaft down the center of most lighthouses where the weight travels, which causes the lens to rotate.

Faking Box—A wooden box where a Lyle gun's shot line was coiled in layers around wooden pins. The pins were mounted on a removable frame. When the pins were removed, the line was free-standing, ready to be paid out without entanglement when fired by the Lyle

Howard Underhill, first officer-in-charge of the Point Reyes Lifeboat Station, knew the terms described in our glossary well, 1927. (Point Reyes National Seashore)

gun. To "fake" a rope is to loop it, as is done around the pegs in a faking box.

Fixed Light—A steady, non-flashing beam.

Fog Bell—A bell used as a fog signal. See *Bell House.*

Fog Signal—A device at a station used to provide a loud, patterned sound during foggy weather to aid mariners in establishing their position or to warn them away from a danger. Often called a "foghorn", a somewhat inaccurate term since whistles, bells, explosives, sirens, gongs, cannons, etc., also have served as fog signals.

Fog Signal Station—A station with more or less the same collection of buildings as a light station except that there was no lighthouse; the fog signal served as the sole aid to navigation.

Keeper—Usually the attendant at a light station. Also refers to the officer-in-charge of a life-saving station.

Lamp—The oil lighting apparatus inside a lens. Early lamps usually had several circular wicks and had to be trimmed and fed several times a night. Glass chimneys were placed over the flame, both to increase brightness and to direct smoke up to a lure and out of the lantern room.

Lantern Room—The glassed-in room at the top of a lighthouse containing the lens.

Lead Line—A rope with an attached lead weight used to determine the ocean's depth.

Lens Apron—A full-length linen apron worn by early-day keepers while working in the *lantern room.* Lens aprons prevented lint and dust off the keeper's clothing from coming into contact with the lens.

Lens Lantern—Large marine lantern, occasionally mounted outside a building at a light station to serve as the light. Unlike lenses, which were housed in a lantern room, lens lanterns were self-contained and were placed outside buildings. Lens lanterns were also commonly used on *lightships.*

Life Car—A small, submarine-like boat completely sheathed in metal and having a small hatch for entry. It could be drawn between ship and shore in much the same manner as a breeches buoy. Sometimes called a surfcar.

Lifeboat—In the U.S. Life-Saving Service, a self-bailing and self-righting pulling boat with air compartments. Manned by six oarsmen and a coxswain who often used a steering oar. Lifeboats were heavier and larger than surfboats and were generally launched from a launchway or cart rather than by hand.

Lifeboat Station—Usually a Coast Guard station with a launchway and equipped primarily with motor lifeboats. Originally, nearly all stations had 34 or 36-foot motor lifeboats which were launched from marine railways. The term was occasionally used by the U.S. Life-Saving Service also.

Life-Saving Station—Established by the U.S. Life-Saving Service, most stations were equipped with pulling (oar-powered) *lifeboats* and surfboats, which were launched through the surf by hand or by using a specially designed wagon called a *boat carriage.* These stations usually lacked true launchways since they were frequently located on beaches having heavy breakers which would have destroyed a marine railway.

Light Station—Refers not only to the lighthouse, but to all of the buildings at an installation having a lighthouse. Light stations often had a fog signal building, oil house, carpenter shop, blacksmith shop, cistern, water house, laundry shed, etc., in addition to the lighthouse itself. Some light stations have had more than one lighthouse.

Lighthouse Tender—Ship used to supply light and fog signal stations, maintain buoys, and service lightships. Today, similar vessels are called *buoy tenders.*

Lightship—A moored vessel which marked a harbor entrance or a danger such as a reef. Lightships were usually equipped with a light, fog signal, and radio beacon. Under the Coast Guard, they were generally painted red with large, white lettering proclaiming the location they mark, e.g., Blunts Reef, Columbia River, or San Francisco. When the regular lightship returned to port for maintenance, a lightship marked *Relief* replaced it.

Lure—A large, inverted funnel in a lantern room which trapped smoke from the *lamp* and directed it up the chimney to escape via the *ball* vent atop the roof.

Lyle Gun—A small cannon used to shoot an 18-pound weighted projectile, with a line attached, from shore to a shipwreck.

Motor Lifeboat—A self-bailing and self-righting powered lifeboat designed to operate in heavy surf. In the U.S. Coast Guard, such boats were 34, 36, 44, or 52 feet in length and were called for duty under the most extreme sea conditions. The 44 and 52 foot classes are active at Coast Guard stations today.

Mushroom Anchor—A large anchor shaped like a mushroom and used on almost all modern Coast Guard lightships.

Oil House—A small building, usually of concrete or stone, used to store oil for the lighthouse lamps. Oil houses were built after kerosene came into use as an illuminant. Kerosene was so flammable that it could no longer be stored in or immediately adjacent to the lighthouse as had been the practice with less dangerous oils. Most California oil houses had flat roofs.

Patrol Boat—A Coast Guard rescue boat, usually of 82 to 110 feet in length, frequently used for such duties as searching for missing vessels, towing disabled craft, and transferring personnel at offshore light stations.

Pulling Boat—A boat which was rowed, especially a pulling lifeboat or pulling surfboat.

Radio Beacon—A radio-sending device which transmits a coded signal by which a mariner can determine his position using his own radio-direction-finding apparatus.

Sandpounder—Slang term for early beach patrolmen who walked their patrols.

Shot—A measurement of anchor chain length. One shot equals 90 feet.

Siren—A fog signal in which steam or compressed air is forced through slots in a rapidly spinning disk, thus producing a loud noise.

Surfboat—In the U.S. Life-Saving Service, a clinker-built pulling boat designed for use in heavy surf. Surfboats had to be lightweight so they could be launched by hand from remote beaches.

Surfman—The Life-Saving Service crew who manned the pulling boats, stood lookout duty, and walked the beach patrols. Most life-saving stations had six to eight surfmen in the crew, all under the command of a station keeper. Sometimes still very appropriately used as a term for Coast Guard motor lifeboat crewmen.

Vertical Mushroom Trumpet Fog Horns—A fog horn mounted vertically with a mushroom-shaped cover which directs the sound horizontally in all directions. In contrast, shore stations usually have horizontally mounted horns pointing in one or two directions away from shore. Often used on lightships.

Watch Room—The room where a light keeper stood watch. In a lighthouse, the watch room was usually either directly beneath the lantern room or beside the tower entrance. Fog signal buildings often had watch rooms as well.

Whistle—A fog signal through which steam or compressed air was forced. Fog whistles are classified by their diameter, i.e., a 12-inch whistle is 12 inches in diameter.

Wickie—Term for a light keeper, originating in the recurrent task of trimming the wicks.

BIBLIOGRAPHY

Adamson, H.C., *Keepers of the Lights* (New York: Greenberg, 1955)

Bingham, Helen, *In Tamal Land* (San Francisco: Calkins Publishing House, 1906)

Carse, Robert, *Keepers of the Lights* (New York: Scribner, 1969)

Conklin, Irving D., *Guideposts of the Sea* (New York: Macmillan, 1939)

Delgado, James, *Shipwrecks of the Golden Gate* (San Francisco Maritime Museum, 1984)

Edwards, E. Price, *Our Seamarks* (London: Longmans Green, 1884)

Engel, Norma, *Three Beams of Light* (San Diego: Tecolote Publications, 1986)

Flint, Willard, *Lightships and Lightship Stations of the United States Government* (Washington, D.C.: U.S. Coast Guard Headquarters, 1989)

Gates, Jon Humboldt, *Night Crossings* (Eureka, CA: Pioneer Graphics, 1986)

Gibbs, James A., *Sentinels of the North Pacific* (Portland: Binfords & Mort, 1955)

Gibbs, James A., *Shipwrecks of the Pacific Coast* (Portland: Binfords & Mort, 1971)

Gibbs, James A., *West Coast Lighthouses* (Seattle: Superior, 1974)

Gibbs, James A. and Chad Ehlers, *Sentinels of Solitude: West Coast Lighthouses* (Portland: Graphic Arts Center, 1981)

Gibbs, James A., *Lighthouses of the Pacific* (West Chester, PA: Schiffler, 1986)

Halberstadt, Hans, *U.S.C.G.: Always Ready* (Novato, CA: Presidio, 1986)

Hartman, Tom, *Guinness Book of Ships and Shipping Facts & Feats* (Guinness Superlatives Limited: Middlesex, UK)

Holland, Francis Ross, Jr., *America's Lighthouses* (Brattleboro, Vermont: Stephen Greene Press, 1972)

Lott, Arnold S., *A Long Line of Ships, Mare Island's Century of Naval Activity in California* (Annapolis: U.S. Naval Institute, 1954)

Marshall, Don B., *California Shipwrecks* (Seattle: Superior, 1978)

Mason, Jack, *Point Reyes Historian* (Inverness, CA: various years)

National Transportation Safety Board Marine Accident Report, "Near Capsizing of the Charter Passenger Vessel Merry Jane, Bodega Bay, CA" (Washington, D.C.: National Transportation Safety Board, 1986)

Osborne, Ernest and Victor West, *Men of Action* (Bandon, OR: Bandon Historical Society, 1981)

Perry, Frank, *East Brother: History of an Island Light Station* (Pt. Richmond, CA: East Brother Light Station, Inc., 1984)

Putnam, George R., "Beacons of the Sea," *National Geographic* (Vol. 24, no. 1, January 1913)

Putnam, George R., *Lighthouses and Lightships of the United States* (Boston: Houghton Mifflin, 1917)

Putnam, George R., "New Safeguards for Ships in Fog and Storm," *National Geographic*, August, 1936

Putnam, George R., *Sentinel of the Coasts: The Log of a Lighthouse Engineer* (New York: W.W. Norton, 1937)

Scheina, Robert L., *U.S. Coast Guard Cutters & Craft of World War II* (Annapolis: Naval Institute Press, 1982)

Shanks, Ralph, "Lighthouses of Marin," *Old Marin with Love* (San Rafael, CA: Marin County American Revolution Bicentennial Commission, 1976)

Shanks, Ralph, *Lighthouses of San Francisco Bay* (San Anselmo, CA: Costaño Books, 1976)

Shanks, Ralph, "The United States Life-Saving Service in California," *Sea Letter* (San Francisco: National Maritime Museum, No. 27, Spring 1977, and No. 31, Summer 1980. Two-part article.)

Shanks, Ralph, *Lighthouses & Lifeboats on the Redwood Coast* (San Anselmo, CA: Costaño Books, 1978)

Shanks, Ralph, "Tenders: Unsung Heroes," *The Keeper's Log* (U.S. Lighthouse Society, San Francisco: Winter, 1987)

Stevenson, D. Alan, *The World's Lighthouses Before 1820* (London: Oxford University Press, 1959)

Toogood, Anna Coxe, *Historic Resource Study: A Civil History of Golden Gate National Recreation Area and Point Reyes National Seashore* (Denver: National Park Service, 1980)

U.S. Coast Guard, *The Coast Guardsman's Manual* (Annapolis: U.S. Naval Institute, 1967)

U.S. Coast Guard, "Evolution of the Lighthouse Tower" by Robert Scheina, in "Lighthouses Then and Now," Supplement to "Commandants' Bulletin" (Washington, D.C.: 1989)

U.S. Coast Guard, *Historically Famous Lighthouses* (Washington, D.C.: G.P.O., 1972)

U.S. Coast Guard *Light List, Pacific Coast and Pacific Islands* (Washington, D.C.: G.P.O., various years)

U.S. Coast Guard, *Notice to Mariners* (San Francisco: various dates)

U.S. Department of Commerce, *United States Coast Pilot, Pacific Coast, 10th ed.* (Washington, D.C.: G.P.O., 1968)

U.S. Life-Saving Service, *Annual Reports* (Washington, D.C.: G.P.O., 1878-1914)

U.S. Lighthouse Board, *Annual Reports* (Washington, D.C.: G.P.O., 1852-1939)

U.S. Lighthouse Service, *Bulletin* (Washington, D.C.: G.P.O., various years)

U.S. Lighthouse Society, *The Keeper's Log*, Wayne Wheeler, editor (San Francisco: 1984-1989)

Weiss, George, *The Lighthouse Service* (New York: AMS Press, 1974)

Wilson, T.G., *The Irish Lighthouse Service* (Dublin: Allen Figgis, 1968)

Farewell to the wooden 36-foot Coast Guard motor lifeboats. Number 36542 leaves Bodega Bay bound toward Point Reyes. 1975 (R. Shanks)

ACKNOWLEDGEMENTS

It is largely because of the helpfulness of the following people and institutions that this book could be written. They are listed in no particular order since all played vital roles. A sincere thank you to everyone!

It is worthy of note that without the magnificent help of the Coast Guard, this book could never have been written.

U.S. Lighthouse Service keepers and families: Wayne, Martha and Nancy Piland; Edith Jordan Hall Simons; Irving D. Conklin; J. Milford and Louise Johnson; Walter Fanning; Radford Franke; Esther Gonzales; Peggy Mayeau; Ole and Bernice Lunden; Barbara Hicks Clough; Bill and C. Isabel Owens; Harry Miller; and Laverne Dornberger.

U.S. Coast Guard 11th and 12th District's: Public Affairs Office, especially Jim Boyd, Paul Mobley, and Milt Duby. Aids to Navigation Office, especially O.F. De Graaf, Commander Dale Foster and Com. J.D. Blackett. Point Bonita Light Station, especially Jack Dusch, Bob Grass and Harry Lent. Officers and crew of the Bodega Bay Lifeboat Station, especially Mark Galusha, David Kissling, and Scott Richardson; officers and crew of Fort Point Lifeboat Station, especially Harry Hoffman, Senior Chief Rick Dixon, Mark Dobney, and Barry Duke. Base San Francisco Buoy Depot, Yerba Buena Island. Joseph Picotte of East Brother Light Station. Jim Demerin of Point Blunt Light Station.

Rear Admiral Richard Bauman, USCG; Wayne Wheeler, U.S. Lighthouse Society; Colin MacKenzie, Nautical Research Center of Petaluma, CA; National Maritime Museum and Porter J. Shaw library, esp. Karl Kortum, David Hull, and Ted Miles; Sue Lemmon, shipyard historian, Mare Island Naval Shipyard, Vallejo, CA; Douglas Brooks of the Treasure Island Museum, San Francisco, CA; Ken Black of the Shore Village Museum, Rockland, ME; Beverly Kienitz; Torrey Shanks; Ed Troy; Richard Boonisar; Captain Gene Davis of Coast Guard Museum Northwest in Seattle; Jack Mason Museum; Humboldt State University library, especially Eric Shimps; Bandon Historical Society.

Dave Edwards, Officer-in-Charge, Quillayute River Lifeboat Station, La Push, WA; Ron Ferguson of Alcatraz Island Light Station and Point Reyes Lifeboat Station; Captain Dan Stuhlman and his officers and crew of the buoy tender *Blackhaw*; Master Chief Mike Gaul and Rick Bilbro of Coos Bay Lifeboat Station, OR; Master Chief David Duren, USCGC *Point Ledge*, Noyo River Station, Fort Bragg, CA; Chief Samuel H. Mostovoy and Al Thieme of Point Reyes Lifeboat Station; Master Chief Dan Sutherland, USCG Ret.; CDR Bill Ehrman, USCG, Ret.; Carl Christensen; Capt. Cornelius Sullivan, U.S. Life-Saving Service; Chief Garner and Thora Churchill of Humboldt

Bay Lifeboat Station. U.S. Coast Guard Academy Museum, especially Paul Johnson and staff; Robert Scheina, Coast Guard historian; National Archives.

Dewey Livingston, Don Neubacher, and Armando Quintera of Point Reyes National Seashore; Greg Moore, Golden Gate National Park Association; Jim Delgado, National Park Service; Charles Hawkins and JoAnn Jeong, Fort Point National Historic Site; Craig Dorman, Alcatraz Island, Golden Gate National Recreation Area; Cape Hatteras National Seashore; Steve Czarniecki, Fire Island National Seashore; Cape Cod National Seashore; Tom Laverty, Twin Lights State Park, NJ; Bancroft Library, University of California, Berkeley; California Historical Society Library, San Francisco; California State Library, Sacramento; Independent-Journal Library, San Rafael, California; Public Libraries of Marin County, Oakland, San Francisco and Vallejo; Richmond City Museum, Richmond, CA; San Francisco Maritime Museum; U.S. Army Museum, Presidio of San Francisco; North Bay Photo; B&B Photo; The Graphics Group; Miller-Freeman Publications; McNaughton & Gunn, printers.

The kindnesses extended by numerous other individuals and institutions are also gratefully appreciated.

Editor Lisa Woo Shanks atop Chesapeake Light Tower off Cape Henry, Virginia.

ABOUT THE EDITOR

Lisa Woo Shanks began her career with the National Park Service at Golden Gate National Recreation Area in San Francisco. She assisted in the planning of the Park Service's acquisition of Point Bonita lighthouse and has worked as a ranger on the National Park Service's historic ships at Hyde Street Pier in San Francisco. She has joined her husband on motor lifeboats, offshore lighthouses, and numerous Coast Guard small craft from Los Angeles Harbor, California, and Coos Bay, Oregon, to Boon Island, Maine and Chesapeake Light, Virginia. She is responsible for the publication planning, design, artwork and editing of this book. Lisa Shanks was also editor of the *North American Indian Travel Guide*. She is a soil conservationist for the USDA Soil Conservation Service and has authored technical material for the vineyard industry. Mrs. Shanks holds a degree in Natural Resource Planning and Interpretation.

Author Ralph Shanks on board Coast Guard motor lifeboat Intrepid. *Coos Bay, Oregon.*

ABOUT THE AUTHOR

Ralph Shanks is a maritime historian specializing in the history of the Coast Guard, the Lighthouse Service and the Life-Saving Service. He has been trained at California lighthouses since age eight and this is his third book on lighthouses and Coast Guard search and rescue operations. His earlier books include *Lighthouses of San Francisco Bay* and *Lighthouses and Lifeboats on the Redwood Coast*. His articles on the Life-Saving Service have been published by the National Maritime Museum. Mr. Shanks has been a consultant on lighthouse and lifeboat station preservation and history for the National Park Service, Coast Guard, Bureau of Land Management, California State Department of Parks and Recreation, and others. He believes in gaining first hand knowledge of his subject and has been at sea in over a dozen types of Coast Guard vessels and has operated lighthouses and handled motor lifeboats. He is a teacher in the San Rafael City Schools in San Rafael, CA, and his love of Coast Guard history is only exceeded by his love of his wife Lisa and his family. Besides his maritime history work, Mr. Shanks is interested in Native American cultures and wrote the *North American Indian Travel Guide*. He has a masters degree in sociology.